SOCIAL RESEARCH ETHICS

Also edited by Martin Bulmer

CENSUSES, SURVEYS AND PRIVACY (1979)
SOCIAL POLICY RESEARCH (1978)
SOCIOLOGICAL RESEARCH METHODS (1977)
(all The Macmillan Press)

SOCIAL RESEARCH AND ROYAL COMMISSIONS (1980)
MINING AND SOCIAL CHANGE: DURHAM COUNTY IN THE
TWENTIETH CENTURY (1977)
WORKING CLASS IMAGES OF SOCIETY (1975)

SOCIAL RESEARCH ETHICS

an examination of the merits of covert participant
observation

Edited by

Martin Bulmer

Lecturer in Social Administration
London School of Economics and Political Science

First published 1982 by
THE MACMILLAN PRESS LTD
London and Basingstoke
Companies and representatives
throughout the world

ISBN 0 333 29198 0 (hard cover)
ISBN 0 333 29199 9 (paper cover)

Typeset by
CAMBRIAN TYPESETTERS
Farnborough, Hants

Printed and bound in Hong Kong

Contents

Part Three

ON THE PHILOSOPHY AND ETHICS OF COVERT
METHODS

Part Four

CONCLUSION

Preface

This book is intended to be a contribution both to the discussion of ethics in social research in general, and to the debate about the pros and cons of covert or secret participant observation in particular. How social science is conducted, and how it conducts itself, are matters of proper public and professional concern which a collection such as the present one is designed to illuminate.

There are several reasons for considering such analysis timely. Scientists, including social scientists, have wide responsibilities in conducting research, not only to further the ideal of scientific truth but (in research involving human subjects) to pay attention to questions of informed consent, responsibility for the well-being of research subjects and the relative importance of risk and benefit arising from the research. In biomedical research, such considerations have been in the forefront for many years. Medical experiments, for example, are not undertaken without prior ethical review. The growing tendency, particularly in the United States, to extend this biomedical model to the behavioural and social sciences is creating a situation of a new kind, where the practices of social scientists are increasingly required to come under review by peers in their own and other disciplines. The creation of Institutional Review Boards at universities and research institutes means that the social researcher in the last quarter of the century faces a different situation from that he did at mid-century. The scale and perhaps the prestige of social science has grown, but so have the checks on its unhindered practice.

A second reason for concern is the need to be conscious of

the good name of social science. In most matters to do with responsibility, privacy, confidentiality and ethical practice, social scientists have themselves been in the forefront in drawing attention to the implications of particular research methods. The record is not unblemished, but criticism of doubtful practice is more likely to come from fellow professionals than from outsiders. Social scientists need to be kept up to the mark ethically, by constantly examining and re-examining their work.

This anthology is a re-examination in the sense that its topic is by no means new. The book consists of six original chapters and six chapters previously published in out-of-the-way places. It deliberately does not include any of the well-known articles of the 1960s, several of which are most conveniently collected in W. J. Filstead's anthology of material on qualitative methodology published in 1970. Social science does not stand still, and in the 1980s the ethical assessment of covert methods has to be revised in the light of intervening research, five examples of which are presented here. The present work is also intended to complement more recent general discussions of the ethics of social research by John Barnes and by Edward Diener and Rick Crandall.

Covert methods are not very widely used in social science research, being neither common nor typical of most sociological inquiry. When they have been used, however, they have usually provoked more or less fierce ethical controversy, highlighting sharply general issues about social science and the human condition. This is a healthy situation, indicating responsibility and creativity among social researchers. Ethical issues are not to be fought shy of or avoided because they are difficult and intractable. Social research involves the researcher in ethical decision-making, which poses dilemmas and faces him or her with risks. To these kinds of problems the present collection is addressed.

It remains to thank those who helped to make the present collection what it is. Two admirable secretaries in the LSE Department of Social Science and Administration, Gay Grant and Bridget Atkinson, typed parts of the manuscript with precision and speed. Several people, particularly John Barnes, Jennifer Platt, Paul Reynolds, Edward Shils and Donald

Warwick, discussed aspects of social research ethics at different points in time. For detailed comments on the opening and closing chapters I am grateful to Robert Burgess, Nigel Fielding, Simon Holdaway and Roger Homan. None of those mentioned, however, are to be held responsible for the editor's own views on research morality.

London   MARTIN BULMER
April 1980

Contributors

DR SISSELA BOK is a philosopher who teaches ethics and decision-making in medicine at the Harvard Medical School. She is the author of *Lying: moral choice in public and private life* (1978) and of numerous articles on medical ethics. She has worked in hospitals on human experimentation committees, has been a member of the Ethics Advisory Board to the US Secretary of Health, Education and Welfare and was recently Vice-President of the Hastings Center, Institute of Society, Ethics and the Life Sciences at Hastings-on-Hudson, NY.

MARTIN BULMER teaches the methodology of social research and the applications of social research to public policy-making in the Department of Social Science and Administration at the London School of Economics and Political Science. Previously he taught at the University of Durham and worked in the Population Statistics Division of the Office of Population Censuses and Surveys, London. He is a member of the Ethics Committee of the Social Research Association. He has also edited *Social Research and Royal Commissions* (1980), *Censuses, Surveys and Privacy* (1979), *Social Policy Research* (1978) and *Sociological Research Methods* (1977).

DR NORMAN K. DENZIN is Professor of Sociology at the University of Illinois at Urbana. He has also taught at the University of California at Berkeley. His major teaching and research interests include symbolic interactionism, research methodology and the sociology of deviance. He is the author of *The Research Act in Sociology* (1970), *Childhood Sociali-*

sation (1978), editor of *Studies in Symbolic Interactionism* (1978, 1979) and several anthologies as well as many articles in scholarly journals.

DR KAI T. ERIKSON is Professor of Sociology and American Studies at Yale University, and also serves as editor of *The Yale Review*. His publications include *Wayward Puritans: a study in the sociology of deviance* (1966) and *Everything in Its Path: destruction of community in the Buffalo Creek flood* (1976), which was published in Great Britain under the title *In the Wake of the Flood*.

DR NIGEL FIELDING is Lecturer in Sociology and Applied Social Studies in the Department of Sociology at the University of Surrey. His main teaching interests are in the sociology of deviance and control, the sociology of law, and in qualitative social research methods. In addition to his work on the NF, he has carried out research on control and support in the work of probation officers, and is engaged in research on the training and socialisation of recruits to the police. The research reported in Chapter 5 was carried out during his doctoral study at the London School of Economics. His publications include *The National Front* (1981) and various articles reporting his research on the NF and on probation officers.

DR JOHN F. GALLIHER is Professor of Sociology at the University of Missouri at Columbia, where he teaches courses in criminology and the sociology of law. He has written on the social and cultural origins of criminal laws and on the ethics of social science research. He has published widely in socio-legal journals, including *The American Sociologist, Social Problems, Crime and Social Justice* and *Contemporary Crises*. His most recent article on ethics is 'Social Scientists' Ethical Responsibilities to Superordinates: Looking Upward Meekly', *Social Problems* 27 (1980).

DR SIMON HOLDAWAY is Lecturer in Sociology in the Department of Sociological Studies at the University of Sheffield. Before taking up his present post in 1975 he worked as a police officer for eleven years, during which time he was seconded to read sociology at Lancaster University. He graduated in 1973, returning to his force for two years, during which time he carried out research. He is the author of a number of articles on the police and editor of *The British Police* (1979). During the academic year 1979–80 he was a Nuffield Social Science Research Fellow and warmly thanks the Nuffield Foundation for their generous assistance in enabling him to write up his research free from teaching and administrative duties. Apart from the police, his interests lie in the area of the sociology of religion, deviance and adult socialisation. He is currently training to be a worker priest with the Anglican Church.

DR ROGER HOMAN is Senior Lecturer in Sociology and Education at Brighton Polytechnic. His main current teaching interests are in the Sociology and Politics of Education. His PhD thesis (University of Lancaster, 1978) was entitled *A Sociological Analysis of the Language-behaviour of Old-time Pentecostals*. He has also done research on Victorian sabbatarianism, the Society of Dependents, the Socialist Workers' Party and aspects of political socialisation in western and communist societies. His publications include articles in the *British Journal of Sociology*, *The Sociological Review*, *Comparative Education*, *A Sociological Yearbook of Religion in Britain*, and the *International Journal of Political Education*.

DR PAUL DAVIDSON REYNOLDS is Professor of Sociology at the University of Minnesota in Minneapolis-St Paul. His main teaching interests are related to graduate programmes in applied sociology and on courses related to the extent to which social science provides an understanding of everyday life. He has done experimental research on small group processes, survey research on criminal victimisation, analysis of ethical codes adopted by social science associations, and is planning a multi-factor survey of adult daily life. He has published *Ethical Dilemmas and Social Science Research* (1979), *A Primer in Theory Construction* (1971), several articles on ethics, and has written various reports on victimisation and evaluation of community agencies.

DR D. L. ROSENHAN is Professor of Psychology and Law at Stanford University, California. He is primarily concerned with experimental research in social psychology, with the issue of context, and the manner in which these concerns integrate with law. He has conducted research in the social psychology of institutions, in personality (particularly affective) processes and in prosocial behaviour. His publications include three books and some eighty articles.

EDWARD SHILS is Distinguished Service Professor in the Committee on Social Thought and in the Department of Sociology at the University of Chicago. He is also a member of Peterhouse, University of Cambridge. He founded and edits *Minerva*, and was a founding member of the editorial board of the *Bulletin of the Atomic Scientists*. His books include *The Torment of Secrecy* (1956), *Center and Periphery: essays on macrosociology* (1975) and *The Calling of Sociology and Other Essays on the Pursuit of Learning* (1980). With Talcott Parsons he is the co-author of *Towards a General Theory of Action* (1951).

DR DONALD P. WARWICK is an Institute Fellow at the Harvard Institute for International Development and a Lecturer on Sociology and on Education at Harvard University. He offers courses on Comparative Organizations, Program Implementation, and Ethics and Public Policy. He has conducted research on a broad range of topics, including the effects of shift work on workers and their families; the impact of higher education on student values; the growth and persistence of public bureaucracy; and educational planning in Latin America. His current research centres on the formulation and implementation of population policies in the developing countries; the implementation of development programmes in Indonesia; and the bureaucratic and political contexts of state-owned enterprises. He is author of *The Teaching Ethics in the Social Sciences* (1980) and *A Theory of Public Bureaucracy* (1975); co-author of *The Sample Survey: theory and practice* (1975), *Persistence and Change: Bennington College and its students after twenty-five years* (1967), and *Shift Work: the social, psychological and physical consequences*

(1965); and co-editor of *The Ethics of Social Intervention* (1978) and *Comparative Research Methods* (1973). He has also published chapters and articles on the ethics of population control, the ethics of deception, the politics and ethics of cross-cultural research, and national development.

Part One

Introduction

1 Ethical Problems in Social Research: the case of covert participant observation

Martin Bulmer

Introduction

The scientific community has responsibilities not only to the ideals of the pursuit of objective truth and the search for knowledge, but also to the subjects of their research. Whether human subjects in the physiological laboratory, patients in the medical school, students in the psychological laboratory or members of the public whom the sociologist encounters while out in the field, the researcher has always to take account of the effects of his actions upon those subjects and act in such a way as to preserve their rights and integrity as human beings.[1] Such behaviour is ethical behaviour.

Ethics is a matter of principled sensitivity to the rights of others. Being ethical limits the choices we can make in the pursuit of truth. Ethics say that while truth is good, respect for human dignity is better, even if, in the extreme case, the respect of human dignity leaves one ignorant of human nature.[2]

This book examines ethical issues that arise in the conduct of social research. It does so by means of case studies of the use of covert or secret participant observation, a research procedure which has aroused sharp ethical debate in the past[3] and which poses clearly many of the ethical dilemmas which can face the social researcher. Though occasional references will be made to ethical considerations in biomedical and psychological research,[4] the main focus is upon social science, whose research procedures differ significantly from those used in dealing with laboratory subjects or patients undergoing clinical trials. Covert participant observation is not even a very common research technique, but its use brings out most clearly some of the ethical principles which guide the conduct of social research.

Definitions

What is meant by 'covert' or 'secret' participant observation? The term is used here to refer to research using participant observation methods,[5] where the researcher spends an extended period of time in a particular research setting, concealing the fact that he is a researcher and pretending to play some other role. In such a situation, the identity of the researcher and knowledge of his work is kept from those who are being studied, who have no knowledge that they are being studied.

In this respect covert participant observation is analogous to situations in which political organisations are infiltrated by agents provocateur or spies working for bodies hostile to that organisation. A recent example is provided by the following case.

In January 1980 it was revealed in the British press that the former Deputy-Director of the International University Exchange Fund (IUEF), an independent body based in Geneva offering support for political change in Southern Africa and scholarships for South African refugees, had been a captain in the South African police working for the South African government through the period since he had ostensibly 'fled' South Africa as a political refugee, and thereafter became an employee of IUEF. When the story broke, the policeman concerned fled from Switzerland and returned to South Africa, where he gave press interviews saying that many people would now be alarmed about information which he might have revealed while working as an under-cover agent for the South African police.[6]

The parallel between covert observation and the activities of spies is underlined by similar sorts of jokes about small extremist political groups, the majority of whose members are under-cover police spies, and small extremist religious sects, the majority of whose members are sociologists of religion studying them covertly. Joseph Conrad's description of agents provocateur as 'some species of authorised scoundrelism'[7] suggests that covert participant observers may also be criticised for behaving unethically. The activities of police informants and spies have been examined in detail by G. T. Marx, whose analysis suggests several further parallels with the covert observer.[8]

The methodological literature on participant observation contains a number of discussions of the different roles which the participant observer may play in the field. Traditionally, 'secret' observation has been contrasted with 'open' observation. Gold, for example, distinguished between the roles of 'complete observer' and 'participant-as-observer'.[9] Such a simple dichotomy is misleading, as Roth pointed out nearly twenty years ago.[10] Dissimulation, the giving of misleading information, lack of total 'openness', deceit and lying are a feature of many different types of social relationship, including social research.[11] In observational studies where the observer does not conceal his identity, he may nevertheless fail to be completely open and frank about his or her purposes and interests. Covert participant observation is defined for present purposes as referring to research situations where the real identity of the observer as a social researcher (like that of the Deputy-Director of IUEF as a government spy) remains secret and entirely unknown to those with whom he is in contact. The researcher in that situation purports to be a complete participant, and is in fact something else.

Some classic cases

Brief descriptions of several classic cases will make clear some of the features of covert observation.

(1) FRANZ BOAS ALLEGES SPYING ON THE PART OF ANTHRO-
    POLOGISTS

In 1919, Franz Boas, the dominant figure in American anthropology, wrote to *The Nation* that '[b]y accident, incontro-
vertible proof has come to my hands that at least four men
who carry on anthropological work, while employed as
government agents, introduced themselves to foreign governments as representatives of scientific institutions in the United
States, and as sent out for the purposes of carrying out
scientific researches. They have not only shaken the belief in
the truthfulness of science, but they have also done the
greatest possible disservice to scientific inquiry . . . The very
essence of (the scientist's) life is the service of truth . . . A
person who uses science as a cover for political spying, who
demands himself to pose before a foreign government as an
investigator and asks for assistance in his alleged researches
in order to carry on, under this cloak, his political machinations,
prostitutes science in an unpardonable way and forfeits the
right to be classed as a scientist.'[12] The allegations related to
'research' in Central America, including one anthropologist
for whom Boas had personally provided an introduction.
Boas argued that whereas soldiers, diplomats, politicians and
businessmen might set patriotic devotion above everyday
decency, the scientist's calling, the search for truth, made
certain very special demands. Boas's allegations were not well
received by his professional colleagues, mainly for reasons to
do with his own power and influence, internal tensions within
anthropology, and post-First World War anti-German feeling,
which are fully described by Stocking.[13] The case is of
interest as an extreme instance of alleged covert observation.

(2) BRUNO BETTELHEIM ANALYSES THE CONCENTRATION-
    CAMP EXPERIENCE

In 1938, following the German invasion, the Austrian scholar
Bruno Bettelheim was interned in a Nazi concentration camp.
To cope with the physical and psychological trauma which it
involved, he decided to study the social and psychological
dynamics of camp life, in order to keep himself alive. He
therefore devoted much time while in the camp to the

observation of the behaviour of both guards and inmates, and attempted to understand it. Why, for example, did guards sometimes behave brutally and sometimes reasonably humanely? Why did some camp inmates adopt the values and beliefs of the Nazis, while others became 'human corpses'? How did inmates adapt to the constant threat of physical and psychological terror? Bettelheim did not of course tell anyone what he was doing. After a year in two camps, he was released in 1939 and went to America. His (now classic) account of his experiences — written from the standpoint of analytic psychology — was rejected by several professional journals (whose editors believed its data exaggerated or unverifiable) before being published in the *Journal of Abnormal and Social Psychology* in 1943.[14] Subsequently he wrote more fully of his experience in *The Informed Heart*.[15] This classic research was 'done' using the methods of secret participant observation, albeit of an extreme and unique kind.

(3) SOCIOLOGISTS STUDY THE AMERICAN AIRMAN

In the early 1950's three American sociologists, Mortimer Sullivan, Stuart A. Queen and Ralph Patrick, studied the process of training new airmen (other ranks) in the American Air Force.[16] To do this, it was decided that a research officer should 'enlist' as a basic trainer. He would behave and be treated as a fully-fledged participant. His identity, mission and role would only be known to the researchers, and to no one else, not even his commanding officer. To carry out this research, the 'trainee' 'enlisted' and was 'discharged' under an assumed name, with falsified education. In the nine months prior to enlistment he developed a 'new personality', was coached in the ways of adolescent subculture, given the age of nineteen rather than his real age of twenty-six, lost 35 pounds in weight and underwent minor plastic surgery to alter his appearance. He cultivated a new 'biography', inventing a fictitious family history consonant with his new research personality. The study was justified on the grounds that it was the only way 'to gather a body of previously unavailable information and to interpret it in a way that might be helpful both to the military and to social scientists'.[17]

(4) A SOCIAL PSYCHOLOGIST STUDIES THE MENTAL HOSPITAL

Around 1950 William Caudill, an American anthropologist with interests in psychology, took part in a research project to study some of the social and medical problems of life in a mental hospital as seen from the patient's point of view. He was admitted to the hospital in the role of a patient. Known only to two senior members of staff, he was admitted as a *bona fide* patient resident in the hospital, and was treated there for two months. The story which he invented to tell his psychotherapist (who did not know that he was there as a covert observer) was that 'he had recently been trying to finish the writing of a scholarly book, but felt that he was not getting ahead; worry over his work drove him to alcoholic episodes ending in fights; he was withdrawn and depressed, and had quarrelled with his wife, who had then separated from him. Beyond these fictions, the observer gave a somewhat distorted picture of his own life, in which he consciously attempted to suppress his own solutions to certain problems and to add a pattern of neurotic defences.'[18] In an article published shortly after, the research team claimed that this use of covert observation, despite its (ethical and personal) disadvantages, yielded a rich body of research data concerning the social situation of patients on the ward, many of which were previously unrecognised.[19]

The Debate Over Ethics

These four cases demonstrate many of the features of covert observation which will be discussed in later chapters of the book. The research described by Rosenhan in Chapter 2, for example, bears some resemblance to that carried out by Caudill. The research discussed by Holdaway in Chapter 4 bears some slight resemblance to the army research by Sullivan *et al.* The questions which all four cases raise include: Are such research methods ethical? Are they justifiable in order to further the cause of social science? Do the benefits to be derived from such research outweigh the risks involved? Do the ends justify the means?

Different answers have been given to these questions in the debate over the ethics of covert observational methods which has gone on over the last quarter of a century.[20] The very liveliness of this debate, to which this book is intended to be a further contribution, suggests that there are no simple and universally-agreed answers to these questions. It is misleading to dichotomise the positions taken up too sharply, but the clearest statements have been made by those who attack or defend such methods most vehemently.

One of the most effective attacks was made by Kai T. Erikson in 1967 in 'A Comment on Disguised Observation in Sociology', in which he argued that 'the practice of using masks in social research compromises both the people who wear them and the people for whom they are worn, and in doing so violates the terms of a contract which the sociologist should be ready to honour in his dealings with others'.[21] Four kinds of relationship are involved. First, the sociologist has responsibilities to the subjects of research. Secret research can injure other people in ways that cannot be anticipated in advance or compensated for afterwards. The method has at least *some* potential to do (unforeseeable) harm. If subjects know they are being studied, at least they have agreed to expose themselves to possible harm. To study them secretly is ethically comparable to a doctor who carries out medical experiments on human subjects without their agreement. Second, the sociologist has responsibilities to his colleagues. Covert observation is liable to damage the general reputation of sociology and close off further avenues for research. For this reason, covert observation should be of concern to all sociologists. Third, most of those who get involved in covert observation are graduate students. Since covert research poses serious ethical problems and often results in personal stress for the observer, it is unreasonable to use a method, the burden of which will fall upon those still dependent upon their academic elders. The sociologist's relationship to his students should proscribe its use.

Erikson's final and strongest argument is that covert research is bad science. The complexities of human social interaction are but imperfectly understood. To believe that it is possible to conceal one's identity from others by playing a

covert role is highly problematical. It is by no means clear
that those who do research in this way really succeed in
becoming full participants accepted as such by others. The
rationale of the method therefore falls away, and the quality
of the data collected by its use is liable to bias, distortion and
error. In summary, Erikson's position is that '(1) it is unethical
for a sociologist to deliberately misrepresent his identity for
the purpose of entering a private domain to which he is not
otherwise eligible; and (2) it is unethical for a sociologist to
deliberately misrepresent the character of the research upon
which he is engaged'.[22]

The contrary view, that covert research is a necessary,
useful and revealing method, has been argued forcefully by
Jack D. Douglas in *Investigative Social Research*.[23] Douglas
explicitly disavows ethical judgements upon the methods he
uses, and does not discuss 'the tortured moral arguments'
over covert methods. His reason for doing so is that '[a]nyone
who really knows what goes on in American society, and who
has any sense of fairness and practicality, will immediately
recognise that all of our [research] methods are by comparison still genteel and relatively harmless'.[24]

The prime objective of sociology should be the search for
the truth. What is the social context in which truth is to be
sought? Conventional accounts of participant observation
stress the need to co-operate with informants, establish trust,
create empathy between researcher and subject, and be
relatively open about what one is doing. Such conventional
procedures rest upon a consensual view of society in terms of
social order. In fact, the nature of contemporary society is
best described by a conflict model. 'Profound conflicts of
interest, values, feeling and action pervade social life . . .
Conflict is the reality of life; suspicion is the guiding principle
. . . It's a war of all against all and no one gives anyone anything
for nothing, especially for the truth.'[25]

The social researcher is therefore entitled and indeed
compelled to adopt covert methods. Social actors employ lies,
fraud, deceit, deception and blackmail in dealings with each
other, therefore the social scientist is justified in using them
where necessary in order to achieve the higher objective of
scientific truth. The model for investigative social research is

provided by 'spies, counterspies, police, detectives, prosecutors, judges, psychiatrists, tax collectors, probation officers . . . investigative journalists' and others who all seek to uncover, for various purposes, different aspects of the workings of modern society.[26] One particular journalistic exposé, Woodward and Bernstein's work on Watergate, is seen as exemplifying this approach.[27]

It is not argued by Douglas that the social researcher should *always* use such methods; co-operative methods are also sometimes appropriate. Part of the standard repertory of sociological research practices should, however, be the use of undercover observational methods in some circumstances for some purposes. The end of science overrides criticisms which might be made of the means used to that end.

Such contrasting ethical standpoints are not peculiar to participant observation research in particular, nor to sociology in general. The problems faced by sociologists are shared by many other practitioners — for example, doctors and clergymen — some of whom have very well developed ethical guidelines for decision-making.[28] The ethics of social research are not therefore peculiar, but they do provide an instructive case study of some of the dilemmas which face the scientist trying to reconcile different objectives. The complexity of ethical decision-making is recognised in this collection by the variety of views put forward about the merits of covert observation. Some, such as Edward Shils, adopt a position close to that of Erikson. Others, such as John F. Galliher, tend towards the position argued by Douglas, though their own standpoint is distinct. Sissela Bok takes an intermediate position and emphasises the difficulties of framing absolute moral rules for research behaviour.

The contributions to the debate are organised in two groups. First, there are five chapters describing and discussing the ethics of actual covert studies, involving researchers posing as mental patients, homosexual lookouts, members of the police, and members of political and religious groups. These chapters both bring out the dilemmas of the covert role and point up sharply the ethical issues involved. Some, such as D. L. Rosenhan, believe that covert methods are justified. Others, such as D. P. Warwick, do not believe that they are. The second group of five chapters carries on the debate in more general terms, though still in relation to empirical studies, again displaying a wide variety of views, most sharply in the exchange between Norman Denzin and Kai Erikson. In conclusion, the editor tries to draw some of the threads together and presents his own personal assessment.

Part Two

Empirical Field Research using Covert Methods

2 On Being Sane in Insane Places*

D. L. Rosenhan

If sanity and insanity exist, how shall we know them?

The question is neither capricious nor itself insane. However much we may be personally convinced that we can tell the normal from the abnormal, the evidence is simply not compelling. It is commonplace, for example, to read about murder trials wherein eminent psychiatrists for the defence are contradicted by equally eminent psychiatrists for the prosecution on the matter of the defendent's sanity. More generally, there are a great deal of conflicting data on the reliability, utility and meaning of such terms as 'sanity', 'insanity', 'mental illness', and 'schizophrenia'.[1] Finally, as early as 1934, Benedict suggested that normality and abnormality are not universal.[2] What is viewed as normal in one culture may be seen as quite aberrant in another. Thus, notions of normality and abnormality may not be quite as accurate as people believe they are.

To raise questions regarding normality and abnormality is in no way to question the fact that some behaviors are deviant or odd. Murder is deviant. So, too, are hallucinations. Nor does raising such questions deny the existence of the personal

* Reprinted from *Science* **179**, 19 January 1973, pp. 250–8, with the permission of the publisher and the author. © American Association for the Advancement of Science 1973.

anguish that is often associated with 'mental illness'. Anxiety and depression exist. Psychological suffering exists. But normality and abnormality, sanity and insanity, and the diagnoses that flow from them may be less substantive than many believe them to be.

At its heart, the question of whether the sane can be distinguished from the insane (and whether degrees of insanity can be distinguished from each other) is a simple matter: do the salient characteristics that lead to diagnoses reside in the patients themselves or in the environments and contexts in which observers find them? From Bleuler, through Kretchmer, through the formulators of the recently revised *Diagnostic and Statistical Manual* of the American Psychiatric Association, the belief has been strong that patients present symptoms, that those symptoms can be categorised and, implicitly, that the sane are distinguishable from the insane. More recently, however, this belief has been questioned. Based in part on theoretical and anthropological considerations, but also on philosophical, legal, and therapeutic ones, the view has grown that psychological categorisation of mental illness is useless at best and downright harmful, misleading and pejorative at worst. Psychiatric diagnoses, in this view, are in the minds of the observers and are not valid summaries of characteristics displayed by the observed.[3,4,5]

Gains can be made in deciding which of these is more nearly accurate by getting normal people (that is, people who do not have, and have never suffered, symptoms of serious psychiatric disorders) admitted to psychiatric hospitals and then determining whether they were discovered to be sane and, if so, how. If the sanity of such pseudopatients were always detected, there would be prima facie evidence that a sane individual can be distinguished from the insane context in which he is found. Normality (and presumably abnormality) is distinct enough that it can be recognised wherever it occurs, for it is carried within the person. If, on the other hand, the sanity of the pseudopatients were never discovered, serious difficulties would arise for those who support traditional modes of psychiatric diagnosis. Given that the hospital staff was not incompetent, that the pseudopatient had been behaving as sanely as he had been outside of the hospital, and that it had never been previously suggested that he belonged in a psychiatric hospital, such an unlikely outcome would support the view that psychiatric diagnosis betrays little about the patient but much about the environment in which an observer finds him.

This chapter describes such an experiment. Eight sane people gained secret admission to 12 different hospitals.[6] Their diagnostic experiences constitute the data of the first part of this article; the remainder is devoted to a description of their experiences in psychiatric institutions. Too few psychiatrists and psychologists, even those who have worked in such hospitals, know what the experience is like. They rarely talk about it with former patients, perhaps because they distrust information coming from the previously insane. Those who have worked in psychiatric hospitals are likely to have adapted so thoroughly to the settings that they are insensitive to the impact of that experience. And while there have been occasional reports of researchers who submitted themselves to psychiatric hospitalisation[7], these researchers have commonly remained in the hospitals for short periods of time, often with the knowledge of the hospital staff. It is difficult to know the extent to which they were treated like patients or like research colleagues. Nevertheless, their reports about the inside of the psychiatric hospital have been valuable. This chapter extends those efforts.

Pseudopatients and Their Settings

The eight pseudopatients were a varied group. One was a psychology graduate student in his 20s. The remaining seven were older and 'established'. Among them were three psychologists, a pediatrician, a psychiatrist, a painter, and a housewife. Three pseudopatients were women, five were men. All of them employed pseudonyms, lest their alleged diagnoses embarrass them later. Those who were in mental health professions alleged another occupation in order to avoid the special attentions that might be accorded by staff, as a matter of courtesy or caution, to ailing colleagues.[8] With the exception of myself (I was the first pseudopatient and my presence was known to the hospital administrator and chief psychologist and, so far as I can tell, to them alone), the presence of pseudopatients and the nature of the research program was not known to the hospital staff.[9]

The settings were similarly varied. In order to generalise the findings, admission into a variety of hospitals was sought. The 12 hospitals in the sample were located in five different states on the East and West coasts. Some were old and shabby, some were quite new. Some were research-oriented, others not. Some had good staff—patient ratios, others were quite understaffed. Only one was a strictly private hospital. All of the others were supported by state or federal state funds or, in one instance, by university funds.

After calling the hospital for an appointment, the pseudo-patient arrived at the admissions office complaining that he had been hearing voices. Asked what the voices said, he replied that they were often unclear, but as far as he could tell they said 'empty', 'hollow', and 'thud'. The voices were unfamiliar and were of the same sex as the pseudopatient. The choice of these symptoms was occasioned by their apparent similarity to existential symptoms. Such symptoms are alleged to arise from painful concerns about the perceived meaninglessness of one's life. It is as if the hallucinating person were saying, 'My life is empty and hollow'. The choice of these symptoms was also determined by the *absence* of a single report of existential psychoses in the literature.

Beyond alleging the symptoms and falsifying name, vocation, and employment, no further alterations of person, history, or circumstances were made. The significant events of the pseudopatient's life were presented as they had actually occurred. Relationships with parents and siblings, with spouse and children, with people at work and in school, consistent with the aforementioned exceptions, were described as they were or had been. Frustrations and upsets were described along with joys and satisfactions. These facts are important to remember. If anything, they strongly biased the subsequent results in favor of detecting sanity, since none of their histories or current behaviors were seriously pathological in any way.

Immediately upon admission to the psychiatric ward, the pseudopatient ceased simulating *any* symptoms of abnormality. In some cases, there was a brief period of mild nervousness and anxiety, since none of the pseudopatients really believed that they would be admitted so easily. Indeed, their shared fear was that they would be immediately exposed as frauds and greatly embarrassed. Moreover, many of them had never visited a psychiatric ward; even those who had, nevertheless had some genuine fears about what might happen to them. Their nervousness, then, was quite appropriate to the novelty of the hospital setting, and it abated rapidly.

Apart from the short-lived nervousness, the pseudopatient behaved on the ward as he 'normally' behaved. The pseudo-patient spoke to patients and staff as he might ordinarily. Because there is uncommonly little to do on a psychiatric ward, he attempted to engage others in conversation. When asked by staff how he was feeling, he indicated that he was fine, that he no longer experienced symptoms. He responded to instructions from attendants, to calls for medication (which was not swallowed), and to dining-hall instructions. Beyond such activities as were available to him on the admissions ward, he spent his time writing down his observations about the ward, its patients, and the staff. Initially these notes were written 'secretly', but as it soon became clear that no one much cared, they were subsequently written on standard tablets of paper in such public places as the dayroom. No secret was made of these activities.

The pseudopatient, very much as a true psychiatric patient, entered a hospital with no foreknowledge of when he would be discharged. Each was told that he would have to get out by his own devices, essentially by convincing the staff that he was sane. The psychological stress associated with hospital-isation were considerable, and all but one of the pseudo-patients desired to be discharged almost immediately after being admitted. They were, therefore, motivated not only to behave sanely, but to be paragons of co-operation. That their behavior was in no way disruptive is confirmed by nursing reports, which have been obtained on most of the patients. These reports uniformly indicate that the patients were 'friendly', 'co-operative', and 'exhibited no abnormal indica-tions'.

The Normal Are Not Detectably Sane

Despite their public 'show' of sanity, the pseudopatients were never detected.

Admitted, except in one case, with a diagnosis of schizophrenia[10] each was charged with a diagnosis of schizophrenia 'in remission'. The label 'in remission' should in no way be dismissed as a formality, for at no time during any hospitalisation had any question been raised about any pseudopatient's simulation. Nor are there any indications in the hospital records that the pseudopatient's status was suspect. Rather, the evidence is strong that, once labeled schizophrenic, the pseudopatient was stuck with this label. If the pseudopatient was to be discharged, he must naturally be 'in remission'; but he was not sane, nor, in the institution's view, had he ever been sane.

The uniform failure to recognise sanity cannot be attributed to the quality of the hospitals for, although there were considerable variations among them, several are considered excellent. Nor can it be alleged that there was simply not enough time to observe the pseudopatients. Length of hospitalisation ranged from 7 to 52 days, with an average of 19 days. The pseudopatients were not, in fact, carefully observed, but this failure clearly speaks more to traditions within psychiatric hospitals than to lack of opportunity.

Finally, it cannot be said that the failure to recognise the pseudopatients' sanity was due to the fact that they were not behaving sanely. While there was clearly some tension present in all of them, their daily visitors could detect no serious behavioral consequences — nor, indeed, could other patients. It was quite common for the patients to 'detect' the pseudopatients' sanity. During the first three hospitalisations, when accurate counts were kept, 35 of a total of 118 patients on the admissions ward voiced their suspicions, some vigorously. 'You're not crazy. You're a journalist, or a professor [referring to the continual note-taking]. You're checking up on the hospital.' While most of the patients were reassured by the pseudopatient's insistence that he had been sick before he came in but was fine now, some continued to believe that the pseudopatient was sane throughout his hospitalisation.[11] The fact that the patients often recognised normality when staff did not raises important questions.

Failure to detect sanity during the course of hospitalisation may be due to the fact that physicians operate with a strong bias toward what statisticians call the type 2 error.[5] This is to say that physicians are more inclined to call a healthy person sick (a false positive, type 2) than a sick person healthy (a false negative, type 1). The reasons for this are not hard to find: it is clearly more dangerous to misdiagnose illness than health. Better to err on the side of caution, to suspect illness even among the healthy.

But what holds for medicine does not hold equally well for psychiatry. Medical illnesses, while unfortunate, are not commonly pejorative. Psychiatric diagnoses, or the contrary, carry with them personal, legal, and social stigmas.[12] It was therefore important to see whether the tendency toward diagnosing the sane insane could be reversed. The following experiment was arranged at a research and teaching hospital whose staff had heard these findings but doubted that such an error could occur in their hospital. The staff was informed that at some time during the following 3 months, one or more pseudopatients would attempt to be admitted into the psychiatric hospital. Each staff member was asked to rate each patient who presented himself at admissions or on the ward according to the likelihood that the patient was a pseudopatient. A 10-point scale was used, with a 1 and 2 reflecting high confidence that the patient was a pseudopatient.

Judgements were obtained on 193 patients who were admitted for psychiatric treatment. All staff who had had sustained contact with or primary responsibility for the patient — attendants, nurses, psychiatrists, physicians, and psychologists — were asked to make judgements. Forty-one patients were alleged, with high confidence, to be pseudo-patients by at least one member of the staff. Twenty-three were considered suspect by at least one psychiatrist. Nineteen were suspected by one psychiatrist *and* one other staff member. Actually, no genuine pseudopatient (at least from my group) presented himself during this period.

The experiment is instructive. It indicates that the tendency to designate sane people as insane can be reversed when the stakes (in this case, prestige and diagnostic acumen) are high. But what can be said of the 19 people who were suspected of being 'sane' by one psychiatrist and another staff member? Were these people truly 'sane', or was it rather a case that in the course of avoiding the type 2 error the staff tended to make more errors of the first sort — calling the crazy 'sane'? There is no way of knowing. But one thing is certain: any diagnostic process that lends itself so readily to massive errors of this sort cannot be a very reliable one.

The Stickiness of Psychodiagnostic Labels

Beyond the tendency to call the healthy sick — a tendency that accounts better for diagnostic behavior on admission than it does for such behavior after a lengthy period of exposure — the data speak to the massive role of labeling in psychiatric assessment. Having once been labeled schizophrenic, there is nothing the pseudopatient can do to overcome the tag. The tag profoundly colors others' perceptions of him and his behavior.

From one viewpoint, these data are hardly surprising, for it has long been known that elements are given meaning by the context in which they occur. Gestalt psychology made this point vigorously, and Asch[13] demonstrated that there are 'central' personality traits (such as 'warm' versus 'cold') which are so powerful that they markedly color the meaning of other information in forming an impression of a given personality.[14] 'Insane', 'schizophrenic', 'manic-depressive', and 'crazy' are probably among the most powerful of such central traits. Once a person is designated abnormal, all of his other behaviors and characteristics are colored by that label. Indeed, that label is so powerful that many of the pseudopatients' normal behaviors were overlooked entirely or profoundly misinterpreted. Some examples may clarify this issue.

Earlier I indicated that there were no changes in the pseudopatient's personal history and current status beyond those of name, employment, and, where necessary, vocation. Otherwise, a veridical description of personal history and circumstances was offered. Those circumstances were not psychotic. How were they made consonant with the diagnosis of psychosis? Or were those diagnoses modified in such a way as to bring them into accord with the circumstances of the pseudopatient's life, as described by him?

As far as I can determine, diagnoses were in no way affected by the relative health of the circumstances of a pseudopatient's life. Rather, the reverse occurred: the perception of his circumstances was shaped entirely by the diagnosis. A clear example of such translation is found in the case of a pseudopatient who had had a close relationship with his mother but was rather remote from his father during his early childhood. During adolescence and beyond, however, his father became a close friend, while his relationship with his mother cooled. His present relationship with his wife was characteristically close and warm. Apart from occasional angry exchanges, friction was minimal. The children had rarely been spanked. Surely there is nothing especially pathological about such a history. Indeed, many readers may see a similar pattern in their own experiences, with no markedly deleterious consequences. Observe, however, how such a history was tranlated in the psychopathological context, this from the case summary prepared after the patient was discharged.

> This white 39-year-old male . . . manifests a long history of considerable ambivalence in close relationships, which begins in early childhood. A warm relationship with his mother cools during his adolescence. A distant relationship to his father is described as becoming very intense. Affective stability is absent. His attempts to control emotionality with his wife and children are punctuated by angry outbursts and, in the case of the children, spankings. And while he says that he has several good friends, one senses considerable ambivalence embedded in those relationships also.

The facts of the case were unintentionally distorted by the staff to achieve consistency with a popular theory of the dynamics of a schizophrenic reaction.[15] Nothing of an ambivalent nature had been described in relations with parents, spouse, or friends. To the extent that ambivalence could be inferred, it was probably not greater than is found in all human relationships. It is true the pseudopatient's relationships with his parents changed over time, but in the ordinary context that would hardly be remarkable — indeed, it might very well be expected. Clearly, the meaning ascribed to his verbalisations (that is, ambivalence, affective instability) was determined by the diagnosis: schizophrenia. An entirely different meaning would have been ascribed if it were known that the man was 'normal'.

All pseudopatients took extensive notes publicly. Under ordinary circumstances, such behavior would have raised questions in the minds of observers, as, in fact, it did among patients. Indeed, it seemed so certain that the notes would elicit suspicion that elaborate precautions were taken to remove them from the ward each day. But the precautions proved needless. The closest any staff member came to questioning these notes occurred when one pseudopatient asked his physician what kind of medication he was receiving and began to write down the response. 'You needn't write it,' he was told gently. 'If you have trouble remembering, just ask me again.'

If no questions were asked of the pseudopatients, how was their writing interpreted? Nursing records for three patients indicate that the writing was seen as an aspect of their pathological behavior. 'Patient engages in writing behavior' was the daily nursing comment on one of the pseudopatients who was never questioned about his writing. Given that the patient is in the hospital, he must be psychologically disturbed. And given that he is disturbed, continuous writing must be a behavioral manifestation of that disturbance, perhaps a subset of the compulsive behaviors that are sometimes correlated with schizophrenia.

One tacit characteristic of psychiatric diagnosis is that it locates the sources of aberration within the individual and only rarely within the complex of stimuli that surrounds him. Consequently, behaviors that are stimulated by the environment are commonly misattributed to the patient's disorder. For example, one kindly nurse found a pseudopatient pacing the long hospital corridors. 'Nervous, Mr X?' she asked. 'No, bored,' he said.

The notes kept by pseudopatients are full of patient behaviors that were misinterpreted by well-intentioned staff. Often enough, a patient would go 'berserk' because he had, wittingly or unwittingly, been mistreated by, say, an attendant. A nurse coming upon the scene would rarely inquire even cursorily into the environmental stimuli of the patient's behavior. Rather, she assumed that his upset derived from his pathology, not from his present interactions with other staff members. Occasionally, the staff might assume that the patient's family (especially when they had recently visited) or other patients had stimulated the outburst. But never were the staff found to assume that one of themselves or the structure of the hospital had anything to do with a patient's behavior. One psychiatrist pointed to a group of patients who were sitting outside the cafeteria entrance half an hour before lunchtime. To a group of young residents he indicated that such behavior was characteristic of the oral-acquisitive nature of the syndrome. It seemed not to occur to him that there were very few things to anticipate in a psychiatric hospital besides eating.

A psychiatric label has a life and an influence of its own. Once the impression has been formed that the patient is schizophrenic, the expectation is that he will continue to be schizophrenic. When a sufficient amount of time has passed, during which the patient has done nothing bizarre, he is considered to be in remission and available for discharge. But the label endures beyond discharge, with the unconfirmed expectation that he will behave as a schizophrenic again. Such labels, conferred by mental health professionals, are as influential on the patient as they are on his relatives and friends, and it should not surprise anyone that the diagnosis acts on all of them as a self-fulfilling prophecy. Eventually, the patient himself accepts the diagnosis, with all of its surplus meanings and expectations, and behaves accordingly.[5]

The inferences to be made from these matters are quite simple. Much as Zigler and Philips have demonstrated that there is enormous overlap in the symptoms presented by patients who have been variously diagnosed,[16] so there is enormous overlap in the behaviors of the sane and the insane. The sane are not 'sane' all of the time. We lose our tempers 'for no good reason'. We are occasionally depressed or anxious, again for no good reason. And we may find it difficult to get along with one or another person — again for no reason that we can specify. Similarly, the insane are not always insane. Indeed, it was the impression of the pseudopatients while living with them that they were sane for long periods of time — that the bizarre behaviors upon which their diagnoses were allegedly predicated constituted only a small fraction of their total behavior. If it makes no sense to label ourselves permanently depressed on the basis of an occasional depression, then it takes better evidence than is presently available to label all patients insane or schizophrenic on the basis of bizarre behaviors or cognitions. It seems more useful, as Mischel[17] has pointed out, to limit our discussions to *behaviors*, the stimuli that provoke them, and their correlates.

It is known why powerful impressions of personality traits, such as 'crazy' or 'insane', arise. Conceivably, when the origins of and stimuli that give rise to a behavior are remote or unknown, or when the behavior strikes us as immutable, trait labels regarding the *behaver* arise. When, on the other hand, the origins and stimuli are known and available, discourse is limited to the behavior itself. Thus, I may hallucinate because I am sleeping, or I may hallucinate because I have ingested a peculiar drug. These are termed sleep-induced hallucinations, or dreams, and drug-induced hallucinations, respectively. But when the stimuli to my hallucinations are unknown, that is called craziness, or schizophrenia — as if that inference were somehow as illuminating as the others.

The Experience of Psychiatric Hospitalisation

The term 'mental illness' is of recent origin. It was coined by people who were humane in their inclinations and who wanted very much to raise the station of (and the public's sympathies toward) the psychologically disturbed from that of witches and 'crazies' to one that was akin to the physically ill. And they were at least partially successful, for the treatment of the mentally ill *has* improved considerably over the years. But while treatment has improved, it is doubtful that people really regard the mentally ill in the same way that they view the physically ill. A broken leg is something one recovers from, but mental illness allegedly endures forever.[18] A broken leg does not threaten the observer, but a crazy schizophrenic? There is by now a host of evidence that attitudes toward the mentally ill are characterised by fear, hostility, aloofness, suspicion, and dread.[19] The mentally ill are society's lepers.

That such attitudes infect the general population is perhaps not surprising, only upsetting. But that they affect the professionals — attendants, nurses, physicians, psychologists, and social workers — who treat and deal with the mentally ill is more disconcerting, both because such attitudes are self-evidently pernicious and because they are unwitting. Most mental health professionals would insist that they are sympathetic toward the mentally ill, that they are neither avoidant nor hostile. But it is more likely that an exquisite ambivalence characterises their relations with psychiatric patients, such that their avowed impulses are only part of their entire attitude. Negative attitudes are there too and can easily be detected. Such attitudes should not surprise us. They are the natural offspring of the labels patients wear and the places in which they are found.

Consider the structure of the typical psychiatric hospital. Staff and patients are strictly segregated. Staff have their own living space, including their dining facilities, bathrooms, and assembly places. The glassed quarters that contain the professional staff, which the pseudopatients came to call 'the cage', sit out on every dayroom. The staff emerge primarily for caretaking purposes — to give medication, to conduct a therapy or group meetings, to instruct or reprimand a patient. Otherwise, staff keep to themselves, almost as if the disorder that afflicts their charges is somehow catching.

So much is patient–staff segregation the rule that, for four public hospitals in which an attempt was made to measure the degree to which staff and patients mingle, it was necessary to use 'time out of the staff cage' as the operational measure. While it was not the case that all time spent out of the cage was spent mingling with patients (attendants, for example, would occasionally emerge to watch television in the dayroom), it was the only way in which one could gather reliable data on time for measuring.

The average amount of time spent by attendants outside of the cage was 11.3 per cent (range, 3 to 52 per cent). This figure does not represent only time spent mingling with patients, but also includes time spent on such chores as folding laundry, supervising patients while they shave, directing ward clean-up, and sending patients to off-ward activities. It was the relatively rare attendant who spent time talking with patients or playing games with them. It proved impossible to obtain a 'percent mingling time' for nurses, since the amount of time they spent out of the cage was too brief. Rather, we counted instances of emergence from the cage. On the average, daytime nurses emerged from the cage 11.5 times per shift, including instances when they left the ward entirely (range, 4 to 39 times). Late afternoon and night nurses were even less available, emerging on the average 9.4 times per shift (range, 4 to 41 times). Data on early morning nurses, who arrived usually after midnight and departed at 8 a.m., are not available because patients were asleep during most of this period.

Physicians, especially psychiatrists, were even less available. They were rarely to be seen on the wards. Quite commonly, they would be seen only when they arrived and departed, with the remaining time being spent in their offices or in the cage. On the average, physicians emerged on the ward 6.7 times per day (range, 1 to 17 times). It proved difficult to make an accurate estimate in this regard, since physicians often maintained hours that allowed them to come and go at different times.

The hierarchical organisation of the psychiatric hospital has been commented on before,[20] but the latent meaning of that kind of organisation is worth noting again. Those with the most power have least to do with patients, and those with the least power are most involved with them. Recall, however, that the acquisition of role-appropriate behaviors occurs mainly through the observation of others, with the most powerful having the most influence. Consequently, it is understandable that attendants not only spend more time with patients than do any other members of the staff — that is required by their station in the hierarchy — but also, insofar as they learn from their superiors' behavior, spend as little time with patients as they can. Attendants are seen mainly in the cage, which is where the models, the action, and the power are.

I turn now to a different set of studies, these dealing with staff response to patient-initiated contact. It has long been known that the amount of time a person spends with you can be an index of your significance to him. If he initiates and maintains eye contact, there is reason to believe that he is considering your requests and needs. If he pauses to chat or actually stops and talks, there is added reason to infer that he is individuating you. In four hospitals, the pseudopatient approached a staff member with a request which took the following form: 'Pardon me, Mr [or Dr or Mrs] X, could you tell me when I will be eligible for grounds privileges?' (or '. . . when I will be presented at the staff meeting?' or ' . . . when I am likely to be discharged?') While the content of the question varied according to the appropriateness of the target and the pseudopatient's (apparent) current needs the form was always a courteous and relevant request for information. Care was taken never to approach a particular member of the staff more than once a day, lest the staff member become suspicious or irritated. In examining these data, remember that the behavior of the pseudopatients was neither bizarre nor disruptive. One could indeed engage in good conversation with them.

The data for these experiments are shown in Table 2.1 separately for physicians (column 1) and for nurses and attendants (column 2). Minor differences between these four institutions were overwhelmed by the degree to which staff avoided continuing contacts that patients had initiated. By far, their most common response consisted of either a brief response to a question, offered while they were 'on the move' and with head averted, or no response at all.

The encounter frequently took the following bizarre form: (pseudopatient) 'Pardon me, Dr X. Could you tell me when I am eligible for grounds privileges?' (physician) 'Good morning, Dave. How are you today?' (Moves off without waiting for a response.)

It is instructive to compare these data with data recently obtained at Stanford University. It has been alleged that large

TABLE 2.1 *Self-initiated contact by pseudopatients with psychiatrists and nurses and attendants, compared to contact with other groups*

Contact	Psychiatric hospitals		University campus (nonmedical)	University medical center Physicians		
	(1) Psychiatrists	(2) Nurses and attendants	(3) Faculty	(4) 'Looking for a psychiatrist'	(5) 'Looking for an internist'	(6) No additional comment
Responses						
Moves on, head averted (%)	71	88	0	0	0	0
Makes eye contact (%)	23	10	0	11	0	0
Pauses and chats (%)	2	2	0	11	0	10
Stops and talks (%)	4	0.5	100	78	100	90
Mean number of questions answered (out of 6)	*	*	6	3.8	4.8	4.5
Respondents (No.)	13	47	14	18	15	10
Attempts (No.)	185	1283	14	18	15	10

*Not applicable

and eminent universities are characterised by faculty who are so busy that they have no time for students. For this comparison, a young lady approached individual faculty members who seemed to be walking purposefully to some meeting or teaching engagement and asked him the following six questions.

(1) 'Pardon me, could you direct me to Encina Hall?' (at the medical school: ' . . . to the Clinical Research Center?').

(2) 'Do you know where the Fish Annex is?' (there is no Fish Annex at Stanford).

(3) 'Do you teach here?'

(4) 'How does one apply for admission to the college?' (at the medical school: ' . . . to the medical school?').

(5) 'Is it difficult to get in?'

(6) 'Is there financial aid?'

Without exception, as can be seen in Table 2.1 (column 3), all of the questions were answered. No matter how rushed they were, all respondents not only maintained eye contact, but stopped to talk. Indeed, many of the respondents went out of their way to direct or take the questioner to the office she was seeking, to try to locate 'Fish Annex', or to discuss with her the possibilities of being admitted to the university.

Similar data, also shown in Table 2.1 (columns 4, 5, and 6), were obtained in the hospital. Here too, the young lady came prepared with six questions. After the first question, however, she remarked to 18 of her respondents (column 4), 'I'm looking for a psychiatrist', and to 15 others (column 5), 'I'm looking for an internist'. Ten other respondents received no inserted comment (column 6). The general degree of cooperative responses is considerably higher for these university groups than it was for pseudopatients in psychiatric hospitals. Even so, differences are apparent within the medical school setting. Once having indicated that she was looking for a psychiatrist, the degree of cooperation elicited was less than when she sought an internist.

Powerlessness and Depersonalisation

Eye contact and verbal contact reflect concern and individuation; their absence, avoidance and depersonalisation. The

data I have presented do not do justice to the rich daily
encounters that grew up around matters of depersonalisation
and avoidance. I have records of patients who were beaten by
staff for the sin of having initiated verbal contact. During my
own experience, for example, one patient was beaten in the
presence of other patients for having approached an attendant
and told him, 'I like you'. Occasionally, punishment meted
out to patients for misdemeanors seemed so excessive that it
could not be justified by the most radical interpretations of
psychiatric canon. Nevertheless, they appeared to go unques-
tioned. Tempers were often short. A patient who had not
heard a call for medication would be roundly excoriated, and
the morning attendants would often wake patients with,
'Come on, you m-----f-----s, out of bed!'

Neither anecdotal nor 'hard' data can convey the overwhelming sense of powerlessness which invades the individual
as he is continually exposed to the depersonalisation of the
psychiatric hospital. It hardly matters *which* psychiatric
hospital — the excellent public ones and the very plush private
hospital were better than the rural and shabby ones in this
regard, but, again, the features that psychiatric hospitals had
in common overwhelmed by far their apparent differences.

Powerlessness was evident everywhere. The patient is
deprived of many of his legal rights by dint of his psychiatric
commitment.[21] He is shorn of credibility by virtue of his
psychiatric label. His freedom of movement is restricted. He
cannot initiate contact with the staff, but may only respond
to such overtures as they make. Personal privacy is minimal.
Patient quarters and possessions can be entered and examined
by any staff member, for whatever reason. His personal
history and anguish is available to any staff member (often
including the 'grey lady' and 'candy striper' volunteer) who
chooses to read his folder, regardless of their therapeutic
relationship to him. His personal hygiene and waste evacuation
are often monitored. The water closets may have no doors.

At times, depersonalisation reached such proportions that
pseudopatients had the sense that they were invisible, or at
least unworthy of account. Upon being admitted, I and other
pseudopatients took the initial physical examinations in a

semipublic room, where staff members went about their own business as if we were not there.

On the ward, attendants delivered verbal and occasionally serious physical abuse to patients in the presence of other observing patients, some of whom (the pseudopatients) were writing it all down. Abusive behavior, on the other hand, terminated quite abruptly when other staff members were known to be coming. Staff are credible witnesses. Patients are not.

A nurse unbuttoned her uniform to adjust her brassiere in the presence of an entire ward of viewing men. One did not have the sense that she was being seductive. Rather she didn't notice us A group of staff persons might point to a patient in the dayroom and discuss him animatedly, as if he were not there.

One illuminating instance of depersonalisation and invisibility occurred with regard to medications. All told, the pseudopatients were administered nearly 2100 pills, including Elavil, Stelazine, Compazine and Thorazine, to name but a few. (That such a variety of medications should have been administered to patients presenting identical symptoms is itself worthy of note.) Only two were swallowed. The rest were either pocketed or deposited in the toilet. The pseudopatients were not alone in this. Although I have no precise records on how many patients rejected their medications, the pseudopatients frequently found the medications of other patients in the toilet before they deposited their own. As long as they were cooperative, their behavior and the pseudopatients' own in this matter, as in other important matters, went unnoticed throughout.

Reactions to such depersonalisation among pseudopatients were intense. Although they had come to the hospital as participant observers and were fully aware that they did not 'belong', they nevertheless found themselves caught up in and fighting the process of depersonalisation. Some examples: a graduate student in psychology asked his wife to bring his textbooks to the hospital so he could 'catch up on his homework' — this despite the elaborate precautions taken to conceal his professional association. The same student, who had trained for quite some time to get into the hospital, and who had looked forward to the experience, 'remembered' some drag races that he had wanted to see on the weekend insisted that he be discharged by that time. Another pseudo-patient attempted a romance with a nurse. Subsequently, he informed the staff that he was applying for admission to graduate school in psychology and was very likely to be admitted, since a graduate professor was one of his regular hospital visitors. The same person began to engage in psychotherapy with other patients — all of this as a way of becoming a person in an impersonal environment.

The Sources of Depersonalisation

What are the origins of depersonalisation? I have already mentioned two. First are attitudes held by all of us toward the mentally ill — including those who treat them — attitudes characterised by fear, distrust and horrible expectations on the one hand, and benevolent intentions on the other. Our ambivalence leads, in this instance as in others, to avoidance.

Second, and not entirely separate, the hierarchical structure of the psychiatric hospital facilitates depersonalisation. Those who are at the top have least to do with patients, and their behavior inspires the rest of the staff. Average daily contact with psychiatrists, psychologists, residents, and physicians combined ranged from 3.9 to 25.1 minutes, with an overall mean of 6.8 (six pseudopatients over a total of 129 days of hospitalisation). Included in this average are time spent in the admissions interview, ward meetings in the presence of a senior staff member, group and individual psychotherapy contacts, case presentation conferences, and discharge meetings. Clearly, patients do not spend much time in inter-personal contact with doctoral staff. And doctoral staff serve as models for nurses and attendants.

There are probably other sources. Psychiatric installations are presently in serious financial straits. Staff shortages are pervasive, staff time at a premium. Something has to give, and that something is patient contact. Yet, while financial stresses are realities, too much can be made of them. I have the impression that the psychological forces that result in depersonalisation are much stronger than the fiscal ones and that the addition of more staff would not correspondingly improve patient care in this regard. The incidence of staff meetings and the enormous amount of record-keeping on patients, for example, have not been as substantially reduced as has patient contact. Priorities exist, even during hard times. Patient contact is not a significant priority in the traditional psychiatric hospital, and fiscal pressures do not account for this. Avoidance and depersonalisation may.

Heavy reliance upon psychotropic medication tacitly contributes to depersonalisation by convincing staff that treatment is indeed being conducted and that further patient contact may not be necessary. Even here, however, caution needs to be exercised in understanding the role of psychotropic drugs. If patients were powerful rather than powerless, if they were viewed as interesting individuals rather than diagnostic entities, if they were socially significant rather than social lepers, if their anguish truly and wholly compelled our sympathies and concerns, would we not *seek* contact with them, despite the availability of medications? Perhaps for the pleasure of it all?

The Consequences of Labeling and Depersonalisation

Whenever the ratio of what is known to what needs to be known approaches zero, we tend to invent 'knowledge' and assume that we understand more than we actually do. We seem unable to acknowledge that we simply don't know. The needs for diagnosis and remediation of behavioral and emotional problems are enormous. But rather than acknowledge that we are just embarking on understanding, we continue to label patients 'schizophrenic', 'manic-depressive', and 'insane', as if in those words we had captured the essence of understanding. The facts of the matter are that we have known for a long time that diagnoses are often not useful or reliable, but we have nevertheless continued to use them. We now know that we can not distinguish insanity from sanity. It is depressing to consider how that information will be used.

Not merely depressing, but frightening. How many people, one wonders, are sane but not recognised as such in our psychiatric institutions? How many have been needlessly stripped of their privileges of citizenship, from the right to vote and drive to that of handling their own accounts? How many have feigned insanity in order to avoid the criminal consequences of their behavior, and, conversely, how many would rather stand trial than live interminably in a psychiatric hospital — but are wrongly thought to be mentally ill? How many have been stigmatised by well-intentioned, but nevertheless erroneous, diagnoses? On the last point, recall again that a 'type 2 error' in psychiatric diagnosis does not have the same consequences it does in medical diagnosis. A diagnosis of cancer that has been found to be in error is cause for celebration. But psychiatric diagnoses are rarely found to be in error. The label sticks, a mark of inadequacy forever.

Finally, how many patients might be 'sane' outside the psychiatric hospital but seem insane in it — not because craziness resides in them, as it were, but because they are responding to a bizarre setting, one that may be unique to institutions which harbor nether people? Goffman[4] calls the process of socialisation to such institutions 'mortification' — an apt metaphor that includes the processes of depersonalisation that have been described here. And while it is impossible to know whether the pseudopatients' responses to these processes are characteristic of all inmates — they were, after all, not real patients — it is difficult to believe that these processes of socialisation to a psychiatric hospital provide useful attitudes or habits of response for living in the 'real world'.

Summary and Conclusions

It is clear that we cannot distinguish the sane from the insane in psychiatric hospitals. The hospital itself imposes a special environment in which the meanings of behavior can easily be misunderstood. The consequences to patients hospitalised in such an environment — the powerlessness, depersonalisation, segregation, mortification, and self-labeling — seem undoubtedly countertherapeutic.

I do not, even now, understand this problem well enough to perceive solutions. But two matters seem to have some promise. The first concerns the proliferation of community mental health facilities, of crisis intervention centers, of the human potential movement, and of behavior therapies that, for all of their own problems, tend to avoid psychiatric labels, to focus on specific problems and behaviors, and to retain the individual in a relatively non-pejorative environment. Clearly, to the extent that we refrain from sending the distressed to insane places, our impressions of them are less likely to be distorted. (The risk of distorted perceptions, it seems to me, is always present, since we are much more sensitive to an individual's behaviors and verbalisations than we are to the subtle contextual stimuli that often promote them. At issue here is a matter of magnitude. And, as I have shown, the magnitude of distortion is exceedingly high in the extreme context that is a psychiatric hospital.)

The second matter that might prove promising speaks to the need to increase the sensitivity of mental health workers and researchers to the *Catch 22* position of psychiatric patients. Simply reading materials in this area will be of help to some such workers and researchers. For others, directly experiencing the impact of psychiatric hospitalisation will be of enormous use. Clearly, further research into the social psychology of such total institutions will both facilitate treatment and deepen understanding.

I and the other pseudopatients in the psychiatric setting had distinctly negative reactions. We do not pretend to describe the subjective experiences of true patients. Theirs may be different from ours, particularly with the passage of time and the necessity process of adaptation to one's environment. But we can and do speak to the relatively more objective indices of treatment within the hospital. It could be a mistake, and a very unfortunate one, to consider that what happened to us derived from malice or stupidity on the part of the staff. Quite the contrary, our overwhelming impression of them was of people who really cared, who were committed and who were uncommonly intelligent. Where they failed, as they sometimes did painfully, it would be more accurate to attribute those failures to the environment in which they, too, found themselves than to personal callousness. Their perceptions and behavior were controlled by the situation, rather than being motivated by a malicious disposition. In a more benign environment, one that was less attached to global diagnosis, their behaviors and judgments might have been more benign and effective.[22]

3 *Tearoom Trade:* Means and Ends in Social Research*

Donald P. Warwick

We're so preoccupied with defending our privacy against insurance investigators, dope sleuths, counterespionage men, divorce detectives and credit checkers, that we overlook the social scientists behind the hunting blinds who're also peeping into what we thought were our most private and secret lives. But there they are, studying us, taking notes, getting to know us, as indifferent as everybody else to the feeling that to be a complete human being involves having an aspect of ourselves that's unknown.

Nicholas von Hoffman,
The Washington Post

Any man who remains in a public restroom for more than five minutes is apt to be either a member of the vice squad or someone on the make. As yet, he is not suspected of being a social scientist.

Laud Humphreys, *Tearoom Trade:
Impersonal Sex in Public Places,* p. 26

* Reprinted from *The Hastings Center Studies* 1, 1973, pp. 27–38, with the permission of The Hastings Center and the author. © Institute of Society, Ethics and the Life Sciences, 360 Broadway, Hastings-on-Hudson, NY 10706, USA 1973.

In the mid 1960's Laud Humphreys undertook an intensive sociological study of male homosexual activities in public restrooms. The results were published in 1970 in *Tearoom Trade*. (A 'tearoom' is a location in which homosexual encounters are reputed to take place.) Humphreys' methods were varied and painstaking, ranging from direct observation of homosexual acts in restrooms to a follow-up survey with men who were observed in these acts. That they were also controversial is made evident by the statement of Nicholas von Hoffman attacking the scope and methods of Humphreys' study and the growing intrusiveness of social research.

Humphreys' research provides a case study in the impact of social research on human freedom. I have chosen *Tearoom Trade* as an example partly because it is recent and controversial, partly because of its varied methodology, and partly because the author and his defenders comment explicitly on its research ethics. It is admittedly an extreme example in many respects, and it is far from typical of social scientific research. Most social scientists and social research institutes go to great lengths to avoid deception, misrepresentation, possible harm to respondents, and other problems arising in Humphreys' study of homosexuals. Because their continuing success depends precisely on maintaining the confidence and good will of the participating public, large survey research institutes are particularly scrupulous in this regard. Nevertheless, though *Tearoom Trade* is not typical, it is instructive in pointing up issues of ethics which arise in lesser degree in many other studies.[1]

The Sociologist as Watchqueen

To grasp the implications of Humphreys' research one must have a clear picture of his stragegy and tactics. Once he chose to train his sights on the problem of impersonal sex, he had to gain entry to the society of male homosexuals. Social deviants inside restrooms and elsewhere develop careful defenses against outsiders, including special gestures and extreme caution with strangers. After spending some time exploring various public restrooms, Humphreys discovered a relatively simple and convenient *entree* to observation: the role of 'watchqueen'.

> Fortunately, the very fear and suspicion of tearoom partici-
> pants produces a mechanism that makes such observation
> possible: a third man (generally one who obtains voyeuristic
> pleasures from his duties) serves as a lookout. Such a
> 'watchqueen', as he is labeled in the homosexual argot,
> coughs when a police car stops nearby or when a stranger
> approaches. He nods affirmatively when he recognises a
> man entering as being a 'regular'. Having been taught the
> watchqueen role by a cooperating respondent, I played the
> part faithfully while observing hundreds of acts of fellatio.[2]

To record the full details of his observations Humphreys made use of a 'Systematic Observation Sheet'. Space was provided for the time and place; the weather; the age, dress, general appearance, and automobile of the participants; their specific role in the activities; and a floorplan of the restroom. To be sure that the information was fresh, Humphreys took field notes *in situ* with the aid of a portable tape recorder hidden under a carton in the front seat of his car.

Through patient time-and-place sampling of selected sites he came up with a list of 134 active participants in fellatio. He also identified each participant (except two walkers) with an automobile and duly recorded its state and licence number. He then sought to learn more about these men by finding their names, addresses, and the year and make of their cars in state license registers. 'Fortunately, friendly policemen gave me access to the license registers, without asking to see the numbers or becoming too inquisitive about the type of "market research" in which I was engaged.'[3] With various kinds of attrition the final sample of identifiable tearoom participants dwindled to 100.

From the beginning Humphreys felt it important to do more than observe the minutiae of male homosexuality in tearooms. He also wanted to explore the social origins and present circumstances of the participants. The sample of 100 names and addresses provided an excellent opportunity to collect this information — if he could gain access to the individuals involved. Before moving to a fullscale household survey he spent a Christmas vacation recording a description of each individual's residence and neighborhood. But some questions could be answered only by personal interviews.

The author admits that this last stage of his data-collection efforts raised serious ethical problems. 'I already knew that many of my respondents were married and that all were in a highly discreditable position and fearful of discovery. How could I approach these covert deviants for interviews?'[4]

The solution was again ingenious. While conducting his own research Humphreys also held another position in which he was responsible for developing an interview schedule to be used in a 'social health survey' of a random sample of males in the community. 'With permission from the survey's directors, I could add my sample to the larger group (thus enhancing their anonymity) and interview them as part of the social health survey.'[5] The resulting 'random sample' consisted of addresses of 50 homosexual and 50 control respondents.

For various reasons Humphreys was anxious to interview the homosexual group himself, but he was also concerned that he might be recognised. To minimise this possibility he waited at least one year from the date of the original contacts, and changed his hair style, dress and car. He claims that none of the respondents recognised him or seemed unduly suspicious about the 'health survey', despite the fact that it contained questions about marital sexuality. It is possible, however, that a few respondents were better at disguising their emotions than the investigator was in detecting them.

The findings of the study were reported in two forms: statistical tables with the usual controls for occupation, marital status, age, etc.; and vignettes serving as case studies. The author claims that he went to unusual lengths to protect the confidentiality of the results without distorting them in the process. 'The question I have always asked myself in this connection is: Could the respondent still recognise himself without having any others recognise him? I may have failed in a few cases to meet the first part of this standard, but I am confident that I have not failed to meet the second.'[6]

How, then, should we evaluate the overall ethics of Humphreys' study or, for that matter, any piece of social scientific research? The task would be easier if we could dismiss the study as worthless sociology or incompetent research, but it is neither. The problem is that there are no well-developed and generally acceptable ethical standards for judging serious research. It is not just that social scientists disagree among themselves on ethics but that the conceptual-isation of ethical problems in research remains at a very low level, with some notable exceptions.[7] As a step toward improving the state of the art I suggest the concept of human freedom as one yardstick for assessing research. How would it apply to the Humphreys study?

Human Freedom

The notion of human freedom offers a useful vantage point for judging the impact of social research on both individuals and the larger society. It suggests a broader range of ethical criteria than the commonly-used yardsticks of 'privacy' and 'dignity', while it seems more manageable from a conceptual standpoint than the idea of 'rights'.

Human freedom may be defined for present purposes as *the capacity, opportunity and incentive to make reflective choices and to act on these choices*. This definition includes two elements on which there is substantial agreement among writers on freedom: (1) the individual's ability to choose among alternatives and to originate action; and (2) circum-stances in the environment which are favourable to the suggestion of alternatives and the execution of action. To be free a man must have certain qualities within himself which permit him to choose and act, and also live in an environment which aids choice and does not impede his actions. Hence we may distinguish between *personal freedom* and *environmental freedom*.[8]

Personal freedom, which might also be termed psychological or dispositional freedom, is built on personality tendencies which help the individual to make reflective choices and to act on these choices. Viewed positively, it consists of the ability and will to choose and act within the matrix of the opportunities provided by the society within which one lives. Viewed negatively, it is the absence of fear, anxiety, defense mechanisms and other psychic qualities which impair rationality or impede action. *Environmental freedom*, in turn, comes close to the concept of liberty in Anglo-American philosophy and law. It includes both the absence of external impediments to individual action and the presence of conditions, such as information, aiding reflection and choice.

To be fair to social research it is important to conceptualise freedom in a manner that permits improvements as well as impairment. Too often discussions of ethics and the social sciences view research as a process which can only *limit* human freedom through such means as deception or invasions of privacy. What we need now is a kind of benefit/cost matrix permitting estimates of the net gains and losses for freedom involved in a given study.

Freedom for Whom?

Whose freedom should be considered, and what weight, in judging the ethics of social research? In the case of research involving human subjects at least four parties are involved: the individual participant (subject, respondent), the researcher, the larger society, and the researcher's profession. Many of the ethical problems in research spring from conflicts between the freedoms of these four parties. The researcher will usually place strong emphasis on the freedom of scientific inquiry. Social scientists typically justify incursions into the private life of participants on the grounds that free men have the right to know, that scientific knowledge is the basis of social progress, or that the specific knowledge generated by their research will contribute to the alleviation of some pressing social problem. But these claims may conflict with the individual citizen's desire for a sense of dignity and a private sphere of existence. Similarly, the investigator's research procedures may enhance his freedom of inquiry at the expense of other members of his own and perhaps related professions. If Humphreys' study contributes to public suspicion about the trustworthiness of social scientists, as I think it does, then my freedom and that of my professional colleagues to do our kinds of research will suffer accordingly. Hence one of the most difficult problems facing the social sciences is how to assign priorities when the freedoms of various parties are incompatible. As T. R. Vaughan writes:

> There is no natural law to which the scientist can appeal. Like others, he bases his decisions on personal predilections and particular values. But one person's predilections — be he scientist or saint — are not perforce more natural than another's. The proclivity among scientists to minimise, if not ignore, competing social ethics, and to define science in some independent sense, is quite widespread. In short, the scientist typically subscribes to the notion that the end of knowledge justifies the scientific means.[9]

The debate stirred up by *Tearoom Trade* aptly illustrates the conflict between the freedom of the researcher and that of other parties. Especially instructive in this regard was the exchange between Nicholas von Hoffman of the *Washington Post* and the editors of *Trans-Action,* Irving Louis Horowitz and Lee Rainwater. Von Hoffman's argument is well-stated in his final sentence. 'No information is valuable enough to obtain by nipping away at personal liberty, and that is true no matter who is doing the gnawing. John Mitchell and the conservatives over at the Justice Department or Laud Humphreys and the liberals over at the Sociology Department.' Horowitz and Rainwater (who were listed by Humphreys as advisors to his research) responded in an editorial entitled 'Sociological Snoopers and Journalistic Moralizers'. Von Hoffman is portrayed there as a journalistic poacher who had invaded the sacred preserves of sociology. His main intent is not to question the ethics of social research, but to give sociology a few knocks to keep it in place. He is thus linked to 'clergymen, politicians, and intellectuals generally' who are envious of sociology's rising power because it is a threat to their own.

Social Research and the Individual Participant

Some of the most critical questions of ethics in social research deal with its impact on the individual participant, such as the respondents in Humphreys' study. Following the approach to freedom suggested earlier, we can point to positive as well as negative effects of the research process on such individuals.

Benefits

What are some of the ways in which social research might enhance the personal freedom of the participant? Let us take survey research as an example. Critics of this method commonly emphasise the inconvenience and intrusions associated with surveys, but they overlook a number of satisfactions which it can provide.

First, individuals who know something about surveys may find in them an opportunity for self-expression. People often derive satisfaction from providing information or expressing an opinion on subjects in which they are interested. Often this satisfaction is enhanced when the resulting information may have some effect on the policies of a nation, community or employer. Another positive effect may stem from inter-personal response — the satisfaction found in sharing important events in one's life with a sympathetic listener. In Humphrey's study twelve of the men observed in public restrooms agree to be interviewed in some detail about their background and experiences. The author's account suggests that these men, who were told the purpose of the study, may have found it helpful to discuss their lives and problems with an outsider. A third positive quality is the sheer intellectual challenge of some studies. Respondents will often agree to be interviewed to satisfy their curiosity about what goes on in surveys and polls or to reduce loneliness and boredom. Fourth, the interview may lead to insights which are helpful and rewarding. There is some evidence, for example, that interviews following upon personal or social disasters, such as suicides among family members or deaths caused by tornadoes, help the respondent to make sense of highly confusing experiences. These four conditions can be considered positive contributors to individual freedom to the extent that they provide the individual with opportunities for self-expression or contribute to a reduction of fear and anxiety.

Costs

Every method of social research using live human subjects entails certain potential risks or hazards to the freedom of the individuals involved. Foremost among these are deception, invasions of privacy, and harmful uses of the research findings.

Deception. Humphreys' research provides a unique case study of deception. The concatenation of misrepresentation and disguises in this effort must surely hold the world record for field research. Consider the following:

(1) In the initial stages the author spent several months passing as a deviant ('another gay guy') in private gatherings, gay bars, an annual ball, a local bathhouse, movie theaters, and tearooms. 'On one occasion, for instance, tickets to an after hours party were sold to the man next to me at a bar. When I asked to buy one, I was told that they were "full up". Following the tip of another customer, I showed up anyway and walked right in.'[10] All of this was to tool up for passing in closer quarters.

(2) Humphreys misrepresented his identity while serving as 'watchqueen' in the public restrooms. While carrying out his duties in this role he gave no indication to the lead actors about his real reasons for being there. He defends his actions on the following grounds:

> Since one's identity within the interaction membrane of the tearoom is represented only in terms of the participant role he assumes, there was no misrepresentation on my part as an observer: I was indeed a 'voyeur', though in the sociological and not the sexual sense. My role was primarily that of watchqueen, and that role I played well and faithfully. In that setting, then, I misrepresented my identity no more than anyone else.[11]

Humphreys gives himself away with his comments on being a 'voyeur'. It is clear that he represented himself to the participants as a voyeur in the *sexual* sense, and made himself credible in that role by acting as the good and faithful watchqueen. Also, it is plain that he did misrepresent his identity more than others, save visiting policemen or blackmailers.

The men who came to the tearooms saw each other accurately — as individuals seeking a certain type of satisfaction with anonymity and little commitment. Humphreys came there *primarily* as a sociologist carrying out research on deviance.

(3) Humphreys disguised the fact that he was making an oral record of his observations by hiding a tape recorder in the front seat of his car. The point of this procedure was to avoid the possibility that those frequenting nearby tearooms would discover his true identity.

(4) He deceived the police about the nature of his study ('market research') in order to gain access to automobile license registers.

(5) In carrying out the household survey he allowed a year to lapse from the time of the original contacts and changed his appearance, attire, and automobile to avoid being recognised as the watchqueen. Is this deception? The author denies any false representation in this procedure, resorting again to the 'two hats' argument. 'I wore only one of two possible hats, rather than going in disguise.'[12] The only problem is that while changing hats he also changed the hair styles, looks, and clothes beneath them and switched cars.

(6) Presumably when he introduced the study he told the respondents that they were part of a random cross-section sample chosen to represent the whole metropolitan area, that this was a 'social health survey of men in the community', and that they were anonymous. If so, the first point is a grave misrepresentation of the actual sampling procedures, the second is at best misleading and incomplete, while the third is simply untrue (he knew their names). There would be fewer problems, on the other hand, if the respondents were told that the information was confidential, rather than anonymous. Though Humphreys does not go into detail about his procedures, he implies that the participants were promised anonymity.

(7) In a larger sense, both Humphreys and the project director of the 'social health survey' may have distorted that study by allowing a sub-sample of 50 homosexuals to be blended into the total cross-section. Random (probability) sampling is generally understood to include only those processes of selection in which the units of the sample are chosen

by 'chance' methods. Though Humphreys tried to adhere to this canon in choosing his own sample, it is hard to see how these individuals could be treated in one moment as persecuted social deviants and in the next as representative males in the metropolitan area.

Humphreys justifies his research tactics on the grounds of 'situation ethics'.

> As I learned during the time I administered examinations in Christian Ethics to candidates for the priesthood, questions that arise in regard to means are always relative. There are no 'good' or 'bad' methods — only 'better' or 'worse' ones. Neither interview schedules nor laboratory experiments nor participant observation can be neatly classified as involving either 'open' or 'disguised' approaches. I have never known an interviewer to be completely honest with his respondents; were this so, the whole concern with constructing an 'effective' questionnaire could be dropped. Neither does any researcher ever have adequate insight for a perfect representation of his identity; it is always a matter of greater or lesser misrepresentation.[13]

This statement invites several comments. First, it is grossly misleading to imply that Christian ethics as a whole has embraced the absolute relativism of extreme situation ethics. Even a casual reading of recent work on the ethics of research should lay this notion to rest.[14] Second, and more serious, by the author's logic there is no *intrinsic* evil in any research procedure, including the medical experimentation carried out in Nazi Germany, the use of torture to determine the character of human behavior under extreme stress, or the injection of live cancer cells into healthy subjects without their knowledge or consent. None of these methods is *bad* — only *worse* in comparison with others. Admittedly the situation and circumstances are important considerations in evaluating the ethics of research, but Humphreys seems to rule out any notion of inviolable rights for the individual. This position seems curious in view of his absolute moral outrage at the situation of homosexuals in contemporary society. Third, the author is guilty of ethical sleight-of-hand in equating the seriousness of outright deception with situations in which researchers are not 'completely honest' with their subjects or try to construct an 'effective' questionnaire. Here we are very much in the realm of the relative, but important distinctions can still be drawn. For example, I know of no ethical theory holding that the individual should be *completely* honest with others in human interaction. Even if such honesty were possible, one could argue that it is destructive, and therefore unethical, to reveal all of our misgivings, hostilities, and affections toward others when first meeting them. It is possible, on the other hand, to provide survey respondents with a basically accurate statement on the scope and purposes of the research. They may not know much about survey research or the intricacies of data processing, but they can be given a fair idea of what they are getting into. This situation of roughly accurate but less than complete understanding is rather different than one in which the investigator deliberately misrepresents a study by leaving out important information about how and why the respondent was chosen, as in Humphreys' research.

Privacy. Privacy is related to personal freedom in the sense that certain aspects of the self are seen as inviolable or subject to discussion only under the most restricted conditions. A crucial part of freedom consists of the capacity and opportunity *not* to reveal or even discuss certain beliefs, attitudes and behaviors. The question raised by *Tearoom Trade* and other social research is how far the social scientist can intrude into the inner reaches of the self without jeopardising freedom. This problem is highlighted in the quotation by Nicholas von Hoffman at the beginning of this article.

The response to von Hoffman's criticism by the editors of *Trans-Action* is instructive. At first they are unwilling to take his charges seriously, and attempt to undercut them by an *ad hominem* counterattack.

> Von Hoffman seems to mean this to be a statement about the right to privacy in a legal sense, but it really represents a denial of the ability of people to understand themselves and each other in an existential sense. This denial masks a fear, not that intimate details of our lives will be revealed

to *others*, but rather that we may get to know *ourselves* better and have to confront what up to now we did not know about ourselves.[15]

In other words, von Hoffman's concern about the privacy of others covers up a deep fear of his own unconscious aroused by Humphreys' data.

Later, however, they admit that the study does involve a conflict between two goods: the right to know and the right to privacy. They then offer several lines of defense for Humphreys' methods. First, Humphreys had as much right as anyone else to be in the restrooms since they were public. This is true enough, except that the point of *Tearoom Trade* is to show that tightly private interaction networks develop in public places. Second, those who frequent tearooms run the risk 'that they have among them people who have ulterior purposes . . . The fact that in this instance there was a scientific rather than a criminal or sexual "ulterior motive" does not necessarily make it more hideous or more subject to criticism, but perhaps less so.'[16] This is certainly damning by faint defense. Third, it is Humphreys' obligation as a sociologist to pursue the truth, to create countervailing knowledge about homosexuality (against the police), and to demystify 'the shadowy areas of human experience'. Presumably these ends justify the means chosen, though the authors do not say precisely why or how far they would extend such legitimising power. Fourth, the law itself is vague from the definition of privacy and incidents constituting invasions of privacy. Until such definitions are clarified, Humphreys' research should not be criticised for invading privacy. One might counter by pointing out that changes and clarifications in the law are usually brought about in *response* to debate and criticism. In short, it is hard to escape the conclusion that, whatever the current state of legal definitions of privacy, Humphreys intruded much too far into the lives of the men he observed and studied. From now on tearoom participants must be on the alert not only for blackmailers and policemen, but for sociologists in voyeur's clothing.

Misuse of Information. One of the greatest fears plaguing any conscientious social scientist is that information collected with good intentions or given him in good faith by others will be used against them or bring them harm. The data collected by Humphreys could have been used either for purposes of blackmail or criminal prosecution. During the process of data-collection and analysis the master list of names was stored in a safe-deposit box, and then was later destroyed. (One would conclude from reading *Tearoom Trade* that the master list was still in the safe-deposit box. I learned about its destruction only through personal correspondence.) A critical problem with these and other social science data is that they enjoy no legal protection or privilege. This situation arises, of course, with hundreds of sociologists, social workers, newspaper reporters, and others who possess potentially damaging information. However, Humphreys was running unusual risks by collecting the kind of data he did. This is one of the few social scientific studies which would have lent itself directly to a grand jury investigation. Homosexuality, especially in public restrooms, is clearly a more sensitive and explosive subject than many of the topics on which social scientists collect potentially damaging data. Also, its sensitivity and potential harm to respondents were heightened by the fact that it dealt primarily with one city.

A second and equally grave problem is the anxiety produced among the individuals studied by the fact that *someone knows*. Probably some of the men are aware that they were studied as a result of the publication of *Tearoom Trade*. Moreover, unless they have read the book, they may not know of the precautions taken with the data and, even if they did, they would not know that the master file containing their names had been destroyed. Thus some may rightly wonder whether Humphreys or someone else will somehow reveal their indiscretions and thereby damage or destroy their reputation. It might be objected that the social scientist should not be responsible for the irrational fears of those he studies. My reply is that any conscientious professional person *must* be concerned about the anxiety he creates in people as a result of his work. This concern should be especially great when a researcher imposes himself on others for his own ends, without their knowledge. The men in the tearoom did not, after all, *ask* to be studied or helped.

Social Research and the Society

The intrusions of social research are commonly justified by the benefits it brings to the larger society. The census and sample surveys, for example, play a vital role in supplying governments with data needed for economic and social planning or action programs. However, social research must also be set in the context of a rising tendency to collect more data on individuals and groups, and increasing sophistication in the storage, retrieval, and analysis of these data. The growing prevalence of such research has raised doubts about the conventional liberal assumptions concerning the inherent value of information. These assumptions are clearly reflected in the *Trans-Action* editorial defending the research by Laud Humphreys.

> Sociologists have tended to assume that well-intentioned people fully accept the desirability of demystification of human life and culture. In the age of Aquarius, however, perhaps such a view will be recognised as naive.[17]

> The only indictment seems to be among those who are less concerned with the right to know than they are with the sublime desire to remain in ignorance. In other words, the issue is not liberalism or conservatism or privacy vs. publicity, but much more simply and to the point, the right of scientists to conduct their work as against the right of journalists to defend social mystery and private agony.[18]

The logic here is amazingly facile: the more information we have about society, the happier we will be. Those who collect it are contributing to the alleviation of social misery; those who oppose it force the oppressed to live on in agony. While some degree of demystification may contribute to human freedom, it seems absurd to assume that extreme demystification produces social bliss. Men in every age — including the social scientists of the present — need illusions to be free, if only the illusion of destroying the illusions of others.

Another possible reactive effect of social research is to reinforce the tendency of individuals to be wary and to live 'for the record'. Arthur Miller states one side of the problem as follows:

As the populace becomes increasingly aware that a substantial number of facts are being preserved 'on the record', people may start to doubt whether they have any meaning apart from the profile in the computer's files. As a result, they may begin to base their personal decisions, at least in part, on whether it will enhance their record image in the eyes of third parties who have control over important parts of their lives.[19]

Complaints along these lines have already been lodged against the secret files maintained by federal agencies on political dissenters. The kind of research carried out by Humphreys raises a similar problem: an increased fear among ordinary citizens that someone, be he a social scientist or a credit checker, is watching. An important part of human freedom is the ability to withdraw into our home or other private domain and feel that we will not be observed. To the extent that social scientists engage in covert observation, however noble the cause, this freedom will be reduced. It is only in a totalitarian society that one must constantly look over his shoulder or check under his bed to be sure that he is not being observed and heard. The social scientist will say, of course, that covert observation is still rare, and that it is often justified by the higher cause it serves, such as helping homosexuals. However, this argument can be applied with equal force by the FBI, salesmen posing as survey researchers, and credit checkers entering suburban homes under various guises. Everyone feels that *his* cause is of paramount importance, and that the abuses wrought by *his* intrusion are minimal. At this stage we must be concerned not only about the impact of the single intrusion, but also with the cumulative effects of thousands of acts of prying on the quality of human life.

The Researcher and the Research Professions

Humphreys' study further raises the question of the balance between the freedom of the individual researcher and that of his colleagues in allied professions. We might draw an analogy between social research and the growth of industry. Both

make use of scarce resources, and both may create environmental pollution preventing further expansion. The resources
consumed in social research include money, personnel,
public tolerance, and the good will of the participants — all
of which are finite. Just as the emission of industrial wastes
can pollute rivers, lakes, and the atmosphere, so can the
abuse of social research contaminate the environment for
other users. The most common and harmful abuses are the
sheer overexposure of the public to all types of research, and
illegal activities, deception, misrepresentation, or other
offensive behaviors on the part of researchers.

Viewed in this context the net effect of Humphreys' study
on the research environment is likely to be negative.
Undoubtedly public reaction to *Tearoom Trade* will be
strongly affected by the subject matter and the way in which
the findings are presented. Many readers, finding the whole
topic revolting, will channel their distaste against the author
and sociology in general. Indeed, Humphreys invites this
reaction by lacing the text with graphic detail that does not
seem to be called for by his scientific goals. Even so, I would
strongly defend Humphreys' right to study this topic, however controversial it might be. My objections are not to the
topic but to the tactics. Humphreys, however, sets himself
above considerations of appearances and public opinion.

> Concern about 'professional integrity', it seems to me, is
> symptomatic of a dying discipline. Let the clergy worry
> about keeping their cassocks clean; the scientist has too
> great a responsibility for such compulsion.[20]

Recent experience with field interviewing suggests that this
'public be damned' attitude is producing a growing backlash
against social research. Field directors of large survey organisations in the United States report that it has become increasingly difficult to obtain a high response rate in central city
areas. The reasons for this situation are complicated, but
fears of deception and misrepresentation, or sheer fatigue
with surveys, are certainly part of the problem. A study in
the United States shows that as of 1964, 250 communities in
34 states had passed legislation restricting the activities of

survey interviewers.[21] The degree of control varies from complete prohibition to the requirement that interviewers register with local law enforcement officials. It is reasonable to expect that the greater the nuisance value of social research, and the more social scientists are perceived as untrustworthy, the more difficult it will be to carry out any kind of field study. Indeed, a *lack* of concern for professional integrity may spell the death of field research.

There is always a danger that remarks such as these will be interpreted as a plea for safe, bland, non-controversial research which is controversial offensive to the public because of its subject matter, and studies which create ill-will, suspicion, and resentment because of Machiavellian methodology. C. Wright Mills carried out a great deal of research which was offensive to political conservatives because of its subject matter and conclusions, but to my knowledge he never engaged in deception or misrepresentation. Social scientists have not only a right but an obligation to study controversial and politically-sensitive subjects, including homosexuality, even if this brings down the wrath of the public and government officials. But this obligation does not carry with it the right to deceive, exploit, or manipulate people. My concern with backlash centers primarily on the alienation of ordinary individuals by research methods which leave them feeling that they have been cheated, deceived, or used. If social scientists set themselves, and their methods above society, they must be prepared to take the consequences. The brief history of the social sciences suggests that it is abuses of ordinary people, such as research subjects, rather than political controversy *per se* which generate pressures for legal restrictions on research.

Conclusions

We come, then, to the most basic question of all about Humphreys' study: should he have done it? The author himself asks:

> Are there, perhaps, some areas of human behavior that
> are not fit for social scientific study at all? Should sex,
> religion, suicide, or other socially sensitive concerns be
> omitted from the catalogue of possible fields of social
> research.[22]

Most of us in the social sciences would answer no, but these
are the wrong questions. The real issue at stake is not
whether male homosexuality or any other subject should be
studied, but whether the methods used are ethically justified.
In other words, does the end justify the means in social
research?

Humphreys clearly feels that *his* ends justify the means he
used. These ends, aside from the usual aim of increasing
scientific knowledge, center about improving the lost of
homosexuals in American society. One way to do so, he
argues, is to gather data which can be used as a contervailing
force against police repression of this group. He does not
make explicit, however, how this knowledge will benefit the
individuals in question, nor does he consider the hypothesis
that it could be used by the police to improve their means of
control. But perhaps his most basic argument is that
increased knowledge about homosexuality will stir a concern
in the larger society and perhaps lead to changes in present
repressive laws and practices. He writes:

> We are not, however, protecting a harrassed population by
> refusing to look at them. At this very moment my writing
> has been interrupted by a long distance call, telling me of
> a man whose career has been destroyed because he was
> 'caught' in a public restroom. . . . The greatest harm a
> social scientist could do this man would be to ignore him.
> Our concern about possible research consequences for our
> fellow 'professionals' should take a secondary place to
> concern for those who may benefit from our research.[23]

The author's concern for the suffering individual is
admirable, but his logic and ethics are not. Several assumptions in this passage are particularly dubious. First, the
notion that social scientists do positive harm to suffering

individuals by *not* studying them suggests a rather inflated sense of professional self-importance. I also wonder if the tearoom participants would agree that they would have been harmed by being left alone. Second, what is the factual basis for assuming that *Tearoom Trade* will ultimately alleviate the risks and suffering of male homosexuals in public restrooms? While this book has apparently been well-received in homosexual circles, my impression is that a widespread reading by the larger public might well produce negative rather than positive results.

But even if we grant that this research will ultimately help homosexuals, we come back to the very basic question of means and ends. Should every social scientist who feels that he has a laudable cause have the right to deceive respondents about the nature of surveys, engage in covert observation, and resort to other kinds of trickery? Should the same rights be extended to credit-checkers and the FBI, or do social scientists have special rights in the society? If a right-wing social scientist felt that the type of sociology practiced by Humphreys and advocated by his defenders constituted a threat to individual rights, and that these social scientists themselves needed help, would he be justified in sending covert observers to spy on their private lives? Whose causes are the right causes in social research? Neither Humphreys nor the editors of *Trans-Action* address themselves to these questions. They take the righteousness of their causes for granted, and assume that all men of good will should do likewise.

In sum, there are three ethical objections to the research tactics reported in *Tearoom Trade*. First, the researcher took advantage of a relatively powerless group of men to pursue his study. Had Humphreys passed as a voyeuristic gardener or chauffeur for a prominent family he would have been subject to legal and other kinds of retaliation. The men in the tearooms could not fight back. A critic might argue that Humphreys' subsequent acceptance by homophile organisations, including his election to a position on the National Committee for Sexual Civil Liberties, testifies to the fact that he did not exploit the people he studied. However, the men he studied are probably not represented in these organisations because of the covert nature of their activities. Even if they were, one could still object to the manipulations and deception of research subjects for whatever end. Second, through his research tactics Humphreys reinforces an image already prevalent in some circles that social scientists are sly tricksters who are not to be trusted. The more widespread this image becomes, the more difficult it will be for any social scientist to carry out studies involving active participants.

The third and strongest objection is that the use of deception, misrepresentation, and manipulation in social research encourages the same tendencies in other parts of society. A democratic nation is ultimately built upon respect for constitutional processes and restraint in the use of means. If one group arrogates to itself the right to use non-constitutional means for advancing its ends others will do likewise. The same lesson applies to the social sciences. If we claim that our causes justify the use of deception and manipulation, those advocating contrary causes will apply the same logic to their choice of means. When the issue of wire-tapping first came before the Supreme Court some forty years ago, Justice Brandeis warned against the damage that would be wrought by letting the government violate the law in the name of the law. He also warned that the doctrine of the end justifying the means would bring terrible retribution to the country. About the same time Aldous Huxley wrote, 'The end cannot justify the means for the simple and obvious reason that the means employed determine the nature of the ends produced.' Social research involving deception and manipulation ultimately helps produce a society of cynics, liars and manipulators, and undermines the trust which is essential to a just social order.

4 'An Inside Job': a case study of covert research on the police*

Simon Holdaway

In August 1975, after eleven years' service, I resigned from the British Police. Departure was bound to be difficult, despite my looking forward to new work as a university lecturer. This chapter is concerned with the ethics of my covert research, work conducted in the course of employment as a police sergeant in a busy, urban police sub-division. First, the setting of the research will be explained, including the assumptions I brought to it. After this, the methods used in the project, from access to publication, will be discussed with particular reference to ethical questions raised in the field-work situation and now, some five years after leaving the police service.

Ethics and Fieldwork – Some Assumptions

I worked as a constable for five years before secondment to Lancaster University. Study for 'A' level examinations and, later, undergraduate work in sociology combined with my commitment to Christian social ethics and, not unimportantly, marriage to a graduate in social science to spur my

* Original material © Simon Holdaway 1982.

desire to understand the institution I had joined from secondary school and the nature of the social structure of which it was a part. Although the conceptualisation of many highly questionable police practices as 'the occupational culture of policing' was analytically helpful, my moral distaste for such practices was not dulled.

From an early stage, I learned two things about sociology. First, it is not a final arbiter in ethical decision-making. Secondly, a direct fit between social policy and theoretical inference drawn from sociological research is rare. These statements might seem blindingly obvious — yet in much of our discipline a background of utopian simplicity lies behind a foreground of sociological complexity. However, we know that totally 'value-free' sociology is a myth. I am aware that if academic curiosity was a driving force behind my research, so that curiosity was tempered by moral concern to weigh police practice and, in the longer term, change it. The point is whether ethics are the tail that wags the researching dog; in participant observation, an issue decided contextually.[1]

When I returned to my force from university I had ideas of beginning a research project but also felt some measure of commitment to the police service, for they seconded me to study and shared some part in the first-class degree I was awarded. I also thought that they would be interested in the skills I had acquired during the course of my studies. In fact, the three senior officers of the division in which I was to work were uninterested in such matters; indeed, at initial interviews on return from university it was clear that they knew virtually nothing of my background. They told me that there would be no time for 'research' and that I should 'get into policing again'. For example, the officer in charge of my sub-division did not know that I was joining his staff until he received a call from the divisional office telling him that I was on the way to his station by car from the chief officer. He greeted me: '. . . the last thing I want is men with beards. I spend half my time telling men to get their hair cut' — continuing, 'You will have no time for research, we have to get on with policing the ground and haven't time for experiments. What I want is people who can lead men.'

I left for my station feeling intense frustration, hurt and

not a little anger. Despite having read numerous articles on the method of participant observation, not least, ways of gaining access to research, I found myself torn between opportunities for research and commitment to the police service. But such a beginning was parabolic; ethical decision-making is rarely a dispassionate, wholly objective enterprise.

It took some time to realise the pertinence of the senior officer's remarks that I should 'get into policing again', for they were urging me to rediscover that 'common-sense' of police work, the very theme of my research. This was also highly relevant to developments in published research on the police and, more generally, the sociology of deviance and social control. At Lancaster, I made particular study of symbolic interactionism and Schutz's social phenomenology, together with the associated method of participant observation. My understanding of deviance and social control was greatly influenced by the 'labelling perspective', agreeing with Park's dictum — at that time, in theory if not practice — that the sociologist 'should get the seat of his pants dirty with real research'.[2]

In 1973, the year I rejoined my force, two strands of thought dominated discussions of deviance and social control. On the one hand, a conflict theory of deviance, greatly influenced by Marxism, offered a placing of the labelling process within a social structural framework.[3] On the other hand, many were concerned with the issues raised by phenomenology and ethnomethodology, using the rule-based character of social life as a starting point of analysis. Despite their potential for using sensitive fieldwork methods, both perspectives were dominated by voluminous theoretical discourse which rarely pitted itself against data from conversation, observation or any source other than armchair debate. As far as work on the police was concerned, it seemed that the use of participant observation to gather some empirical evidence was a basic and necessary feature if either of these dominant strands were to prove their relevance.

Research on the police led me to the same conclusion. Banton's pioneering study, conducted mainly by interview but also involving observation, had been published for some time. Maureen Cain's doctoral thesis, based on some of

Banton's conclusions, was published in 1973. It indicated the defensiveness, interdependency, action orientation and virtual illegality of some central aspects of policing by the lower ranks of an inner city area. It was also apparent from Cain's report that, although researched several years before publication, her findings were highly pertinent to contemporary policing. While it was obvious that Cain had penetrated behind the 'front' of policing, more research of the occupational culture was required and, in order to do that, it would be necessary to document the handling of suspects in the charge room, their detention in the station, a far greater number of arrests and other 'crime-oriented' incidents than Cain had observed. I was also less than satisfied with a remark that Cain had spent a good deal of time cooking meals for the officers in their canteen and resting in parked vehicles — it crossed my mind that some management of the researcher might have been going on.[4]

Although separated by a different structural context, American research also demonstrated the importance of seeking to document policing in practice. Westley had researched the use of violence by an American force and Skolnick the discretionary powers of a specialist vice squad — virtually all the published research indicated that the legal framework of policing shielded a rather different practice and that it was the lower ranks who had the organisational power to work in the way they thought fit. I found myself in a situation where I could probe the occupational culture in a unique manner, adding to this body of knowledge.[5]

Two further points were important. First, a chief officer of my force interviewed me and suggested that I keep a diary which would provide a focus of interest during my routine work. I agreed with him, but did not ask how that diary might be used. Second, after I registered as a self-financed, part-time graduate student at a major university, my supervisor supported my ideas of a covert project but warned me strongly that the police, along with the Roman priesthood, were two occupations which, when studied by sociologists who have more than an intellectual curiosity in them, present sharp ethical problems.

I have now, so to speak, presented a case study in ethical

decision-making, articulating a number of personal moral values, the relevance of sociological research on the police, preferences in theory and social research methods and other information to aid the decision of what form any research should take. Six major options were open:

(A) Seek the permission of the chief officer to research, giving full details of method and intention.
(B) Seek permission as above, so phrasing the research description that it disguised my real intentions.
(C) Seek permission of lower ranks, later requesting more formal acceptance from senior officers.
(D) Do no research.
(E) Resign from the police service.
(F) Carry out covert research.

I chose the final option without much difficulty. From the available evidence, it seemed the only realistic option; alternatives were unrealistic or contained an element of the unethical which bore similarity to covert observation. I believe that my senior officers would have either refused permission to research or obstructed me. Option B is as dishonest a strategy as covert research, if the latter is thought dishonest. For example, if I were a Marxist and wanted to research the police and declared my Marxism, I know that I would be denied research access; yet to 'front' myself in a different research guise is surely dishonest. Option C could not have been managed. D denies the relevance of my studies and Option E would have been its logical progression — yet I felt an obligation to return to the police who had financed my study.

I chose covert research. My access to the police was not simply for the purpose of research for I was and had been a police officer for a considerable number of years. Unlike Festinger, Humphreys, Lofland or Rosenhan, I was legally employed by the police, without funding from a research-oriented organisation and already very familiar with the institution I was rejoining.[6] Any deception involved at this early stage of access was moderated; indeed, I would argue that my course of action was the only viable one.

Further factors influenced and strengthened my decision. As a legally empowered police officer I was the member of a powerful institution of our society and I would, though not exclusively, deal with the less powerful. The argument that all individuals have a right to privacy, that is to say freedom from observation, investigation and subsequent publication based on the investigation, is strong but it should be qualified when applied to the police.

Research. and my previous experience of the police demonstrated the power of the lower ranks, not least their resistance to external control of their work. Any effective research strategy would have to pierce that protective shield if it was to be successful. This much is true of research on many organisations; however, the necessity of covert research is strengthened by the central and powerful situation of the police within our social structure. The police are said to be accountable to the rule of law, a constitutional feature which restricts their right to privacy, but which they neutralise by the maintenance of a protective occupational culture. When such an institution is highly secretive and protective its members restrict any right to privacy they already have. It is crucial that they are researched.[7]

It might be argued that senior police officers could use management techniques to change the practices found amongst lower ranks. Again, research and my own experience confirmed that in the police, managerial control is minimal and it would be highly restrictive to place one's data in the hands of senior officers, believing that they could alter the practice of policing by the lower ranks. In these circumstances, all ranks in the police restrict their right to privacy and the opportunity to deal with their own affairs. The covert researcher of the police has to be reminded that he is working within an extremely powerful organisation which requires its public and private practice to be revealed on the basis of first-hand observation. In part, therefore, my covert observation was justified by an assessment of the power of the police within British society and their demonstrably secretive character.

This, however, is not to argue that covert research is ethical when conducted on so-called 'powerful groups' and unethical when the sociologist acts as 'zoo-keeper' of the powerless. Indeed, when one researches the police, data on the less powerful in our society (not all of it entirely complimentary) is inevitably collected. For example, there were occasions when I was subject to false allegations of violence from black youths. Research of less powerful groups by covert means can suggest rebuttal of 'common-sense' claims of their behaviour. The major point is that an ethical decision should consciously take all the available evidence into account, explore all options and, as far as possible, the likely effects of research on the parties involved. We should remember Roth's point that the final objectives of research are rarely known at an early stage but, nevertheless, the onus is on the researching sociologist to demonstrate why and how they took the decision to research covertly.

Into Research — Defining the Limits

Having made the decision in principle to conduct covert research, I had to face its practical implications. This was none the easier for my being a police sergeant, holding all the legal powers of that office as well as being responsible for the supervision of a large number of officers who would be working according to the rules of the occupational culture. I was not a sociology lecturer masquerading as a schizophrenic, alcoholic, millenarianist, pentecostalist or factory worker; I actually was a police officer who had no idea of when or if he would leave the field setting for other work. That, as will be seen, was the cause of considerable personal stress.

Although my research was the first to be conducted by a serving police officer in Britain, four American studies have been published by sociologists who joined the police, Richard Harris, George Kirkham, Jonathan Rubinstein and John Van Maanen. Harris researched a training school, Rubinstein was trained as a police officer but conducted his research as an unarmed civilian observer, as did Van Maanen. Only Kirkham entered training school and then acted as a police reservist, mainly to check his criticisms of the police against what he considered to be the reality. Neither Harris nor Rubinstein offers full discussion of their problems of observing police work. Van Maanen does give an extremely comprehensive account of his research methods and states that he did not document incidents where the law was broken. However, he does not write of how he actually handled ethical problems. It is left to Kirkham, funded to write by 'Americans for Effective Law Enforcement Inc.', to explain: 'Once quick to drop critical barbs [about the police] I now became extremely sensitive about such remarks – and several times became engaged in heated arguments over them.' In fact, although what Kirkham describes as central to policing might prove an object lesson for academic criticism, he could equally have recalled his lectures on methodology – a better example of 'going native' could not be found. We are left totally unaware of Kirkham's limits of tolerance in ethical decision-making.[8]

Unlike experimental, questionnaire and other highly controlled methods, covert research is highly unpredictable. Those who are being researched control the situation as much as the researcher, and when the context of the research is the police, whose job is highly unpredictable and various, none the less so when the researcher is a serving police officer, the definition of limits of ethical tolerance is a highly significant matter. Codes like those recently adopted by the British Psychological Association deal with predictable and planned research, conditions which are not present in fieldwork – indeed, their absence is the very reason for naturalistic methods to be chosen.

As I began police duty I asked myself what I would do if, as happened to William Westley, a police officer hit a suspect in my presence? What would happen if, as happened to Skolnick, highly questionable techniques of securing an arrest came to my knowledge? These sociologists had to cope with such ethical issues, but they were not police officers also fulfilling supervisory responsibilities.

I soon discovered that contemplating ethical problems which *might* arise spoiled my ability to document with detail. However, the police unknowingly provided me with a pilot study where I was able to learn how to handle such issues – or so I thought – before being transferred to another station and a substantive research project. My chief officer posted me to a small station where, with two other sergeants, I shared charge of about twelve constables. During my first week's duty, I was station officer. A man was arrested for driving whilst unfit through drink and I dealt with the charge. He was exceedingly uncooperative and I suspected that sooner or later he would be hit by a police officer; I took firm control of the situation. For a brief period the prisoner was alone with me, he standing and I sitting on opposite sides of a desk. Suddenly, he dashed for the door and, finding it incorrectly unlocked, ran for the street. I shouted and chased, catching him at the entrance to the station. As I brought him back, other officers arrived. The rules of the occupational culture direct that such a negation of police control should be redressed with physical contact. I did not offer that contact and my colleagues saw that I did not. In this way, I defined a limit of tolerance but only the most cursory of fieldwork notes were recorded.

Three nights later, I dealt with a man who had threatened his wife with a pistol. He pleaded his innocence and a police officer kicked him on the backside, not with force but just to remind him that his explanation was unacceptable. I recorded this incident and omitted that the prisoner had been kicked; it was too sensitive an issue for me to accept.

These situations continued. I recorded in my diary:

> It is still a problem working with another police officer who has very different ideas about civil liberties — patrolling with Sergeant X, in this case. Every time we stopped someone I had to manage a situation in which the possibilities of corners being cut were real. This causes strain for the sociological observer.

That impersonal sociological observer was me and I had to realise that I was actually involved in grappling with these difficult ethical issues.

I also soon learnt that I was gaining access to and recording very private and, I do not use the word lightly, precious moments of people's lives. For example, I was called by two constables — as a result of their shock rather than for any other reason — to deal with the sudden death of a young baby. The mother was utterly distraught, hysterical with grief and she made some remarks about her marriage. Was I to record these remarks? — No.

I well remember wrapping the baby in a blanket and holding it in my arms as, with two silent colleagues, I was driven to the mortuary. The attendant took the child and in a routine fashion 'placed' it into refrigeration. A colleague later said that he felt like 'putting one on the attendant for the way he treated the child'. I later classified the conversations about this incident in the terse category of jokes and stories, for it proved to be the genesis of an idea about the use of humour to manage the personal stress of police work. I should also add that incidents like this one reminded me of what policemen are required to do in the course of their work and that they really are very human — here I take Kirkham's point as something the researcher needs to be reminded of.

During these first two months and thereafter I found that I was accumulating considerable amounts of data but could not make much sense of them. My academic supervisor was supportive and encouraging but I was very dissatisfied with my situation and applied for an academic job which, thankfully, I did not get. One of my former lecturers wrote to me saying, 'It's easier to sustain the effort when you know that your sentence is to end.' He also added that research was 99 per cent perspiration and 1 per cent inspiration. Indeed it was; I wanted an end to my sentence.

Much of my frustration was vented on the senior officers who were reporting on my progress and suitability for substantive promotion to sergeant. I had demonstrated my values to the constables through my own example and when tea mugs belonging to the shift were changed, we were presented with colours to suit our personality — mine was yellow. 'Why yellow?' I asked naively. 'Because you're scared.' This designation did not exclude me from hearing about others' work, but it did exclude me from dealing with some of their work.

If the constables thought I was 'yellow', senior officers found me truculent, and one reported that he doubted if my attitudes suited the police service. I later complained of his insensitivity to another senior officer. He put it that 'You might disagree with Mr . . . but do you disagree with 99 per cent of the officers at the station?' We talked and he later explained, 'There are two important things about police work. First, policemen must be willing to cut corners or else they would never get their job done. Secondly, it's because policemen have been happy to gild the lily that the law has been administered in this country.' He was absolutely correct. I did disagree with him and he knew so.

A new officer soon commanded the division and I was transferred to another station. A colleague I had worked with told me I should have moulded my attitudes to suit my senior officers. Another thought my transfer was because I had not made enough arrests. However, I was posted to a larger station and placed under the supervision of an inspector, working with three other sergeants and about twenty constables. I saw this as an opportunity to build another research project and I knew something of what was in store, for the constables at this station worked in the same manner as those at my previous station. Furthermore, my feelings of frustration were now much tempered.

I was keen to tell new colleagues of my opinions about the use of force, the manner in which evidence is used, the handling of suspects in the police station, and so on. This was done by engaging them in conversation about a particular issue or job they were dealing with, which I would then focus on as a means of making my views known. For example, one of the sergeants on my shift was known to use 'unorthodox techniques' of questioning suspects. I discussed this with him and his remarks conveyed a full description of what he was not willing to do, citing particular examples. This proved to be an exceedingly useful description because I was able to compare it with his subsequent behaviour and that of others. Fortunately, he enjoyed discussing issues and drew on my opinions about sociology. Unknowingly, he became a major 'informant' who was always happy to provide detail of what was happening to particular officers, in particular incidents, and so on.

I had defined my limits of tolerance, my immediate colleagues did not exclude me from information of their actions and I was able to keep on the fringes of incidents which I found questionable. It was noticeable that constables who brought a 'dodgy job' into the charge room would, if they had a choice, ask a colleague to deal with it; sergeants would also intervene and almost protect me if they thought that I would spoil or misunderstand a procedure they wished to control. They never intervened directly but there was this sense in which they protected me and, as they would see it, their subordinates who knew how they would like investigations to be conducted. The senior officers were pleased with my work as a sergeant, negating previous reports made on me but realising that I held views which they did not agree with.

Stress – the Life-blood of Participant Observation

In his account of research in 'Cornerville', William Whyte writes, 'I also had to learn that the field worker cannot afford to think only of learning to live with others in the field. He has to continue living with himself.'[9] Ethical questions raised by covert research create a situation of stress within which the sociologist has to live with himself.

As a serving police officer, I worked alongside others who did not share my assumptions and values, meaning that I was constantly hearing about and occasionally seeing practices which were personally offensive to me. Such, it might be said, is the nature of a nasty world; I had some direct responsibility for such matters for I was, I am again reminded, employed as a police officer. Sometimes, stress caused by ethical problems caused me to avoid a particular situation. For example, following a television documentary about black youth, officers decided to supervise a local youth club as its members went home. Simply listening to the whole relief, including supervisory staff, discussing the situation so troubled me that I left the station in my patrol car and remained on patrol, unobtainable, until I knew that I would not have to deal with any matter arising from their work. In fact, other duties prevented their suggested action.

Stress was also generated because colleagues do not always respect limits of tolerance. An officer might not be familiar with my expectations of conduct in the charge room; he might lose his temper with a suspect, or use legitimate force on a person but exceed what I considered to be the proper limits of that force when being assisted by me. Such situations did arise and were dealt with by advice, admonition and so on. They were stressful.

Third, and linked to the previous point, establishing a covert research role involves a constant process of self-reflection. Gold and others have encouraged us to consider a continuum with overt and covert research at either end.[10] In my research, a constant triadic dialogue took place: that dialogue was a balancing of personal ethical limits with the aims of sociological research and my duty as a police officer. There were occasions when I forgot that I was researching. Indeed, I found that it was necessary to actually state my research interest to myself as I began to work each day. There were times when my administrative duties were spoiled because I was involved in remembering the minutiae of police action. Covert research involves a constant heightening of sensitivity to the possibilities of recording conversation, action or whatever — such activity is exceedingly demanding and can, after a time, become stressful.

There were other times when I 'went native', but when this happened I was often pulled back by a particularly distasteful event. I recorded one such moment after colleagues had been discussing race relations.

I reacted badly to the conversation yesterday and want nothing to do with such sentiments. I remember saying to myself, 'Underneath, these policemen are ruthless and racist'. I seem to have slipped into the mould easily during the last couple of weeks and wonder if I should have been so easy with my feelings. The balance of participant observation is one which can so easily be submerged and forgotten. Now it has been brought before me in glaring lights and all the old issues of ethics, when to speak out, how involved one should get, whose perspective one takes on, loom large.

Fourth, there is the stress of 'being found out'. It has been argued that we all present 'masks' in the context of relationships with others. Covert research is merely making explicit what is present in all that we do.[11] This seems to overstress the place of 'fronts' and the normalcy of secrecy and deception in relationships, which should be sharply contrasted with the pervasive tension between the perception one has of oneself as researcher and, in my case, as a police officer.

I have a good memory for detail — the police taught me that. Each day, I used an official form which any officer might carry in the station and used it to jot down my own shorthand notes. I kept this paper in the back pocket of my trousers and developed the habit of checking to see if it was secure. If I had to leave the station office or charge room to secure privacy for my shorthand, I was always listening for approaching footsteps.

> One afternoon, while working in plain clothes, I got on a bus and wrote some notes. I looked across the aisle and noticed the night duty telephonist sitting next to me.

> On another occasion while at the station I arranged a tutorial with my supervisor over the telephone. When returning to the communications room a constable said to me, 'Switch that tape recorder off, Sarge.' I asked, 'What are you on about?' 'Oh, nothing.' I do not know what was meant and never found out but his remark caused me considerable anxiety.

The stress of covert research might resemble an element of masking in personal relationships, but it is closer to experiencing a relationship with a person who is highly conscious of their self-image and thereby over-sensitive to 'unmasking'.

Finally, friendships with colleagues are formed. When conducting research on the police, publication of sensitive data could result in their careers being ruined, the taking of disciplinary action against them and worse. Although I did not allow this to restrict the data I gathered, it remained with other factors to increase the stress of the research situation.

When these conditions are added to the sheer physical effort involved in shift work, with few days' leave each week, it should be obvious that the covert researcher can easily be overburdened by the task of policing, let alone the completion of demanding research. Illness through stress is documented as a regular feature of policing — the covert researcher will share in that aspect of policing.[12]

Stress in covert research cannot be avoided, it has to be managed to the advantage of the researcher. I used my situation to heighten my consciousness of what was going on around me, not least when potentially stressful incidents were likely to happen. This led me to make a particular study of the police use of physical force, finding that I could tolerate its use more satisfactorily by taking extremely detailed notes. This enabled me to check attitudes against action, while clarifying my own limits of tolerance.

Furthermore, as Bettelheim demonstrated in a far more extreme situation than my own, research can be a strategy for personal survival. After appointment to my lecturership at Sheffield, I was able to remain in the field for a further year. Knowing that I would be leaving for a base from which I could publish and, perhaps, also influence policy concerned with the police, I was able to understand my research as a means of making sense of my situation. We know from Bettelheim's publications that an indeterminate sentence in an extreme situation can, after a lengthy period, result in terrible mental distress. Yet the stress of that same situation can be used to the advantage of the researching sociologist, not least in enabling him to 'live with himself', as Whyte puts it.[13]

Validity and Reliability

Criticisms of the unreliability of participant observer research are legion, but economy of space prevents their full review here. However, the accuracy, validity and reliability of one's findings are of importance to ethics. Clearly, if a research method is shot-through with error, it is unsuitable for the documentation of any group of people. If the researcher is working alone, unable to hold research conferences with colleagues in the field and is, so to speak, an apprentice, the problems of reliability and representativeness are highly significant.

In contrast to the total research experience, recording data is an exceedingly mundane business. I worked within the general rules that I should observe and record as much, even of the seemingly routine and insignificant, as was possible and as many officers in as many contexts as possible. A difficulty encountered early on in my research was the apparent gap between my own rich experience of being a police officer and the flat, highly descriptive snapshots of that 'cine-film reality' within which I was living. In particular, it was difficult to record the often lengthy period between particular incidents. I had to learn to put that issue to one side as I documented all I could. This is not to suggest that participant observation is an entirely random business. Published literature is useful to direct one's attention to particular topics, and I found Maureen Cain's work exceedingly helpful because, although it was completed over a decade before my own work, it described a situation very similar to the one I found myself in. Yet I was also told that the force had changed during my period at university. I began by taking many of Cain's central concepts and developed themes from them. For example, having recognised that policing is a sporadic, essentially actionless job but that, as Cain found, the lower ranks regarded it as highly action-oriented, I documented how personnel constructed a world of action through the use of technology and other devices. This led me to a consideration of story- and joke-telling as a further means of sustaining the police world. In this way, the 'moss of data' gathered as research rolled on.

Other factors are important. I spent two years in fieldwork which meant that I was not under pressure to gather data with a sense of urgency, ending up with a 'smash and grab' ethnography. Furthermore, documenting across time has enabled me to compare the attitudes and actions of individual and groups of officers in seemingly unconnected but, in subsequent analysis, interrelated events. Using a cross-indexed subject and individual officer index, I am able to refer to the documented activities of each officer as well as those of others involved in the same or similar incidents, as well as evidence clustering around a particular theme, involving any number of officers on any number of occasions.

The use of a 'rhetorical question' became a most useful tool of analysis. If I was working on a particular theme, I would test my interest by questioning a number of officers.

One Sunday night I was patrolling with a colleague when a call to a fight came over the radio. The location of the call was too far away and the incident too trivial for a sergeant to attend but we drove towards the scene at high speed. I asked, 'The only reason you drove like that was because you wanted to have a fast drive?' He replied, 'Yes, well, it's a bit of fun, isn't it? It all makes a bit of excitement and gets rid of a headache.'

This offered some verification of a theme I had been considering and I was able to continue developing it. Similar means were used throughout the research.

My academic supervisors were also very helpful because they were able to listen to my stumbling accounts of what I had found — more often than not, what I couldn't make any sense of — and suggested some lines of enquiry I might follow, as well as encouraging the work. This helps the researcher to rethink, away from the immediate pressures of the field. It was therefore important to the validity of the research findings.

Knowing what colleagues think of you is not always pleasant, but it is crucial to participant observation for it permits the researcher to discriminate between reliable and unreliable details of evidence. This was fairly easy as far as senior officers were concerned because I was subject to routine probationary reports — although they understood my views to be different from their own, they thought I had proved myself an adequate sergeant. Lower ranks would let some of their opinions be known in the course of work and usually in the form of a joke.

In response to two exceedingly conscientious British Transport policemen, a colleague remarked, 'Right couple of lawyers we've got out there. They're trying to decide who cautioned him before he was arrested. Must have a sociology degree from Lancaster.'

On another occasion a constable said to me, as he left the canteen, 'I'm going to get a spade now, Sage.' He punched a fist in the palm of his hand.

These gave some indication of how to assess officers' remarks, together with verification from their attitudes and actions in other situations and those of their colleagues.

On one occasion, I used what Schutz called the 'member test of validity'.[14] I submitted an article on police—community relations to the chief officer for permission to publish but, without reason, he refused publication. I read some of the paper to colleagues, who disagreed with my statements that they did not find 'peace-keeping' aspects of police work to be important. But how one would operate Schutz's test and its applicability to any research setting is open to much questioning. However, I have had some exceedingly useful comments on the validity of my work from police officers engaged in extra-mural study. These officers have been from a different force from that where the research was carried out and have been most helpful in pointing to the applicability of my own ideas to another force area.

Finally, although I find Schutz's member test suspect, I rely upon my own membership of the police as relevant to the validity of my research findings. For example, after chasing a number of suspects who had committed a burglary, I returned home to my wife — I had been off duty, unloading shopping at the time I saw the suspects — raging at what I would do to them if I caught them. I was completely 'native', displaying all the attitudes of normal policemanship. In short, I experienced being a policeman and that was of use in realising the necessary empathy for participant observer research.

Into 'Civvy Street' — Analysis and Publication

Leaving the police — after eleven years' service — was comparatively easy, but there was the nagging doubt in my mind that if I published, those who had unknowingly cooperated in my research project could be hurt. Here, despite my criticisms of police action, I agree with Roy Wallis when he writes about his research on the Church of Scientology, 'It seemed to me that a sociologist owed his subjects an obligation not to cause them undeserved harm.'[15]

'Undeserved harm' is not easy to judge and the Official Secrets Act, by which I am bound, was partly designed to prevent such harm. However, as ludicrously restricting as that Act is, I had no intention of submitting my data, containing countless examples of rule-breaking by police officers, to the chief officer. In this sense, I was willing to protect those whom I had observed. Chief officers of police are understandably proud of their ability to manage their force. However, my research, together with other work, demonstrates how the rhetoric of police professionalism embraced by these officers and the organisation of the police combine to prevent and, in some measure, shield lower ranks from effective management. If this was to be demonstrated in my research, I had to circumvent the sanction of the chief officer, which is what I did.

All my publications have rendered the names and places of officers and location of incidents to anonymity. Suitable safeguards have been taken to protect the data themselves. Again, this is to protect individual officers who need not be made an example for their indiscretion by the publication of research findings. This is not to deny their personal moral responsibility, neither is it to deny my own in this matter. However, I take the broader view that my research has relevance to the academic understanding of policing in Britain and, indeed, police policy in our society. I am therefore willing to submerge the moral responsibility of those involved in my research in favour of a broader responsibility to influence change amongst the whole of the British police.

This might sound fanciful, but I have found considerable interest in my research from the national media and policy-oriented research organisations. Retaining the anonymity of my subjects, I avoid publicity which will exploit the spectacular. For example, the publishers of my first article in an academic journal wanted to put a press release on it, which I refused.[16] Publication of another article in a policy-oriented journal did stimulate interest, but that piece also managed to attract the imagination of sub-headline writers in the popular press.[17] Keeping such publicity to a minimum, I have also been able to use my research in conjunction with an independent research agency and given evidence to the Royal Commission on Criminal Procedure, using my data as the basis for that oral evidence. Furthermore, I have acted as consultant and interviewee on a number of television and radio programmes, all concerned with policing policy. I try to write to Members of Parliament offering assistance with questions they might be asking in the House. This type of work, alongside strictly academic publishing, is necessary if the moral responsibility of the reseacher who has decided to submerge the culpability of those he has observed is to be taken seriously. I am certain that such responsibility is present in all research which has implications for policy, but it is all the more so in covert research on the police.

A more difficult matter of responsibility is found in relation to those who the police dealt with during the period of research and may have a grievance against them. I knew of no cases where my own evidence was sufficient to prove a complaint of illegality, but any research on the police which pierces the gloss of police legality will have to cope with moral responsibility towards the offended. Obviously, romanticism should be avoided but, nevertheless, attempts to influence policy change are also carried out with such people in mind.

The impression may be given that I am only concerned with policy issues — this is not the case and my work cannot be interpreted as a vendetta against police policy. Damage done to the reputation of sociology has to be considered, for some members of that highly diverse group of practitioners object to covert research. It is difficult to know which particular group of sociologists one should take notice of but if those who research the police are a pertinent reference group, then I do not find any criticisms of my stance from them; neither do I find criticism of my methodology from editorial boards. Some could argue that my work will prevent further research on the police — it might prevent any further probing of the police world by me but, with the increased interest in police research, I would not be surprised if chief officers denied the force of my own findings and permitted further work by others to disprove my case. Any such research would have to consider the powerful masking of much police practice by lower ranks and find ways of penetrating those masks.

The Risks of Ethical Decision-Making

If there is one feature of the ethics of covert research I wish to convey, it is simply that we should avoid the impression that research ethics are a clear-cut matter, based on a residual, all-embracing type of social scientists' natural law. However we rate our moral credibility, covert research of a legal institution will result in highly contextual decision-making and, if that decision-making is engaged with a sense of responsibility, much stress will have to be endured.

Researchers in this area will benefit from the uncomfortable business of laying bare the dilemmas they face in the field, for without accounts of such matters the credibility of their work is weakened. Indeed, such accounts might also result in creation of a greater sensitivity amongst sociologists who engage in denouncing the unreliability and 'Uncle Tom' character of research of the police. These sombre tones should not shield the fulfilment of covert research, with its benefits for academic and policy-oriented knowledge.

In this chapter I have attempted to argue that my research on the police was based in good ethical decisions but that these decisions do not offer a *carte blanche* authority to the researching of any group. The most significant question to ask when deciding on any research strategy is this: 'If I were to place myself in the situation of those I wish to research, would I object to the covert method?' If we begin with this very human question and pit all our evidence against it, preferably in debate with a number of others concerned with the research, then a good decision might well be made. (I fear that a sociologically-based objection that we cannot stand in another's shoes would be an incredibly facile reply.) In the end, it is the individual researcher who will have to make the decision, accepting the risks it involved. There is much truth in Whyte's remark that they will have to live with that decision — and continue to do so.

5 Observational Research on the National Front*

Nigel Fielding

The Study

Participant observation is not a research strategy appropriate to every research problem. Like other methodologies, it suffers from the defects of its virtues. Its insights arise from the relationships the researcher forges in unfamiliar settings; similarly, deception and fraudulence may be latent products of those relationships. The fact that ethical issues arise from research relationships alerts one to the nub of the method, its reflexivity. This reflexivity, predicated on the notion that meaning is constructed out of interaction, is further manifest in the guilt and self-doubt experienced by practitioners of the technique. Nor does the agonising over deliberately misleading statements of support and implanted expectations of advocacy stem merely from the inbuilt *angst* of a profession painfully aware of its own marginality. While libel laws do concentrate the mind, there remains beneath the cynicism the feeling that at a point lost in past time, one set out with a commitment to truth. That commitment was wedded, impossibly, to an intention not to exploit or to alter the phenomenon brought back, alive and kicking, from reality's dark corners. At the close of research, neither truth nor

* Original material © N. Fielding 1982.

phenomenon have been ideally served. Yet the recognition of the impossibility of achieving a product thus conceived represents the beginning of a more plausible sociology.

I chose to make participant observation a major element of my research strategy for studying the National Front.[1] I was relatively uninterested in the demographic indices of National Front (NF) electoral support, its funds or membership figures. My concern was to understand why NF members believe what they do, and to examine the link between their ideology and their actions in an extreme right-wing racial-nationalist political movement. The ideology's appeal was seen in terms of its ability to solve problems of the individual's experience. Commitment to a particular ideology was seen as a rational choice originating in the individual's assessment of the situation. While the person's analysis may be dubious, that he invests this belief-system with meaning implies that he is capable of perceiving a course of action which has the potential to alter the political situation he regards as unsatisfactory. He possesses a political conscious-ness which distinguishes him from his fellows. The significance of belief in NF ideology lay in its existence, not its quality. Political deviance was the rational, constructive activity of those with a claim to political self-awareness.

The fit between beliefs and action is crucial, as J. Douglas notes: 'Only in this way can we hope to see all the complex convolutions of problematic meanings and the complex, often conflicting patterns (and non-patterns) of actions these convolutions give rise to in everyday life.'[2] As an approach to deviance employing a qualitative methodology, the research sought answers to the questions 'What are the *characteristics* of . . . [the] phenomenon, the forms it assumes, the variations it displays?'[3] The research aimed to delineate the NF ideology as it is expounded by leaders and, further, as it is understood by members. I then examined the fit between these political beliefs and the politico-moral stance of the member, seeking to indicate the linkage between their particular experience of the world and adherence to the ideology. This analysis required detailed information concerning the involvement of activists and ordinary members in political conflict. A vocabulary of motives provided by the ideology and linked to the everyday concerns of members was described. This vocabulary of motives appeared to legitimate and encourage the political action taken by members. Descriptive data pertaining to demographic factors associated with membership, the party's formal organisation and history were also required.

Such analytic requirements dictated an approach to the party employing several methodologies. Material pertaining to formal organisation, formal ideology and commitment of activists was gained from formal and, later, open-ended interviews with party officials. Data on the demographic characteristics of members, the needs satisfied by activism and the understanding of ideology by ordinary members arose from observation of branch meetings and of public marches. Some observation was undertaken with the knowledge of headquarters (HQ) and some as an interested member of the public. The observational material was particularly useful in relation to the needs satisfied by membership. Information relating to political conflict was largely gained from monitoring media coverage of the party and from the party's own paper and magazine. Interviews with opponents and journalists were also employed. Observation provided only relatively incidental material germane to political action; this was a consequence of the mundane character of the branch activities I attended. Other observers have emphasised the party's involvement in violence, but it is my impression that, for the ordinary member representative of the 'average decent patriot' the party seeks to attract, passionate action seldom matches the impassioned rhetoric. Nevertheless, the party's conflict with its opponents formed a continual backdrop, particularly in the conversation of active members.

Having adopted S. Bruyn's scheme for validation of subjective data,[4] which emphasises penetration of the phenomena at a maximum number of organisational levels and over as long a period as possible, the use of these various methods was not phased. Instead, contacts with HQ, observation at branches and on marches, interviews with candidates and opponents took place whenever opportunities arose. This is not to say that a particular site was not systematically studied, but simply that there was not a rigid adherence to a temporal sequence of the sort which exhausts one mode of inquiry before moving to the next. As an example, my approach to one branch began with an interview with its candidate and continued with observation of a demonstration it mounted. As a subscriber to the party's publications, I was then invited to attend a major demonstration with it. At the outset, I adopted a formal researcher role, but moved later to present myself as an interested member of the public. I shall elaborate on my role later in this chapter. I adopted this overall approach because I felt the NF could not be understood as if its adherents were isolated in a world explicable by social class analysis. Its position was to be assessed as a moral posture and its members' interpretations were to be illuminated by an empathic immersion in their world. In the process of 'telling it like it was for them', I could reproduce an account from which outsiders could understand the ideology's persuasiveness to people so placed. From that, better-informed efforts at dissuasion could proceed.

Procedure

Entry to organisations and obtaining permission to study the people one wishes is a problem universal among those sociologists who rise from their desks. However, I feel, with Polsky, that far too many negative noises about research amongst particular groups represent the reluctance of the researcher rather than the real difficulty of entry.[5] Those working in the field of deviance and control have been particularly alert to this in recent years.[6] There are some rules of thumb. Douglas has stressed the need to be constantly alert for potential contacts, to widely discuss one's research with acquaintances. He also presents criteria of time and risk which broadly delineate settings in which attempting to pass is worthwhile. 'One generally chooses to become a member only in a open public setting (that is, one open to the general public) or an organised private setting where he already happens to be a member or can easily become one.'[7] This sensible delineation repudiates the most extreme forms of covert research while leaving a broad compass for investigation. It would, for example, permit both Chambliss' approach to the rackets (as a consumer) and an approach to religious sects, such as the Church of Scientology, which tout for membership in the public arena.

As I have indicated, fieldwork employed several contemporaneous approaches to the NF. My use of covert observation and overt interviewing held in common the presentation of a sympathetic attitude to members. In the overt approach, I still wanted to put respondents at ease as much as possible, and where this involved ignoring gibes about sociology, the Left or long-haired students, or pouring scorn on other observers of the party, then I did so. Likewise in the covert approach, it was necessary to establish that, despite my appearance, I favoured the party and its principles. While elementary security implied keeping covert and overt roles distinct, I did not entirely succeed here. Attending one event as a potential convert, I met by chance my principal respondent from HQ. Yet this potential embarrassment worked to advantage from both 'directions', for the branch members were impressed by my acquaintance with the official, and the official was pleased I was 'spontaneously' attending a party event (see p. 86). Thereafter I sought to blur formal and informal approaches to the party by emphasising my HQ contacts to branch members and my sympathy for the ideology to HQ contacts. I made no effort to alter my name or appearance in either role. It is not possible to determine whether overt or covert work yielded most data, for the straightforward reason that both yielded useful but qualitatively different material. Basic descriptive information about formal organisation and ideology was the essential contribution of the overt material, but from it also arose invitations to observe at party activities. Covert observation yielded information about the attitudes and beliefs of ordinary members, and about the everyday world of fringe politics. Information regarding concepts such as commitment and sacrifices on behalf of commitment was gained from both sources.

To effect entry to unfamiliar groups, one must make one's role compatible with the subjects' expectations and standards, and clearance obtained at one level may not carry over to others. While presenting myself as available for conversion, I found there were a considerable number of people occupying peripheral positions around local branches. It was feasible to attend meetings without becoming a member, although this had to be negotiated periodically. The deception thus entailed represents one of those points where one's credibility rests on one's belief in the self created to play the part of unconverted sympathiser. One may not have the stomach for this but, as Gorden noted, it is rather easy to disguise a retreat from battle as an ethical advance.[8]

As I have stated, a principal tactic used in my approach to both local groups and to HQ officers of the NF was to give the impression of being sympathetic to key points of the ideology. As in Bonilla and Glazer's study of the political attitudes of Chilean university students, respondents were led to believe the researcher agreed with them either by emphasising points of agreement or refraining from expressing disagreement.[9] This bland statement makes of such a tactic a simply mechanical procedure. But there is clearly more involved than the glib manipulation of robotic 'subjects'. J. Barnes has urged that 'there must be some amount of compatability between the values of the scientist and those of the citizens he studies'.[10] Indeed, where the element of deception is too great, it is apparent that the real cost is to the conscience of the researcher, not to the subjects, as in Barnes' example of two anthropologists who 'deceived patients, their relatives and staff in a palliative care unit for the dying'.[11] Such costs may be justified by the value of the data. Rich material was gathered from my observational work on branches, pertaining to social indices of NF support, the social networks binding or failing to bind members, the frustration arising from the stale trappings of routine meetings. Some data concerning social class was available from interviews, but direct observation of branches was the sole source for these other items.

The observational data also augmented that which I was able to gather from my formal approach to the party. After a pilot interview with an NF by-election candidate, I requested an interview with party officials. I identified myself as having a scholarly interest in the practical functioning of British political parties, and my letter led to an invitation to interview a National Directorate member at headquarters. While the description of my interests was purposely bland, it was accurate. At this time I planned a comparative element with extreme Left parties, and early in my formal approach I made it plain that my work was oriented to an academic qualification and possible publication. At this first meeting, an interview schedule was employed, but ensuing visits featured broader discussion, growing informality and an evolution of the attitude towards me of my contacts. I was fortunate in my primary contact, who was aware I was doing research, broadly favoured it, and had some knowledge of sociology. It was through a relationship of gradually increasing trust between us that ensuing HQ contacts were possible. These led to invitations to observe meetings at some branches, and the ill-fated Red Lion Square meeting. Participant observation at another branch enabled my attendance at a major party event, the Remembrance Day march. This was significant in my relation with my primary contact because our chance meeting there was the first time he knew me to attend an NF event outside what he called my 'objective capacity'. At another point, I was asked by an elderly branch member to outline for her the party's principal policies, as it had changed so much. That I passed this test was apparent from the enthusiastic yea-saying by those marching next to us. Arlene Daniels has written of the insight which may arise from observing an organisation while possessing traits which clearly mark one as an outsider. She writes that, 'unlike the stranger who is an immigrant coming to stay, the stranger in this instance encounters a situation fraught with all the opportunities for confidences and intimacies which Simmel describes'.[12] The 'potential convert' role I adopted in the covert approach and the 'sympathetic researcher' role I pursued with officials were both substantially assisted by the perception of my imprecise and transitory status. I also found that stressing my American background enabled me to query matters insiders would be expected to accept. As Daniels noted, the occupancy of a low-status, dependent role ('humble observer', not 'research director') meant many people were 'eager and able to show me any error of my ways'.[13]

While the observer cannot pretend to complete integrity, deception is not absent in other, more detached approaches. For example, in my interviewing, the most important answers often arose from casual asides, rather than the interview schedule. This point also bears on the issue of trust and intrusion, as does my reservation regarding the sensible methodological injunction that it is important to record failures as assiduously as successful forays. Here, again, sociology demonstrates its insidious capability, for even a failure to record a result becomes a form of result itself.[14] For example, I was given an indication of the limit of my relationship with HQ staff, and with my principal contact, when, during the October 1974 General Election, I responded to my contact's complaints of being very busy by offering to help at HQ. While the offer was refused, the reason given, my being present during confidential discussions, indicated the limit of my acceptance by senior officials. My contact's declaration that if it were up to him it would have been alright also showed how far the relation with him had developed.

To suggest that the appreciation of the symbolic meaning of social phenomena is best gleaned from observation rightly carries with it injunctions to sample the culture at different role points and over an extended period of time. Subjective adequacy is partly assessed by the degree of penetration.[15] Seeing the process as one of increasing penetration implies that each new form of the social world one experiences represents the possibility of more accurate findings. For example, when my contact invited me to attend a branch meeting, this represented a logical step further in exposure to the party. I was pleased to be asked to do what I had anyway intended, because it meant positive judgement of me as trustworthy. My welcome into the group was underlined by my contact bringing his wife to meet me and their invitation to visit them at home.[16] By observing different levels of party organisation, and balancing material from HQ with that from branches, I was able to evaluate my interpretations. I also recorded as sensitively as possible the process of all research contacts. For example, in the case of my being invited to a branch meeting, I noted the anxious non-verbal exchanges between the two contacts who extended the offer in negotiating which branch would be suitable.[17]

Tactics which encouraged a closer incorporation of respondents in the research included the feedback of interviews to subjects and records of meetings where I had been a known observer for comments on my transcript. This procedure was useful in developing a relation with HQ staff, while the overt reason for the exercise, correcting transcription errors, was an incidental benefit. Further, the procedure gave me a chance to return to present the carbon. The caution to be borne in mind is that 'citizens may be just as keen to point out errors of interpretation, as they see it, as errors of fact'.[18] The researcher reserves a right to second-guess the subject which the latter lacks, for in research concerned with belief and meaning, disputed interpretation is itself data.

To speak of the production of trust makes apparent that the researcher manipulates the research setting to enable him to discover what he needs to know. In presenting oneself to the subject group and reporting to the public, one cannot be honest to all sides. The approximation one produces appears partial and distorted from any viewpoint, its logic apparent only from one's own. In Dorothy Douglas's account of participant observation,[19] the emphasis is placed on effecting a good performance, on successful 'front management'. Such an approach, in which contacts with subjects are regarded wholly instrumentally, prompts Rock's remark that the sociologist thus described plays with trust in an amoral fashion, 'lying and dissembling at will'. Noting further that ethnography generally bears malignant fruits for the subjects of study, Rock suggests that it is only right for the sociologist to experience feelings of guilt at having, as F. Davis puts it, 'violated the collective conscience of the community'.[20]

The point is that, ultimately, similar 'bad faith' underlies almost any research enterprise. In considering *When Prophecy Fails*, H. Riecken pointed out that the reciprocity of field research makes more apparent the need to deceive. '[I]t is difficult . . . to inquire of an individual how he feels about a matter without having him return the question. . . . Since the beliefs could not be validated . . . by physical reality, the only confirmation available was from social reality. . . . The pressure on observers to take part in the process of mutual support and confirmation was ever present and often strong.'[21] An interesting consequence in small in-groups is the reinforcing effect of the observer's endorsement.

Thus the mechanical demands of participation in certain settings automatically produce deceit. For some, this closes the matter; if the only way of penetrating those settings is to deceive, then such settings should be closed to research. Yet, according to J. Douglas, this expectation emanates from a classical paradigm which 'exudes the small-town Protestant public morality of openness, friendliness and do-gooderism. Everything is open and above-board. . . . Once inside the researcher is expected to establish trust unproblematically with the members and from these relations of trust will flow the truth about what the members are up to.'[22] The reality is that trust is variable, and truth is relative. In Douglas's usage, trust is a device manipulable in order to tease out a truth which transcends the subjects' assertions and which can be 'checked out' against a number of forms of direct experience.

While I concur with his assertion that trust waxes and wanes, that it can disappear in recriminations and is always something to which one's efforts are strenuously directed, I cannot accept his monochromic typification of 'sympathy'. Writing of the classical participant observation paradigm, he declares that 'the almost inevitable stance was assumed to be that of the convert — that is, one of "sympathy". . . . If the group is in some way deviant or stigmatised, when the report is written it tends to show the world that the group studied is not "bad" in the way people thought.'[23] Certainly, the *stance* adopted by the researcher is appreciative — it must be if he is to apprehend the consequences of affiliation. But cannot 'empathy' be as much a device as the evocation of 'trust'? His argument that classical participant observation has tended to solicit 'sympathy' for an unloved group contradicts his later, correct assertion that 'going native' is far less common a problem than is made out in the literature.[24] The unconvincing assertion that in these accounts the subjects' definition of reality is assumed to be 'the only reality which needs to be studied, analysed and presented'[25] fails to acknowledge that very often this only resulted from a need to balance the overwhelming preponderance of analysis from the perspective of the state.

Sociology's special competence arises from its 'capacity to upset common sense' and, apparently, to offend against ethics in the process of laying bare a concealed truth. Sociology, in short, is not nice, and high ethical ideals represent only reluctance to descend from theory and the wilful ignorance of the naive. If we are to illuminate sociology's hidden enterprise we must, as J. Roth writes, collapse the oversimplified distinction between 'secret' and 'non-secret' research. Deceit in research may be seen, like delinquency, as a 'more-or-less' thing, for 'most of us . . . never cease observing the social sphere about us'.[26]

The sociologist has a commitment to the veracity of his description as well as to the persons studied, and he must comprehend both with involvement and detachment. Nevertheless, as Robb wrote of his research on anti-Semitism, 'unless he is particularly insensitive [the researcher] is burdened with the feeling that he is not playing an entirely honest part. He is using a subterfuge to obtain information. . .'.[27] That element of subterfuge is increased in employing the tactic of presenting a positive attitude to a group which one regards sceptically. That I took my primary contact seriously at our first meeting and did not seek to refute his arguments pleased and surprised him. He was delighted when I recognised his voice when he telephoned on his return from abroad. Clues such as the informal ease of interaction, shared jokes, recall of points the other has made and tone of voice are indicative of the growth of the relationship. My relation with him caused me much reflection on the subject of my own politics and friendships. By the time of the Remembrance Day rally, when our time was spent in a jocular commentary on the proceedings which was not entirely functional for relations with other branch members, the relation with my respondent was natural and relaxed.

The cessation of the relation at the close of fieldwork and

resumption of a detached attitude exemplify the difficulty of this research. It is at least as difficult to regard such a person as an object as to so regard oneself. Again, insight can be gained from considering the notion of trust. The guilt which retreat engenders may be more emotional than intellectual. As J. Douglas noted, 'liking' precedes 'trusting' someone. Both parties to a relation may use each other while still preserving friendship. Indeed, we often hope our subjects will be able to make use of us in small ways, and a sophisticated understanding of trust must allow for the subjects' efforts to manipulate us as much as ours to manipulate them.[28]

In publishing sensitive material, there are two chief considerations. First, if a decision is made to publish material which may redound against the group, such as details of criminal convictions or confidential information about finances, it is wise to subject such material to a check sufficiently extensive to give one absolute assurance of its veracity. Second, the subject group can effectively delay publication. The researcher must be very clear on his motives in publication and the effect of publication on the group. Becker has succinctly stated the usual criteria for this decision: 'one should refrain from publishing items of fact or conclusions that are not necessary to one's argument or that would cause suffering out of proportion to the scientific gain of making them public'.[29] As E. Sagarin has argued, it may be necessary to engage in a consideration of the balance of power between the group and the polity; one's political stance may influence a decision whether to publish. [30] While special consideration may need to be given to particular economic or ethnic groups in order to realise the spirit of such principles as 'equal protection',[31] so that 'equal protection' may entail unequal treatment, this decision is one which rests on interpretation, not the unambiguous application of a code.

J. Fichter and W. Kolb approached this decision as a moral challenge as much as a pragmatic consideration, as is clear from the scout-like tone of their analysis. The sociologist who feels obliged to report all the data is diagnosed as being 'in need of the virtues of tolerance, compassion and love'.[32]

The second consideration, determining the extent of potential injury, is only possible if the 'scientist saturates himself' in the group, and the third, the degree to which subjects are members of the 'scientist's moral community', is clearly ambiguous. The difficulties of this moralising approach are several. For example, the typification of the NF is problematic because a number of different perspectives are valid; that is, the NF are both underdogs and repressors. To assert that sociologists determine when to grant 'rights of privacy, respect and secrecy' on the basis of moral verity is simply unrealistic. They do so on the basis of pragmatism — 'what can I get away with' — and instrumentalism — 'will my audience find this plausible' — which act as the only essential limits on the scientist's interpretations of truth. As Becker declares, 'this analysis can be true only when there is some consensus about norms and some community of interest between the two parties'.[33] There may not be a 'necessity of conflict', as Becker goes on to write, but this is closer to the truth than the falsetto issuing from Fichter and Kolb.

Such matters as consideration for the viewpoint of the respondents recede in importance after the close of fieldwork. Attention is diverted to the mundane programme of writing. This underlines the importance of a gradual cessation of field activity. The truce between researcher and subject is tenuous, and one's retreat often signals a resumption of 'normal' hostilities. For example, I had intended to cite all NF members below Directorate level according to pseudonyms in my book, thinking that this was in the best interests of ordinary members. This met with a belligerent response from a senior NF official, who felt there would thus be no means of confirming that I was not simply inventing responses. It was made apparent that any trust built up during the research — my HQ contacts had since left the party — had been entirely eroded. Real names were reinstated and the party was informed. A very thorough reading of the manuscript was undertaken by a libel lawyer engaged by my publisher. Sensitive detail, such as that pertaining to court appearances, required evidence enabling 'absolute verification'. This was obtained by checking press and then court records. Material not confirmed this way was deleted. Only a rather small volume of material was cut this way, since I felt the book's contribution was less in revealing matters of hidden fact (rather little of which comes one's way in undertaking a 'sympathetic' approach) than in its analysis of ideology. I was more resistant to changes of interpretation recommended by the lawyer, which mainly related to choice of wording, but several such changes were also made. This process took about six months. My contract specified that I bore legal costs arising out of any action in relation to the book, and it is recommended that under these circumstances, researchers obtain an insurance against such action.

In the United States, the Supreme Court has recently ruled that social researchers are not 'public figures' and thus enjoy the same legal insulation from defamatory remarks as do ordinary citizens.[34] Beyond law-suits, the researcher's personal security must also be taken into account in research strategy. This is a consequence of the groups sociologists increasingly wish to study. It could be argued that this development tends to supersede the whole question of ethics. Adrift in a sea of relativism, society gets the sociology it deserves. The respondents signal a new branch of the client revolt by charging for interviews and seeking to intimidate the researcher with abusive phone calls. The police arrest researchers as parties to crime in certain extreme cases. The sociologist employs a libel lawyer, a broker to indemnify him and an ex-directory phone number. Free-wheeling interest groups spar with one another, while 'the public', demystified and de-reified, is revealed as a seething mass of predatory coalitions and corrupted losers. In contemporary usage, to say of a particular matter that 'it is academic' is to dismiss it. Surely the ethics of research is now merely 'academic' in that sense?

Discussion

I will suggest two justifications for thinking otherwise. The first is the political justification, which suggests that sociology stands in a radical slot on the value continuum. Here ethics are mediated by a political reading of the subject group. An example is Spencer's approach to the study of the 'military—industrial complex' through an analysis of West Point Military Academy.[35] Under the political justification, the significant ethical questions are one's own political attitude to the group and one's assessment of the research's likely impact on the subjects. Few researchers are able to confront their subject so unambiguously as P. van den Berghe, who stated of his South African work, 'I decided that I should have no scruples in deceiving the government.'[36] More typical and more problematic is the situation Becker describes when he declares that 'the poor, powerless and disreputable seldom complain about the studies published about them . . . because they are seldom organised enough to do so'.[37]

As Duster, Matza and Wellman declare, fieldwork may be the only 'scientific method' for certain kinds of problems, such as housing discrimination.[38] It is appropriate because American society increasingly diverges from the open society enshrined in American mythology.[39] Furthermore, the deception that does occur is singularly mild compared to that practised daily by official and business organisations.[40] It is interesting that a perspective which is so aware of the failings of absolutist claims to truth is so prepared to justify its procedures by recourse to the ideal of truth. Some claims to represent truth are seen as more worthy than others, not in the academic arena but in the market place of ideas. That is, sociological truth competes with other versions adopted by politicians, civil servants and business corporations.[41] I have already noted the problems arising from research on weak and disorganised groups. Further, if the fundamental problem of qualitative research is to determine the social meanings of actions to the actors themselves, the evaluative attitude one assumes in typifying a group either as an overdog or an underdog is hardly conducive to the stimulation of empathy.

Nor is it the case that sociologists cluster at any one point on a spectrum of values. Of course, R. Evans was right in suggesting that the role 'most comfortably assumed by the professional social scientist' is one of objective analysis.[42] But there can be few sociologists left who actually believe they can approach the subject group from any but their own individual perspective. If one accepts Douglas's assertion that

too sharp a distinction has been drawn between empathy —
'ability to feel with the subjects' — and sympathy — 'allowing
one's feelings to affect one's thoughts or analyses' — then the
researcher's emotional involvement with those he spends time
observing needs to be accounted for.[43] One may feel a bond
even to a group with beliefs antithetical to one's own. I was
more inclined during the research to consider certain issues
or arguments which before I would have dismissed. This is a
good thing since it compels one to thorough reflection on
one's analysis. Douglas argues that one ought to avoid
situations one feels deeply about.[44] While this is broadly
sound advice, understanding also flows from feeling, and one
should not be too hasty to distance oneself from the experience of tension between assumed self and researcher. Indeed,
I would be concerned at any observer who declared, 'I tended
to become an "observer" of almost all aspects of my own
life . . . to discuss or express opinions about some political
and social subjects was to risk the loss of rapport with my
respondents.'[45] While he must become familiar with the
subjects' 'lay interpretations', the sociologist must always
have an eye to their inadequacy. All consciousness is partial,
if not false, bar the consciousness of the researcher. Of course
this is no answer, but it does point to the fallacy of the
political justification. Even the limited attention given to
ethical matters in the political justification is rendered
problematic by the difficulty of specifying the 'right' criteria
for identifying subject groups worthy of study.

The second justification adopts criteria internal to the
research discipline. In the search for social knowledge, some
forms of inquiry are justified and others are not. Yet the
criterion used does not relate to the values of the researcher,
but to the conventional experimental criterion of not spoiling
the field for subsequent research. This point is expressed by
Erikson in one of the more influential articles on covert
research. '[W]ith people who have expressed no readiness to
participate in our researches . . . we are in very much the
same ethical position as a physician who carries out medical
experiments on human subjects without their consent. The
only conceivable argument in favour of such experimentation
is that the knowledge derived from it is worth the discomfort

it may cause. And the difficulties here are that we do not know how to measure the value of the work we do or the methods we employ . . .'[46] Erikson's basic point is a strong one. Yet is is a largely practical one. Most researchers have some idea of the value of their work and its policy implications. No matter what method is employed, the research cannot control its later use — Barnes's example of the US Army's use of an anthropological study of Montagnard villagers is telling.[47] Condominas could not possibly have anticipated the misuse of his work, translated out of copyright and applied some years after the close of fieldwork. Finally, one might question the medical analogy Erikson employs. Medical experimentation on human subjects has immediately apparent physical effects on the subject. It is an extreme example. Are we so arrogant as to perceive descriptive and ethnographic fieldwork having similar impact? Duster and Matza have argued that the blanket application of ethical injunctions obscures conflicts of interest.[48] Again, rather than put a countervailing moral principle in line with their belief that privacy is not a right but a privilege accorded the powerful, these authors insist that 'a balance must be reached in each case'. Sociology would look less complex, and more naive, if sociologists were not willing to make such determinations. Perhaps one should not enter the field if one is afraid of getting mud on one's boots.

Nevertheless, I do not think the solution lies in simply turning to the techniques of investigative journalism, as some have argued.[49] Precisely because the NF, like many deviant groups, is easier to research than one may imagine, it is susceptible to bad sociology. In a sense, the personal commitment necessary to observational research encourages a more responsible approach than the adversary techniques recommended by Spencer.[50] I am not suggesting that observation may not entail these procedures, but that employing them without attempting an act of appreciation results in a cynical and cavalier approach.

The appreciative stance begins with the assumption that 'in order to feel that one understands what is "going on" with others, most people try to put themselves in the other person's shoes'.[51] Sociologists have no exclusive claim to this enterprise, for it is a necessary part of everyday life. People commonly form their impression of other people's living from face-to-face interaction. Lofland declares, 'Through taking the role of another face-to-face, one gains a sense of understanding him.'[52] Like journalists, film-makers and other systematic observers of the human scene, qualitative sociologists seek to represent to others what it is like to be a member of specialised groups to which most people lack access. This involves the researcher learning the unfamiliar culture by adopting the way of seeing of insiders. 'In order to capture the participants "in their own terms" one must learn their analytic ordering of the world, their categories for rendering explicable and coherent the flux of raw reality.'[53] The sociologist suspends his own frames of reference and tries to see things in the way insiders do. Out of the dissonance between the new world view and his familiar one, the sociologist may derive insight into the participants' analytic order and its sociological categorisation. Thus I endeavoured to experience the NF members' world on the plane of activity as well as that of ideology.

Of course, the appreciative stance is subject to its own shortcomings. The attempt to see the NF ideology's appeal in terms of its ability to solve problems of the individual's experience raises one (literally) essential weakness of the naturalistic methodology. To the extent that one succeeds in recreating in oneself a consciousness of the world from the standpoint of the NF member, one renders oneself incapable of reporting back. Total belief systems cannot be dismantled into their elements and reassembled without loss. Such an analysis yields a mechanical impression of ideology, shorn of the belief which softens the hard edges of dogma. One cannot appreciate without being merged with the subject of appreciation; an act of appreciation all the while oriented to the giving of a rational account is self-defeating.[54] Of course, one need not insist that because one's understanding is partial it is also worthless.

This problem is aggravated in the study of the 'unloved' group. Certainly the famous problem of going native may be rendered unreal by studying the alien and uncongenial — the necessary tension between distance and intimacy is readily sustained. Yet what fits the observer to regard himself as impervious to conversion limits his assertion of having gained the truth of membership. Consequently, deception is encouraged. In studying the NF, that communion was sought with a group with which honest identification on my part was impossible.[55] From the outset, the experience of participation and the production of a dissonance between subject and object in one's self is deflated, so that it may become merely a device. Only recourse to strong assertions of sociology's right to know can sustain such intellectual philistinism. Other difficulties flow from participation. The observer of the uncongenial group must often reconcile himself to the disparity between the ideology and the apparent decency of many believers. Professing an understanding of the perspective of groups hostile to the values of all those with whom one has sympathy can be a distinctly uncomfortable posture.

Further difficulties arise in research on groups which are hostile to social science and academic study. The extreme Right generally resents academics, whose world view contradicts the simple life of organic harmony. Such considerations again encourage deceit and bear on research strategies which hope to gradually reveal the researcher's purposes. Nor are other conventional ethical injunctions straightforwardly applicable to research on uncongenial groups. For example, R. Gorden has urged researchers to 'help the respondent when possible' in exchange for their co-operation.[56] Such advice poses its own ethical dilemma in relation to groups like the National Front.

The researchers inspired by Jack Douglas have adopted an investigative paradigm which emphasises participation but employs a teamwork strategy and hinges on a conflict model of society. They assert that, insofar as the method permits direct experience of the phenomenon, material thus generated best deserves the tag 'scientific data'.[57] Whether a particular approach employs a conventional interactionist epistemology or Douglas's 'multi-perspectival conflictual' model, it will be intensely concerned with the interpretation of the world by those located in a special position in it. In its methodological orientation to the 'ideal of consonance',[58] interactionism takes the actors part and, in so doing, predicates the actor's rationality. This presumption of rationality bears on the matter of reflexivity. The basis of observation is an implied contract between observer and observed. He must lay his self open to persuasion. He surrenders the safe identity of researcher for that of participant. The act of covert observation, in my case in concert with known observation and interviewing, stimulates the researcher to regard himself as an object. He inevitably poses the question, 'What would I have to be like to believe as these people do?' Again, meaning becomes the focus of inquiry. Simple description of the NF ideology becomes subordinate to answering what needs are fulfilled by these beliefs. The research act becomes a reflexive act, and the researcher's sensitivity, not his adhering to a sterile set of mechanical procedures, becomes the basis of his claim to have adequately represented the phenomenon. Where Douglas would exceed this version is not in the act of immersion but in a concern to 'test out/check out' the accounts offered. To him, a 'contract' which bound the researcher to the subject would have limited duration, applying to an initial stage of research. But it would not lose its force, which is to subject the researcher to direct experience of the culture. One may be entirely cynical about that account and be itching to check out its fit to the action, but the conflict perspective, too, demands that one attempt appreciation.

The need to approach the act of observation in a sensitive spirit of inquiry is made more important by the shift in the model of society in which such inquiry is likely to be placed. Barnes sees the recent interest in research ethics as an 'outcome of a movement away from positivism towards a hermeneutic view of knowledge, and from an evaluation of knowledge as a source of enlightenment to an evaluation in terms of power and property'.[59] In similar vein, Douglas wrote that, 'There are, then, competing models of truth, which must be accepted or rejected on terms other than those of truth.'[60] Douglas proposes that if the sociologist reflects on how he decides the validity of any particular technique, he will recognise that he employs a lay, prescientific notion of truth. 'Otherwise, how would we know when any particular methods used had achieved truth?'[61]

Such a pragmatic approach is appealing and, because it makes direct personal experience the basis of its test of truth, it places radical emphasis on field research. Research proceeding according to Douglas's approach differs from the Chicago School tradition of participant observation by employing a team of observers rather than the usual solo approach. Instead of adopting passive, purposely innocuous or peripheral roles, the researchers become troublesome members of the group or consumers of the service, testing observations by continually probing and prodding at accounts to check where the surface obscures the deep truth below. Scraps of detail which hint at the real phenomenon are alluded to so as to prise out more information from respondents. Instead of approaching subjects on the assumption that their accounts represent the truth of the phenomenon, researchers cultivate and emphasise the conviction that things are seldom what they seem. Douglas's programme 'eliminate[s] the idea of absolute truth and substitutes a more problematic, multi-perspectival conception of truth' which 'makes the researcher, the live and socially situated individual, the ultimate "measure of all things" '.[62] This approach challenges classical participant observation, which 'remained profoundly suspicious of true immersion in the direct experience of everyday life, and insisted on a form of being-with, but not part-of, the member's experience'.[63] What disturbs Douglas most about 'the Chicago school and almost all other field research sociologists' is their reliance on a model of the 'little community' derived from anthropology and which delineates a detached, marginal and aloof role for the observer.

It is this unrealistic typification of the researcher's role which underlies the emphasis on 'ethics' in much debate about field research, and it is this which Douglas most wants to challenge. It is odd then that he sets about challenging participant observation both on the grounds of insufficient immersion (classic participant observation too detached) and on the grounds of being insufficiently probing and sceptical (classic participant observation too sympathetic). Further, the picture he paints of the non-conflictual tendency of classical field research is the opposite of the analyses presented by British sociologists based on solitary participant observation in groups such as the Catholic community in Belfast,[64] working-class youth subcultures,[65] delinquent gangs[66] and the police.[67]

Douglas ultimately negates much of his case by adopting a staged model of inquiry, in which immersion is an important first stage, to be followed by testing out/checking out. But in his assertion that, typically in participant observation, 'the subjects are partially betrayed by revealing more than their public rhetorics, but . . . the readers are also betrayed by not having revealed to them all that one knows to be the truth in a scientific work',[68] we have a clear declaration that, far from substituting 'politics' for 'ethics' as the orienting principle of inquiry, Douglas is laying claim to the scientific mantle. Rather than seeking to radicalise social inquiry, Douglas simply wants to be thorough. There is no intrinsic reason why immersion alone — and solitary participant observation — cannot achieve the same thoroughness as his more manipulative team approach.

However, Erikson raised another, much deeper, reservation: 'we can *impersonate* other modes of behavior with varying degrees of insight and skill, but we cannot *reproduce* them . . .'[69] While we can look for roles that are sufficiently open to permit observation or groups that are relatively amorphous, we never *know* that we have succeeded. Indeed, the best test is still subjective assessment of the act of appreciation. Douglas, as I noted earlier, acknowledges this. 'The crucial first step . . . is the active cultivation of the sense of the problematicness of things. This is not in conflict with our argument that much of basic sociological research should involve, as a second crucial step, the de-focusing that enables one to experience things almost as a member. In this case, the sense of the problematicness is intentionally postponed to the later stage of looking at, questioning and analysing one's experience.'[70] The stimulation of a sense of dissonance is, after all, implicit in the appreciative stance. Put this way, Douglas is back in the participant observation fold, so that his assertion that 'if the sense of problematicness' is never achieved, 'all one presents is an insider account, a member's evocation of his experience' not only appears lame but leaves one wondering just what is so wrong about an 'insider account'.

It may be that what is wrong about it is that the lone researcher who wishes to illuminate a group's beliefs and action without replicating all the suspicions about it felt by outsiders is obliged to shoulder a very heavy burden. He is obliged to accept the persuasiveness of a way of seeing to which the rest of the world is blind. As Manning maintains, 'the scientist in general . . . plays a stranger-role because he suspends his usual system of personal relevances as well as suspending the personal relevances of those he observes. . . . The stranger can be objective. Objective rationality is rare in social life and therefore suspect.'[71] Such a marginal stance arises from what Rock deems 'the predatory character of fieldwork'. It makes little difference whether the researcher adopts a disguised or undisguised role, for either way he 'makes use of conventional appearance for unconventional ends', a puncturing of the trusting assumption of the subject's natural attitude that things are what they seem. In short, 'covert ethnography . . . is based on the lie' and 'even overt observation exploits'.[72]

There must be powerful reasons to proceed with research if one accepts the truth of this position. The sociologist who submits himself to a research act which serves both to bind him closely to a group and to the ultimate betrayal of the relationship he constructs has to be strengthened by some special resolve. That such inhibitions do not emasculate spies and journalists may suffice as justification for some. The suggestion that there may be a parallel with such occupations is strongly rebutted by Erikson, who feels that 'the sociologist has a different relation to the rest of the community'.[73] It is precisely the relation of the sociologist to the community which is debatable. Yet it is far from clear that the public expects the sociologist either to be frank or dispassionate. If we are seriously to explore the attitude of the other party to Erikson's 'contract', we will be compelled to examine just who, amongst the public, gets listened to. In other words, we return to the privilege argument. One may also note the difference in aim of sociologists and spies.[74]

However, the most adequate justification for employing methods which are susceptible to exploitative interpretations is that it produces good sociology. Without the observational methodology, I would have been unable to comment on many of the principal issues pertaining to the NF, such as the relation between beliefs and action, the ideology's fit to members' actual beliefs or the relevance of social class. Without the sympathetic stance, I would have had nothing to go on but the written utterances of the party elite and some interviews. Adopting that stance does not mean that one abandons a critical and inquiring approach, Douglas's 'sense of problematicness'. But playing Riesman's 'other-directed individual' — 'that person who is continually using his interactional radar to adjust his views to the people and situations with which he is dealing'[75] — implies that one has to learn the culture before one is able to pose certain questions. The denial of co-operation to a prominent journalist and the refusal of interview requests by two groups of students during my research highlight the need for a gradual approach to such organisations. Ideally, sensitive fieldwork could effect a process which expands the knowledge of the subject group about society and puts the researcher in an intercalary role.[76] The search for acceptance of the observer role may eventually enable qualm-free covert research. If the subjects and the public can be made to understand that theirs is but one shard of a complex social reality, then social research may be justified. In seeking an acceptable self in the unfamiliar setting, an educational process occurs both for observer and subject. 'Layman and sociologist coach one another in ways that are not at all dissimilar to the forms of conventional interaction. . . . Positions can be clarified, suspicions dispelled, joint histories developed and a common world established.'[77] Fieldwork rests on the sensitive evolution of this relationship.

Conclusion

The drive to make good sociology may be combined with the justification that one is giving the public analysis relevant to the decisions that rest with it. M. Phillipson puts the point well. 'The contribution of sociology . . . through its clarification of man's practical activities, is that it can help the members of a society to pose their own dilemmas more clearly and acutely.'[78] I agree with Becker that it is necessary to make explicit the bases of our judgements,[79] although one must appreciate that because 'almost all the topics that sociologists study . . . are seen by society as morality plays'[80] we must recognise the inevitability of our analysis being perceived as distortion rather than interpretation. Indeed, if one employs one's observational skills, one cannot fail to notice the readiness of the groups thus described to give their own account. Surrounded by advocates, a sociology which fails to retail its own version for fear of 'influencing' the public debate becomes impotent by means of its timidity.

The problem of 'going native' has been much discussed. Becker stated, 'the social scientist . . . unwittingly chooses problems that are not likely to cause trouble or inconvenience to those he has found to be such pleasant companions'.[81] This presupposes that one has found one's subject group 'pleasant associates', which the problem of the uncongenial group renders unlikely, and serves to de-emphasise the sizeable component of acting or deception in observation work. I do not think it an accurate impression of contemporary field research. The opposed problem of betrayal may actually be more common. Perhaps the solution to both is for the sociologist to regard himself as the man in the middle, neither public nor subject. He could seek to function as the interpreter of one side to the other.[82] It is an ambitious project. The danger is that he is liable to achieve the logical culmination of his efforts, becoming an outsider to both sides. I hope my work on the NF helps outsiders to understand its appeal, and that such understanding enables the NF's opponents to persuade those susceptible to membership that the answers to our problems do not lie in racist politics. However, that is only my interpretation.

6   On the Merits of Covert Methods: a dialogue*

Roger Homan and Martin Bulmer

Homan

The work in which I found it necessary to adopt covert methods of observation and interview was an investigation of the language-behaviour of old-time pentecostals. My subjects were members of pentecostal fellowships in England and Wales, Canada and the United States, within which the groupings termed 'old-time' were characterised by their endeavours to sustain the fervour that marked the burgeoning of modern pentecost in the early years of this century and by their absolutist rejection of 'the world': they are distinguished from the 'new' penetcostal style of the second and subsequent generations and the so-called charismatic movement in which sectarian rejectionism and peculiarities of language, behaviour and belief are compromised. My original purpose was to compile a dictionary of esoteric pentecostal language and to explore its social functions in the insulation of the sect from the wider society and in the generation of a sense of sect identity: the functions in which I subsequently became interested included the sustaining of situation definitions involving status differentiation, the allocation of authority and prescriptions of norms of acceptable behaviour.

* Original material © Roger Homan and Martin Bulmer 1982.

So the phenomena that interested me were internal to the pentecostal communities observed and it was important to adopt an unobtrusive and nonreactive method: I wanted to observe and record the language which pentecostals used among themselves, in addition to the form used in communicating to outsiders. Whenever I presented myself as a stranger, I found — predictably — that I was treated as a subject for evangelism and addressed in the everyday language of the uninitiated.

However, the stranger who is a sociologist is rather more problematic a factor in encounters with old-time pentecostals than the stranger who is merely a sinner. During the non-participant phase of my fieldwork, which occupied its first three years, I observed consistent denigrations of education in schools and universities expressed from pentecostal pulpits and in sect literature. Subjects were chiefly suspicious of schools for their teaching of evolution: assaults upon universities were a feature of a more general iconoclasm, the intention of which was to 'bring down the mighty from their seat'. The medical profession, in a similar way, was not so much respected for its achievements as rejected for its limitations. In the campaign to counterbalance the worldly esteem accorded to some respected institutions and professions, old-time pentecostals focus upon death as the time of levelling and upon God as the author of all achievement. Worldly knowledge counts for nothing in relation to divine omniscience; as one crusade speaker said,

> The greatest scholars and the greatest intellectuals think they know it all. They don't know anything at all. They know so very very little.

Undoubtedly, the view of old-time pentecostals arises from the resistance their message has encountered among educated people:

> Education is killing Christianity . . . now head-knowledge gets into religion. It makes young people query the virgin birth. The less education, the more quickly you can accept salvation.[1]

Thus worldly enterprises in knowledge are seen not merely as harmless ventures that miss the point that religion belongs to the heart rather than the head, but as palpable threats to the spiritual life.

The sociologist is even more a bogey-man for old-time pentecostals than the educationist: I discovered among my subjects a generalised view of sociologists as 'communist' inspired or 'atheistic'. It seemed probable that the prevalence of such a perception would prejudice the effectiveness of a fieldworker declaring an identity as sociologist. The problem was whether to make such a declaration and to embark upon the education of one's subjects,[2] to go underground, or to select for participant observation an assembly in new pentecost in which functionaries had appeared to be more informed of sociology and its methods, sympathetic toward them and more receptive of research initiatives. The last of these possibilities was the most straightforward but the least intriguing. However, inveigling old-time pentecostals into co-operating with sociological research seemed not only to be impracticable but also likely to threaten their own perceptions of their behaviour and corporate life. There was an apparent portent in some overt interviews in which respondents declined to answer questions or curtailed the interview on the grounds that there was no point giving answers to one who, being without the experience of salvation, 'would not understand'. For pentecostals, the point is not to observe 'the blessing' but to experience it, and such enterprises as sociological research endanger that experience: 'the letter killeth but the Spirit giveth life'.

My reasons for choosing a covert role, therefore, were largely pragmatic: but I recognised and shall now be arguing that the situation in which I was working was one in which covertness better protected the interests of my subjects than overt methods would have done.

But let me briefly explain the field methods I adopted. Although covert participant observation and interviewing constituted my principal research method, it was by no means exclusive. In the first three years of the research, I observed some fifty-eight pentecostal assemblies and institutions as an overt non-participant, variously using clip-board or tape-recorder, even sitting to make notes when subjects were standing to worship and always explaining my purpose at least to the pastor or elders, albeit in general terms rather than specific detail. Non-participant observation had its usefulness: I was able to experience at first hand negotiations to proselytise me, and I identified and rehearsed roles that I was later able to adopt in participant observation. But my interest was much less in techniques of evangelism than in the internal language of pentecost, and this was withheld in the presence of any stranger in favour of a more public language. This was the basis of the decision to go underground: in order to be able to observe the performance of pentecostal language in its purer forms, a fieldworker must somehow signify that he understands it himself. Accordingly, I used pentecostal forms of the sacred greeting ('Good evening, brother, God bless'), which acts as a kind of password, and I participated in utterances of the so-called praise-phrases ('Praise the Lord', 'Alleluya', 'Amen' and so on).

I was a regular worshipper in a pentecostal assembly for a period of nearly eighteen months. I never gave my testimony, though it was assumed from the fact that I attended weekday prayer meetings and Bible studies that I 'loved the Lord'. I did not verbally profess previous initiation but my behaviour suggested it: as a consequence, preachers who addressed their messages to 'sinners' never looked in my direction. I would lead prayer when called upon to do so, ask questions and offer my own views in discussions, read the lesson as required, make my own requests in chorus time. But I did not rehearse the skills of the nuclear member, such as speaking in tongues or prophesying, and I did not pretend to undergo conversion or submit myself for baptism as did Ken Pryce.[3] In participant observation, I always concealed my research intent: I made neither notes nor recordings in meetings, except where a preacher invited his hearers to write something down. I avoided questions that might betray either ignorance or undue curiosity: I preferred to wait than to guide discussions and conversations towards my research interests.

The conduct of this work has already been the subject of some discussion among professional sociologists. The publication in *The Sociological Review* of an article entitled 'Interpersonal communication in pentecostal meetings'[4] disturbed Bob Dingwall, who protested to Ronald Frankenberg, the editor of *SR*, 'that such a reputable journal has been prepared to associate itself with the ethically dubious practice of covert fieldwork'. Dingwall contended that openness in research was not merely good ethics but good self-interest, and expressed his concern that my 'deceit' would prejudice the reception accorded by pentecostals to any sociologists who entered the field in the future.[5] The issue was subsequently taken up by Rose Barbour, who argued from her own experience of empirical research in a religious community that the adoption of a covert strategy may preclude access to sociologically significant data: unable to find any justification for the conduct of covert research, she concluded that 'Homan made a mistake in adopting this method'.[6] In reply, I admitted to serious misgivings about covertness, largely respecting the investigator as a person, but attempted to defend covert methods as the most considerate among certain kinds of subject.[7] I had some time previously submitted an analysis of my methods to the *British Journal of Sociology*, and this was subsequently published, together with a thoughtful rejoinder from Martin Bulmer, who now takes up the discussion.[8]

Bulmer

There are several criticisms which may be made of your position. Covert observational studies violate the principle of informed consent, which requires that 'the voluntary consent of the human subject [of research] is absolutely essential'. According to this principle, the subject must be competent, informed about the purposes of the research, understanding what he or she is told and giving consent voluntarily and not under any form of duress.[9] This principle is now fully established in biomedical research practice and (in the United States, at least) is being increasingly extended to social research.[10] There are certainly some difficulties in extending this principle from medical to social research — what, for example, constitutes informed consent on the part of a survey respondent?[11] — but equally covert observation is a complete violation of the principle without any extenuating circumstance.

Covert participant observation, looked at from the point of view of the individual subject, may clearly also be a gross invasion of personal privacy. You have quoted with sympathy the strictures of Edward Shils,[12] who elsewhere has argued that

> intrusions on privacy are baneful because they interfere with an individual in his disposition of what belongs to him. The 'social space' around an individual, the recollection of his past, his conversation, his body and his image, all *belong* to him. He does not acquire them through purchase or inheritance. He possesses them and is entitled to possess them by virtue of the charisma which is inherent in his existence as an individual soul — as we say nowadays, in his individuality — and which is inherent in his membership in the civil community. They belong to him by virtue of his humanity and civility.[13]

It may be argued that the benefits of research outweigh the damage which may be done by invading people's privacy. You also argue that in the study of certain types of demonstrative public behaviour, such as prayer, the privacy of the research subjects was better protected by their being unaware that you were doing research, the discomfort of having to interact with you as a researcher being removed. But would the same argument commend itself to members of political groups which had been infiltrated by undercover agents or even agents provocateur?[14] Though the actions of the secret participant observer may be mild by comparison, the same objections can be made to using such methods in both cases.

Homan

I am less certain than you that medical research is an acceptable starting-point for the development of ethical principles to govern sociological enquiry. In addition to the problems of transfer which you mention, I am concerned that the informing of respondents and the acquisition of their consent are often reactive approaches: certainly in my own case, and I believe in many others too, the declaration of research interest would have critically affected the behaviour I intended to observe. I imagine that this is seldom the case in medical research in which the principle of informed consent can be operated without affecting what is to be observed.

Further, the defences of covert methods that I have made at various times have always related to their adoption by scholarly investigators in specific circumstances and I have acknowledged the non-generalisability of my justifications: the critical feature by which I hope I can be distinguished from agents provocateur is intentionality. The methods used by a spy or journalist may not be acceptable for a professional sociologist and vice versa: and those that may be chosen out of consideration for one's subjects in a religious community may be quite unethical in a political cell.

My main reservations about what you say, however, concern the problematic notion of privacy and, in particular, the assumption commonly made that privacy is more threatened by covert than by overt methods. Here it is necessary to explain my position more fully and to recognise that the discussion of subjects' privacy is especially pertinent in the sociological study of religious behaviour. There is something about religion that is rather private: in Western societies at least, the relationship that a man has with his god is in some respects comparable with that which he has with his wife, and we feel sensitive about investigating it too closely. Von Hoffman and Cassidy found the act of invading the privacy of their subjects so 'unbearable' for themselves that they suspended their researches of a black pentecostal assembly:[15] in their case, however, being white and middle class would have precipitated greater strain than I experienced in attending an assembly within a stone's throw of my own home. For my own part, I did not find observation uncongenial: being myself a regular worshipper whose concentration often lapses into observation of fellow members of my own congregation, I find that watching worship comes quite naturally to me. And I suppose that, having over the last fifteen years visited the worship of a great number of denominations and sects out of a curiosity legitimised as scientific enquiry, I have become hardened.

I take it that one of the rights that the claim to privacy asserts is that of freedom from interruption. The enjoyment of free behaviour 'in the Spirit' was axiomatic in the religious practice of my subjects and ministers endeavoured to eliminate all inhibitions, urging their congregations to 'just be free': ecstatic 'praise' utterance was regarded to be both a 'free' expression of the experience of 'joy in the heart' and the discharge of a Christian's duty to God. In testimony and prayer, subjects openly shared their secrets and intimate problems. I accorded to my subjects the right to unselfconscious behaviour in the meetings: where ministers were attempting to remove old inhibitions, I could not be excused introducing new ones. In non-participant observation, the declaration of research intent, whether by formal notification or by the conspicuous use of recording devices, had tended to render worship behaviour selfconscious and thereto rather less meaningful for subjects. The two pentecostal pastors with whom I discussed my research intentions foresaw the potentially disruptive effect of an open declaration and counselled me to withhold my research intent. At least in my situation, therefore, there was a sense in which covertness was less invasive of my subjects' privacy than informed consent.

But further, the privacy of a religious service is itself contentious. I have used in our previous discussion[16] the illustration of my attending football matches on Saturday afternoons: the manifest purpose of my attendance is observation of the skills that are displayed on the pitch, but my attention is invariably drawn to aspects of behaviour on the terraces and I have on occasion written up a field note before or after the game. I have no scruples about making such observations, and to obtain the informed consent of fellow supporters, as by a loudspeaker announcement that there was a sociologist in the crowd, would plainly be ludicrous. Anybody who pays his way through the turnstiles can watch whatever he wants: people go to matches for one or more of several reasons, some posing as supporters to be with their husbands and boyfriends, others mixing observation of crowd behaviour with support of the team. Now, equally, religious assemblies are public occasions legitimately attended for one or more of a number of reasons, and the interest which the assembly has in the visitor is as multifarious at that which the visitor has in the assembly. The noticeboard outside the assembly I joined as participant proclaimed unequivocally, 'All welcome'. The definition of the situation as a private one, therefore, is not based on the perceptions of my subjects but in the principles of sociological fieldwork. In the majority of field studies in the sociology of religion, membership of the observed community is voluntary, and the observed situation is open in the sense that outsiders are free to attend on their own terms. The invasion of privacy is perhaps more problematic in, say, some kinds of educational and psychological research, especially in schools, where subjects are captive and their behaviour relatively involuntary.

Further, the notion of privacy is differentially applied in the critique of sociological method. While covert observation and interviewing are said to penetrate a private domain, little objection has been raised to the method of content analysis. Yet sect literature in the form of weekly magazines, assembly bulletins and missionary newsletters is no more accessible to the stranger or its circulation no less controlled than platform performances in large crusades and conventions in which tape-recording is widely practised. Literature-searching and content analysis are merely forms of a covert non-participant strategy distinguished from observation and interviewing only by the format of observed data. I would question the view of speech and behaviour as private and of literature as public.

But your insistence upon the principle of informed consent, Martin, is not only about one's subjects' entitlement to privacy: it is also about lying or deceit as aspects of the behaviour of professional sociologists, about whether we are willing to become dishonest persons in our search for knowledge. Both you (in your *BJS* rejoinder) and Bob Dingwall (in *Network* 11) concede that lying may be justified in some cases: I guess you have it in mind that deceit is permissible and the means justifiable by the end in the investigation of possibly dangerous organisations such as the National Front. This, again, worries me. That there may be good reason to suspect one organisation of being dangerous or opposed to the public interest (as perceived by the researcher!) says only that its members have failed to keep their cards close to their chests. There may be in the world all kinds of political and religious institutions committing kidnaps, brainwashing, mass suicides and all kinds of outrage. I would be much happier allowing social researchers to infiltrate and investigate such organisations even before there is compelling evidence for suspicion than to inhibit such enquiry on professional and ethical grounds and to observe the consequences of non-intervention: I would prefer the public account of the Jones sect to have taken the form of covert sociological research than press obituary. In such cases as these, scruples about being honest or the reputation of sociology count for little beside the possible benefit of further knowledge.

Bulmer

A different objection to the use of deception in research is that it constitutes a betrayal of trust. If the personal relationships are based upon falsehood, this may harm the subjects of the research. In his recent study of West Indian churches in Bristol, for example, Pryce describes finding himself in such a situation — being a member of two churches at the same time, concealing this fact from the other, and then finding himself with members of both churches simultaneously and being introduced as a recent convert to one. Pryce found himself unable to maintain the deception and withdrew from the second church. He then, however, found himself in a difficult ethical situation with the pastor of the church in which he remained active. He told the pastor of his research interests. This information the pastor concealed from the congregation, but put very strong pressure on Pryce to convert and be baptised in his adopted church. Despite strong personal reservations, this Pryce eventually did, apparently as part of some sort of tacit bargain with the pastor in a semi-covert research situation. Baptism did facilitate subsequent research, for rank and file members of the congregation showed much greater openness to the researcher after it. But they remained in ignorance of his research role.[17]

Pryce's research was only semi-covert. In entirely covert research, the potential betrayal of trust is greater. It is not a satisfactory defence to argue that in published research the identities and location of those studied is concealed. Even if this is done successfully,[18] the preservation of anonymity and confidentiality does not preserve them from harm. If those studied subsequently read or learn of the publication of the research, they must come to terms with the fact that they have been cheated and misled by someone in whom they reposed trust and confidence. Valued behaviour on the part of the (secret) observer in the past — for example, professions of faith, or conversion — must be painfully reinterpreted as merely instrumental and deceitful 'front-work'. Moreover, in some cases the most cherished values and beliefs of the group may be threatened by publication, a fact recognised by anthropologists in the case of some ritual practices, where publication has been managed to avoid, for example, revelations destructive to the traditions of Australian aboriginal society.[19] And regardless of whether individuals may be identified, the publication of a study may cause harm to a group as a *group*. A world too full of pseudo-converts, pseudo-patients, pseudo-students, pseudo-party-members and others playing pseudo-roles will not promote a healthy climate for social science.

Homan

I doubt if such deception as I practised in the field will ever go down in the annals of sociological outrages. I so acted as to avoid being regarded as an outsider or 'sinner': I learnt what behaviour patterns signified allegiance and I purposively practised them. But I did not profess to beliefs which I did not hold: indeed, I regularly exclaimed 'Amen' at the reading of the words with which Jesus instituted the Lord's Supper, 'This is my body', thereby affirming a belief in the real presence not held by my subjects. I could in conscience join prayers for Christians serving prison sentences in the Soviet Union, but protested at the admiration of Ian Smith of

Rhodesia, whom the assembly favoured as a 'born-again believer'. Inasmuch as I refrained from the simulation of tongues utterances (albeit out of fear of being discerned a demon) or submission to baptism, it could be said that I was a participant only on the periphery of the assembly and not a 'nuclear' member.

But there is, of course, a history in sociology and related disciplines of the use of methods even more dishonest and clandestine than mine. Perhaps the most remarkable and controversial case is that of Laud Humphreys,[20] who adopted the role of lookout-voyeur to observe homosexual encounters in men's public toilets and took the registration numbers of his subjects' cars in order to trace and interview them under the pretext of a social health survey. In an earlier and even more intriguing study, Henle and Hubble[21] listened to telephone conversations, eavesdropped in washrooms and stowed themselves under students' beds in order to monitor transactions at tea parties. One of the best known cases in the sociology of religion is, of course, that of Festinger and his colleagues, who joined a group of mystics by professing beliefs they did not hold and even posing as missonaries from outer space whose appearance on earth the mystics were awaiting.[22] As we see from these cases, covert methods may be so practised as to require either the absolute trust of subjects in the investigator (in role as prominent actor) or the subjects' total oblivion of the presence of the person who is the investigator. So trust is not a necessary element in the conduct of covert methods: conversely, overt methods also afford the betrayal of trust, notably at the report and publication stages.

Notwithstanding, I must admit that, upon withdrawal from the field, I was troubled by an acute feelings of having betrayed my subjects and that this has endured. It is not the betrayal of confidential information that has bothered me, for I have always taken pains to avoid that, whether by staying aloof from the more secretive transactions of my subjects in the first place or by refraining to publish data covertly researched that my subjects might have preferred withheld. I have publicly reported covert observations of language-behaviour[23] because these are neutral to the image of pentecost: the only reports I have made that are adverse to this image were observed in overt investigation.

What I have found so uncongenial, however, is the sense of having betrayed feelings and sentiments. I developed a number of friendly relationships with my subjects, and withdrawal from the field necessitated the termination of relationships founded on my side upon developing research interests and on my subjects' side upon affection mixed with ulterior motives to recruit me into more active service. I reciprocated offers of hospitality which helped reduce the strain and I contributed materially to the assembly. But the acceptance of and affection for me betokened by the numerous Christmas cards I received halfway through the observation period caused me a good deal of heart-searching. It did not entirely satisfy me to think that my subjects' motives in the relationship were also veiled and complex.

Indeed, my abiding and retrospective misgivings about covertness tend to relate to the feelings and personal ethics of the researcher rather than to the rights of his subjects. The skills of covert observation and interviewing which I practised in the field carried over to my personal relationships and devotions with detrimental effect. Even drinking coffee with colleagues, I found I was practising covert observation and storing data in the mind to be recorded at the next private opportunity. Whereas in the field my subjects had become my friends, out of it my friends became my subjects. Equally disconcerting for me was the distant scientific interest and detachment that haunted me in my regular Sunday worship. This pervasion of one's life by the arts of undercover practice is perhaps for me the most disturbing feature of covert research. It is for this reason that I would be very reluctant to adopt covert methods again or to commend them to my students, at least until I discover an effective way of preventing the transfer from professional to private life.

Bulmer

You have stated that your initial adoption of a covert strategy was based on pragmatic grounds. Let me, then, offer two pragmatic arguments against the use of covert methods.

The first is not wholly pragmatic, but largely so. It is that the use of covert methods in any particular study is likely to make future research in that locale or in that area either impossible or very difficult, since those studied will react adversely when they learn of the deception that has been practised on them. Whether or not the beliefs of pente-costals about sociology stemmed from prior experience is not stated, but the prospects for future sociologists who identify themselves as such will not be improved if news of your research is widely known among those studied. But the general objection is more compelling. If sociologists adopt covert methods on a large scale, *all* research will become more difficult. Covert studies reinforce 'an image already prevalent in some circles that sociologists are sly tricksters who are not to be trusted. The more widespread this image becomes, the more difficult it will be for any social scientist to carry out studies involving active participants.'[24]

Homan

I fully share your concern that no sociological field should be spoiled by one investigator to the disadvantage of his successors. But once again it is not a simple matter of covert researchers being wholly guilty and overt fieldworkers being innocent. I might even suggest that ecological concern in social research argues as well for nonreactive covert methods as for overt ones that are inevitably obtrusive.

In choosing a research strategy, one of the possibilities open to me was to declare my researcher identity and to educate my subjects in the work I was undertaking. This would have been in line with the principles of practice established by the British Sociological Association, which lay down 'the doctrine of "informed consent" on the part of subjects and [recommend that the sociologist should] take pains to explain fully the objects and implications of his research to individual subjects. The sociologist has a responsibility to explain as fully as possible and in terms meaningful to the subjects what his research is about, who is undertaking and financing it and why it is being undertaken.'[25] One of the major reasons for my not electing this course was its reactivity. My subjects were unaware of the peculiarities of their speech, of the social controls at the disposal of functionaries or of the latent functions of interpersonal communications in prayer performances: to have sensitised subjects of such features in their behaviour would have significantly changed the phenomena being observed: no more would an enlightened ornithologist shoot a rare bird he wanted to study. Not only would the inevitable distancing of subjects from their behaviour detract from or render less valid their own primary purpose in worship, but conscious-ness of controls and communications might dispose subjects to resist or avoid them. Now this applies not only within the period of my own field contact but also at a more general level in that the tendency of sharing sociological insights would be to do away with the experience and behaviour of primitive pentecost. I suppose I am expressing here the mis-giving about education that recurs through D. H. Lawrence's *The Rainbow* and *The Woman Who Rode Away*: but my concern is less a selfless romanticism for blissful ignorance than a selfish desire to preserve subject matter for myself and other sociologists. Because I believe that sociological insight would lead to both unhappiness among my subjects and to the demise of the old-time, I will not offer reports of my observations to the house journals of pentecostal fellowships: to do so, I believe, would be fundamentally insensitive.

In any case, overt methods can also cause damage. In the field in which I was working, the most notable sociologist to have set foot was Bryan Wilson. His pilot work is marked by outstanding insight and is properly accorded enormous respect among sociologists of religion. But the Elim Pentecostal Church rightly or wrongly believes that Dr Wilson took sides with its breakaway faction, the Bible Pattern Church Fellowship, and took counsel from its hierarchy in preference to Elim's.[26] While this belief endures, any sociologists investigating Elim may find or feel that the field relations they can enjoy are prejudiced. Disagreements endure between these two sects and, in presenting myself a sociologist to Elim elders who remembered the initial schism, I was conscious of myself as the representative of a disfavoured profession who was unlikely to be sympathetic:

I found a marked defensiveness among Elim respondents. The major factor in the giving of offence is surely theme rather than method: in treating of the leadership of George Jeffreys, Dr Wilson touched upon a sensitive issue, whereas the language-behaviour that interested me was relatively neutral.

Bulmer

The more substantial pragmatic argument is simply that covert methods are often not necessary and that the same objectives can be achieved by overt or 'open' observational studies. Many accounts of observational research stress that the success of such research depends more on the acceptance of the individual by those he is studying as someone they can trust than on elaborate fronts and role pretence. Some examples of fields where the need for covert methods is debatable — including the study of crime and bureaucracies — were discussed in Chapter 1.[27]

Homan

Yes, anybody who is contemplating covertness in fieldwork must be convinced of the necessity of methods that are both 'dubious' (as Dingwall calls mine) and hazardous (as Barbour suggests). Quite apart from the objections expressed on ethical grounds, overt methods offer decided practical advantages in certain situations and for specific purposes: for example, as Barbour found, overt methods allow the field-worker to play a stranger role, ask questions from a position of ignorance and submit himself to the agencies of recruitment and induction. These benefits must not be under-estimated. Had I been studying techniques of evangelism and counselling or relations between sect members and the wider society, the stranger role might have served me well.

But the principles of field practice established by the BSA allow covert methods 'where it is not possible to use other methods to obtain essential data',[28] and I would insist that the specific purpose and field of my research did not lend themselves to my operating in the stranger or overt investigator role. As I have suggested, performances in pentecostal language-behaviour tend to lapse when the stranger arrives on the scene: the presentation of myself as ignorant enquirer had the effect upon performance of esoteric language that floodlights have upon the nocturnal behaviour of badgers or foxes. I needed a nonreactive method of observation, like infra-red photography: this I realised only in covert participation.

To summarise my position, I would first want to recognise the peculiar conditions of my own research field and purpose, and the limited generalisability of my comments upon the ethical problems arising from the methods I adopted. I would emphasise that I sustain serious misgivings concerning the use of covert methods, but that these relate neither to the supposed rights of subjects nor to the professional status and image of social research but to the effects of the practice of deception upon the researcher himself. Consideration for my subjects, in which I was counselled by two pentecostal ministers whom I used as informal collaborators, argued for the adoption of covert methods. Lastly, many of the practices for which covert methods are criticised (the betrayal of trust, deception, the invasion of privacy, damage to field relations and the reputation of social research) are neither necessary nor exclusive to covert methods: they are both avoidable in covert research and are probable hazards in explicit investigations.

Part Three

On the Philosophy and Ethics of Covert Methods

7 Social Inquiry and the Autonomy of the Individual*

Edward Shils

I

The humanistic contemplation of man has traditionally arisen out of observations gathered in the course of the daily business of life. Having its point of departure in living human beings, it sought no vantage point other than that of ordinary intercourse. Humanistic scholarship confined itself to the analysis of the lives and works of men and women no longer living. Both these modes of the study of man raised many ethical problems, such as the respect due to might and glory, the hierarchy of virtues, the reverence owed to traditional institutions and beliefs, and the value of originality and individuality. When the range and procedure of humanistic study were extended to cover what has come to be called social science, to these problems were added new ones.

Those angular and reluctant heirs of the traditional humanistic study of man, the present-day 'humanities', have taken over only part of this inheritance, the inheritance of humanistic scholarship. They have dealt and still deal with

* Reprinted from D. Lerner (ed.). *The Human Meaning of the Social Sciences*, New York, Meridian, 1959, pp. 114–21, 128–38 and 151–3, with the permission of the editor and author. © Daniel Lerner and Edward Shils 1982.

the 'objectivations' or expressions of the spirit, created in the past and even in the present and having an existence separate from their creators. In the main their materials have not come from living contemporaries, and even where they have, the product of the spirit has been sufficiently discrete from the person who created it that no direct contact with the author has been necessary. Even the study of living languages requires only a minimum of personal contact. The application of psychoanalytic and sociological ideas to the conventional humanistic subject matters has only raised again the older problems.

That branch of the study of man which inquires concretely into man's conduct in society and his actual beliefs, has increasingly tended, ever since its first modern stumblings, toward immediate contact with the sentiments and actions of living human beings. True, there are substantial parts of the study of man today to which this does not apply — for example, economic theory, much of sociological theory, the analysis of economic growth, large parts of comparative religion, and numerous others which use printed and written official documents, officially gathered statistics, published or unpublished, written records of organisations, legal and administrative documents, published books and periodicals, manuscripts, etc. The larger trend, however, has been toward the diminution of the proportion of effort devoted to the study of such sources. The study of man has shifted increasingly toward the assembly of data by direct, deliberate, and orderly observation and by interviewing, which enters in growing measure into spheres of sentiments and intimate personal relations which have traditionally been studied only by retrospection, reflection, and the analysis of discrete works with an objective existence of their own. It is not primarily the novelty of the subject matter that has brought about the change. Essays and maxims on friendship and love, biographies of the dead, editions of the personal correspondence and journals of persons whose life was over, historical reconstructions of the motives and intrigues of politicians and ecclesiastical dignitaries were by no means uncommon, but they were as far as traditional humanistic scholarship went in this sphere. The events studied were either definitely in the past or they were, if contemporaneous, usually studied at a distance from the principals, and above all from their private sphere.

Where, as in the United Kingdom, the direct approach of modern social science was developed in the study of living aborigines or of the lower social and economic classes of one's own society, serious issues did not arise. In the first place, these inquiries did not enter very deeply into the private sphere of their subjects; they confined themselves largely to external economic matters and to publicly observable actions. There was a restraint on curiosity, deriving from the puritanical ethos of the culture from whence the investigators came. There was, furthermore, no obvious problem in intruding on the privacy of savages or workingmen, particularly those at or near the poverty level, because, at bottom, the investigators did not feel that they shared membership in a common moral community with the persons investigated. They possessed no secrets which were sacred to the investigators; they possessed no secrets whose penetration could be expected to arouse discomfiture among the investigators or the circles in which they moved. The situation was little different in the United States. The first large-scale inquiries based on interviewing dealt with slum dwellers, Negroes, immigrants, juveniles on the margin of delinquency, persons with dubious moral standards, *et al.* — people regarded as not possessing the sensibilities which demand privacy or the moral dignity which requires its respect. Moreover, the investigators were inhibited in their curiosity by the wider culture and by the traditions of their discipline.

The shift to the study of the 'respectable' classes came later and in a different atmosphere. Hence, the tradition of direct confrontation of the subject through interviewing became firmly established before there seemed to be any moral problem. This new tradition was, moreover, encouraged by the belief, sometimes held by the investigators or those who conceived, supported, and guided the research, that the results would be applied in the improvement of the welfare of the class of persons being studied. The chief problem of this technique of research therefore appeared to be the overcoming of 'resistance' to being interviewed, i.e., resistance to the disclosure of private matter.

Nonetheless, the creation of techniques for the direct observation of living persons and contemporary institutions, the deepening of intellectual curiosity about the motives and the very tissue of social life, the diminution of inhibitions on intrusiveness into other persons' affairs, and the concomitant formation of techniques for perceiving these deeper and subtler things have precipitated problems of ponderable ethical significance. The ethical values affected by contemporary social research are vague and difficult to formulate precisely. They refer mainly to human dignity, the autonomy of individual judgment and action, and the maintenance of privacy. (To a lesser extent and in a different aspect, they involve the sacredness and majesty of authority and the security of the state and community from external enemies.)

The value of privacy is derived from our belief in the sacredness of individuality.

The sacredness of individuality in the conventional religious sense is based on the belief that men are a special category of God's creatures, having in them a breath of divinity or being capable of absorbing into themselves and of being absorbed into divinity. The so-called secular view omits the element designated as divinity, but retains nearly everything else. It is the sentient, mindful human being whose experiences are not just transient events in time and space but are elements gathered up in memory and transformed by the powers of the mind into a coherent, judging, choosing, discriminating, self-regulating entity, conscious of its selfhood. In its individuality, the human organism develops an ego, a complex bounded system into which the past is assimilated, the future envisaged and sought, and the present made the object of discriminating decisions in which are contained assimilated precipitates of past experience and judgments and choices about the future. Individuality is not, however, just a cognitive system or a system of cathectic (loving and worshiping) orientations. It is constituted by the feeling of being alive, consciously and continuously, by the existence of responsiveness which is part of a highly integrated system. Every response of individuality bears the mark of the uniqueness of the system, which is self-creating and self-sustaining. Individuality is a system with its own rules of directions and rest. This mindful, self-regulating core of the life of a human organism is what is sacred, and it is that which constitutes its individuality. It is this that makes man into a moral entity capable of entering into relationships of personal love and affection, capable of becoming wise, capable of assuming responsibility for his actions and acting on behalf of a civil community.

It is the possession of individuality that renders a human being capable of transcending his individualism in love and friendship and in responsible membership in a civil community. He can, however, transcend his boundaries if he possess and retain them; the transcendence must be discriminating and guided by standards and sensitivities which are integral to the individual. Obviously, there are limitations to the self-regulatory power: the organism within which individuality has its seat brings determinants, and the dispositions and capacities developed in interaction with the early social, primarily familial, environment likewise create a framework which it is not easy to leave behind. Moreover, the weight of cultural tradition, the needs of cooperative undertaking, and the maintenance of social order on a wider scale impose restrictions on the self-regulatory powers of individuality. But they never extinguish it, and the stronger, the richer, and the more elaborate the individuality, the more it can assert its self-regulatory powers. Individuality requires actual autonomy, not only the freedom of action, freedom in the outward movement of the individual, but also immunity from intrusion into areas where the center of selfhood resides. There must be both freedom to move outward and autonomy *vis-à-vis* intrusions or efforts to influence the inner sphere. The sphere of privacy is built up from memories and intentions, by standards, tastes, and preferences, which are constitutive of self-consciousness and which an individual would share only with an intimate, and voluntarily, if he were to share them at all. He might not be in a position to share these elements of his self because he is insufficiently aware of them, even though they are of constitutive significance for the structure of his self-consciousness. But whether he is aware of them or not, their disclosure must be entirely voluntary and deliberate; otherwise his autonomy is infringed upon. Disclosure of the content of the inner realm of individuality should be based on some knowledge of why the disclosure is elicited and a reasonable assent to the reasons for eliciting them.

Modern liberal society is the parent of individuality. It could not develop in a society in which there is no freedom to explore, to experience, and to judge, and in which the individual need not bear some of the responsibility for the consequences of his judgment. The emergence of individuality and the attendant demand for freedom are accompanied, however, by sensitivity and openness to the individuality of others. From this arises one of the problems which modern social research techniques do not create but only complicate.

The individuality of other human beings arouses curiosity; it arouses the desire to be in some sort of contact — whether it be entirely cognitive or cathectic can be left aside at this point. It generates a demand for intrusion into privacy far more powerful than the trivial gossip at a distance which is characteristic of less sensitive phases of human development.

The respect for privacy has taken its place in the constellation of values of modern liberalism. It is, however, a relatively recent addition. It rested for a long time among the undrawn implications of the liberal position and came to the forefront only with the growth of individuality and its appreciation, and the development of a more widespread personal sensitivity. However lately arrived on the scene, it is now fully incorporated. Like the other values of modern liberalism, it is subject to the affinities and the antimonies of every elaborate *Weltanschauung*.

The respect for privacy rests on the appreciation of human dignity, with its high evaluation of individual self-determination, free from the bonds of prejudice, passion, and superstition. In this, the respect for human dignity and individuality shares an historical comradeship with the freedom of scientific inquiry, which is equally precious to modern liberalism. The tension between these values, so essential to each other in so many profoundly important ways, is one of the antimonies of modern liberalism. The ethical problems with which we are dealing here arise from the confrontation of autonomy and privacy by a free intellectual curiosity, enriched by a modern awareness of the depth and complexity of the forces that work in us and implemented by the devices of a passionate effort to transform this awareness into scientific knowledge.

II

The participant-observer technique was once highly esteemed and still has many practitioners in sociological research. It seems to me to be susceptible to considerable ethical abuse. It is wrong for an inquirer ostensibly to take up membership in a community with the intention of conducting a sociological inquiry there without making it plain that that is what he is doing. His self-disclosure might occasionally hamper research he is conducting, but the degree of injury suffered does not justify the deviation from straightforwardness implied by withholding his true intentions. (Furthermore, since sociologists, like most other people, have a certain strength of moral scruple, their subsequent interviewing and observation in the group or community are likely to benefit from having an easy conscience.)

There is, in principle, nothing objectionable about much of the observation of the conduct of other persons. Life in any case is unimaginable without it; it is inevitable as long as human beings live together. It is, moreover, the source of reflective wisdom, and those who do not practice it at all abstain only because they are morally or intellectually defective. The observation which is part of the normal course of life, however, usually is not sought on false pretenses. It is integral to the process of interaction, and when it is focused on actions in which the observer has no immediate part, it is directed to actions which the persons observed perform in the pursuit of their own ends. The observations of everyday life are conducted in relationships which have arisen out of intentions other than observation. The observation has not created the relationship merely for the purpose of observing the other person; to the extent that he has done so he is guilty of manipulation, which, however frequent, nevertheless remains morally obnoxious; nor does it lose its obnoxiousness by virtue of its triviality or harmlessness.

Observation which has within it a large element of manipulation — and this is also common to certain kinds of interviewing and participant-observation and to most projective tests — seem to me to be morally questionable on two grounds. First, on account of the wrongfulness of manipulation itself, and second, on account of the private nature of the subject matter of the disclosures which the manipulating interviewer tries to precipitate. It is an effort to intrude, without a person's consent or his knowing cooperation, into the reserved sphere of his individuality.

Observation which takes place in public or in settings in which the participants conventionally or knowingly accept the responsibility for the public character of their actions and expressions, for example in a parliamentary chamber or in a university seminar or in a public meeting or in a restaurant, a bar, or a café or on the street, is different from observation which seeks to enter the private sphere unknown to the actor. The person who takes on himself the responsibilities of public life has to some extent made a large part of his action public property, although in the case of the mixed public-private situation, e.g., the restaurant, the moral right of privacy should limit the freedom of observation.[1]

The open sphere — the sphere in which the individual by his career has committed himself to publicity — is a legitimate object of observation, as it is of interviewing. The right to observe and to interview in this sphere is justified by the postulate of each individual's responsibility for the actions he undertakes in public places and in public roles. What of the conduct the participants believe to be private to themselves, and would even like to keep secret? The answer depends on whether the action is properly in the public domain. Even though he tries to keep it private or secret, the politician who takes bribes as well as the one who does not, and the administrator who favors a kinsman as well as the one who does not, cannot rightfully claim that his privacy is invaded if a newspaper reporter of a university research worker observes his professional actions or obtains the relevant information by interviewing him or another person about them. On the other hand, the quiet conversation of two friends in a restaurant or bar, the spontaneous intercourse of a family within its own home, the confidential discussion of a governmental committee, or the deliberations of a jury are for a variety of reasons not equally in the open sphere, or in the open sphere at all. In each of these, important events occur which are certainly relevant subject matter for the analyses of the sociologist and the social psychologist. Yet are they justified in entering this sphere through observation?

The propriety of their entry rests in part on the extent to which they do so with the knowing approval of the persons observed. If the social scientists observed what occurred in the relationship but did so with the knowledge and permission of the participants, then the intrusion into privacy can be justified by the assent of the observed. Privacy and even secrecy are positive rights, but the obligation to respect them may properly be suspended by the deliberate decision of the participants whose privacy is in question.[2] Moreover, as long as the knowledge was sought solely for the sake of increasing our general intellectual understanding of human conduct, the moral objection is held within bounds. Likewise, if it is impelled by considerations of public good (and not public curiosity).

But, although there might be some uncertainty regarding the propriety of entering, by permission, into the private sphere, there seems to me to be no doubt at all about the impropriety of unauthorised entry when the persons are observed in situations which they legitimately regard as private to themselves, as persons or as a corporate body. The development of new mechanical devices for observation, such as small soundless motion picture cameras, small, unnoticeable microphones, and other undiscernible sound-recording equipment, has precipitated a very urgent issue, and one on which social scientists should take an unequivocal position. They cannot, on any grounds, approve observations of private behavior, however technically feasible, without the explicit and fully informed permission of the persons to be observed. Such an intrusion into privacy could be justified only as an emergency measure necessary for the maintenance of public order, or the protection of the society as a whole, if it might otherwise be severely threatened.[3] The growth of sociological and psychological knowledge scarcely falls into this class of emergencies, because the real and immediate benefits which it can bring are so small and problematic.

Although the jailing of convicted offenders is justified by the necessities of social order, even the highest scientific curiosity would provide no justification for imprisonment of anyone. *Mutatis mutandis*, the same principle applies to the invasion of the private sphere of the individual or of groups. It is true that in the case of the successfully surreptitious invasion of privacy, no physical harm is done, and none might ever be done, and if the persons observed remain permanently ignorant of the process of observation, they are not even, in fact, embarrassed or inconvenienced. (I assume here that the investigators do not use the data thus gathered in a way which brings subsequent publicity to the particular individuals in question.) Nonetheless, quite apart from consequences, it is a contravention of our moral standards.

In the latter part of 1955, a furor arose in the United States over the installation, by sociological investigators, of microphones in a jury room in Wichita, Kansas. The jurors were not informed of the existence of the microphone or the recording apparatus. It was done with the permission of the trial judge and the lawyers of both litigants. The tape on which the record was made was kept away from any situation in which the individual jurors could be identified by any parties involved in the litigation, their associates, or journalists, and in the typewritten transcript their names were changed so that no particular attributions could be made for any assertions made during the proceedings of the jury. The social scientists involved disclosed nothing of the recorded proceedings to anyone on their own initiative, except to members of the team of investigators. The only breach in complete secrecy in custody of the recording and transcription was committed at the request of the bench.

There are several issues involved here. The first is the deception of the individual members of the jury; the second is the infringement on the confidentiality of collective deliberations which are part of the machinery of adjudication;

the third is the appropriateness of the scrutiny of major institutions by social scientists.

The first question is, in principle, quite simple. The concealment of microphones that would record discussions that jurors had good reason to believe were not being recorded is contrary to honest dealing, and even if the judge and the two lawyers had a crucial responsibility, the social scientists are not thereby exempted from their share of the blame. It must, however, be pointed out that the subject matter of the deliberations was not in the *personally* private sphere of the jurors. Nonetheless, their proceedings were undertaken with the understanding that, although performing *public* functions, they were performing them with the guarentee of *confidentiality*,[4] like those with which private personal relations are conducted. It was therefore an invasion of the fiduciary sphere in the same way that newspapermen invade it when they interview jurors or when they attempt to get government officials and legislators to say what went on in confidential or secret meetings. It differs from the observation of occurrences within a family or between lovers, if their permission to observe them had not been obtained in advance (which are clearly intrusions on privacy), only with respect to the fact that the jury system, like Cabinet meetings, is a matter of genuine public interest and not merely one of titillating public curiosity.

There are other reasons to be considered for denying the permissibility of such action, even if the jurors had agreed in advance to the observation and recording of their deliberations. The confidential or secret character of jury proceedings is traditionally justified by (1) the desirability of completely free discussion as a means of reaching a collective decision; (2) the necessity of avoiding pressure on jurors by nonjurors, which might occur if the course of deliberations were to become known by nonjurors, e.g., litigants, their lawyers, friends and kinsmen of the litigants. The confidentiality of the jurors' deliberations is not the same as the confidentiality of personal private affairs, and the argument for maintaining it must therefore be different. The invasion is an infringement on a convention which, it is claimed, sustains an important public institution. But no harm would be done to the effectiveness of the jury process, firstly, if the record, once taken without the knowledge and permission of the jurors, remained sealed up under the strictest custody of the trial judge until after any period during which appeals could be made had elapsed, and if the control and custody of the record and the transcript were sufficiently rigorous to protect the jurors from pressures or reprisals from persons who might have suffered from their judgments, and secondly, if members of subsequent juries, knowing that their delibera- tions could be recorded, were given absolute assurance by the judge either that no improper use whatsoever would ever be made of the record, or that no record whatsoever was being made.

Nonetheless, although the public order might not be damaged if observations of this sort were made with these safeguards, they would still possess an element of impropriety because they involved subjecting the jurors to deception.

If the jurors had been informed of the arrangements for recording their deliberation and of the secure provision for preventing any breach in confidentiality, and they had agreed to the arrangement, then it would seem to have been permissible.[5] Unfortunately, however, there is no absolute security of such provision. There would be a risk that one or more of the jurors, as jurors sometimes do about the proceed- ings themselves, would talk to an outsider about the recording, and this might be exploited by one of the lawyers in seeking a reversal of the decision; but as jurors cannot be called as witnesses about deliberations in hearings on appeals from decisions by lower courts, so the records of their discussions could likewise be given the same immunity.

The case of the recorded deliberations of the Wichita juries raises questions not only about the permissibility of deception in social research and the right of privacy in private and public roles but also about the susceptibility of sacred institutions to detached inquiry.

III

The public discussion of the recorded jurors' deliberations in the United States devoted little attention to the problems involved in the invasion of the jurors' privacy and not much more to the possible influence of the recording or the research on the effectiveness of the jury system. The response was largely an emotional and unreflective denunciation of the sociological and legal investigators who had had the effrontery to 'tamper' with the jury system. Quite apart from the political motives of the congressional committee which conducted the hearings and of the officials of the Department of Justice, there was a widespread feeling of abhorrence for the very notion of a detached scrutiny of the interior of a 'sacred' institution. The abhorrence, although 'irrational', is not on that account to be condemned out of hand.

The nominally secular modern state has no avowedly 'sacred' sphere, and the churches no longer have the power to prevent anyone outside their jurisdiction from turning an empirically analytical eye onto their sacred objects and actions. Nonetheless, there is a sacred area even of secular societies. The detached and realistic observation of the actual working of certain institutions arouses feelings approaching horror and terror in some persons, just as it exercises the fascination of sacrilege on others. For the secular state, what goes on in these institutions is sacred, and no social scientist would be unqualifiedly free to disclose, even if he were to know as a participant, what goes on in spheres designated as 'secret'. Those who possess secret information are not privileged to disclose it in interviews, and the attempts to learn of it without permission are strictly prohibited under severe penalties, even if the intention is politically innocent and scientifically reasonable.[6]

It would be misleading to account for this horror of penetration into the secrets of vital institutions solely to expediential considerations, such as national security or the protection form skullduggery or the efficiency and effectiveness of the institutions in question. The secular state does not confine its exclusiveness solely to matters which are characterised as necessary for national military security. The meetings of Cabinets, the President's meetings with his advisers, the deliberations of the Supreme Court, the caucuses of party leaders have been closed to scientific inquirers, just as they have been closed to journalists; the reason is not entirely that public knowledge of them would harm the state or subvert public order or diminish the prestige or effectiveness of politicians and administrators, but that persons who wield great power feel a deep urge to keep their deliberations from external knowledge.[7] 'Official secrets' guard not only knowledge and intentions which ought to be kept from foreign enemies but internally 'sacred' things as well.

Even where the society is as populistic as it is in the United States, where the journalists are so inquisitive and where politicians enjoy and are inured to the bright light of publicity, social investigators are denied entry into such spheres. In fact, social scientists usually do not even seek such entry, partly because they believe it would be denied them, and partly, I believe, because they themselves stand in such — seldom acknowledged — awe of the majesty of the powerful, of the sacredness of power, that although their minds are attracted by it, they do not seek direct contact.[8]

Good arguments can be made against continuous publicity about public institutions. It could be claimed that extreme publicity not only breaks the confidentiality which enhances the imaginativeness and reflectiveness necessary for the effective working of institutions but also destroys the respect in which they should, at least tentatively, be held by the citizenry. The former consideration is purely empirical and has a reasonable probability of being right. It stands in contradiction to the liberal—democratic and particularly to the populistic—democratic principles of 'the eyes of the public' constituting the 'virtue of the statesman'. It restricts the freedom of social scientists. The second consideration is genuinely conservative, as it implies that authority must have some aura of the ineffable about it to be effective. It contradicts a postulate of liberalism and of the social science which is a part of liberalism and which has on the whole proceeded on the postulate of unlimited publicity and an easy-going irreverence toward authority.

I think that this latter, more conservative consideration is by no means entirely groundless. But, nonetheless, it should not be carried very far. For one thing, social science, even where it seeks a wide public diffusion of its results, seldom attains it. Most social research reports are works of very restricted circulation.[9] Although it might, under certain conditions, not be desirable that the understanding of man's nature and of the nature of authority, which is forwarded by social science, should be more widely appreciated and shared, that does not happen often enough or intensively enough to endanger any institution or the social system as a whole. Reasonable conservatives have little to fear from the allegedly 'disintegrative' consequences of social research, because it cannot affect the views of great numbers of persons. On the more fundamental issue, although I agree that there must be some feeling of the inherent rightfulness of the principles of justice and authority embodied even in a liberal democratic order, I think that the most rigorously scientific social research (assuming that those performing it are not actually seeking fundamentally to discredit the order they are studying) cannot endanger that order. I do not think that all social order rests on cognitive illusions which the results of scientific social research must dissolve.

I myself see no good reason, therefore, other than expediency, why these 'sacred' secular subjects should not be studied by social scientists or why they should not be studied by legitimate research techniques. I can see no harm that can come from such inquiries, carried on with judicious detachment and presented with discretion. I can see no moral issue here, such as I can see in the case of manipulation by interviewers and observers or in the case of intrusion on privacy.[10]

IV

The reserve forces of Western culture which would inhibit social scientists from seeking to establish a tyranny over their fellow men on behalf of their science and on the basis of it are multifarious; they are also, however, by no means free from ambivalence. On the positive side, there is a very real respect and appreciation for individuality, perhaps even more in the United States than in Europe. There is among men of practical experience a distrust, sometimes excessive, sometimes insufficient, for the theorist, for the scientist with his abstract schemes and doctrines. There is also, in the vast majority of the population, a common decency and sense of moral restraint which is common to our Western culture with its tendency toward moral equalitarianism.

On the other side is the *scientific* attitude, and the impatience with imperfection which are also parts of our cultural inheritance from Bacon, Condorcet, Comte, Marx, down to Bernal and Skinner, and which envisage men of science ruling society, bringing it into order, overcoming man's imperfections by the application of scientific knowledge.

Within the intellectual classes, the same ambivalence exists. On the one hand, the great humanistic tradition to which nothing human is alien, the tradition of the British, French, American, and German Enlightenment, of Locke, Hume, Kant, Jefferson, Franklin, Voltaire, Diderot, *et al.*, who, even where they are not read, continue to exercise a great spiritual influence in heightening the appreciation of the genius in every living human being. On the other side is a cranky, embittered alienation, which accentuates the anti-authoritarianism innate to liberalism. This alienation cuts the individual off from his society and his fellow man and causes him to despise the irrationality and the triviality of ordinary human beings and the symbols and persons they respect. It is exacerbated by a harebrained belief in the ease with which men can be improved and the unreflective conviction that social science is the right means to that improvement.

Within the social science professions themselves, with the exception of political economy, the situation is also quite indeterminate. Unlike the real sciences, no great tradition has yet established itself, commanding universal assent. Something more like chaos reigns there. Social resentment, and scientific enthusiasm, the desire to legitimise themselves by being useful and influential, the alienation from and the fascination with authority, are all forces which potentially could work in the direction of evil. The public opinion which they create among the incoming generation is not always consistent with the true humanism of liberalism. Yet it must be remembered that they are integral parts of our culture and also share in its values in one form or another. Moreover, even the very curiosity which prompts the investigator's intrusion into privacy is the manifestation of a breadth of empathetic imagination, an openness and attachment to other human beings in their essential individuality, that to some extent provides its own inner curb. It is also just to point out that the theoretical orientation which has come to the fore in the past decade is one which makes ample knowledgment of man's moral and rational capacities. The theory of action which is increasingly, in diverse ways, influencing sociological and social psychological research sees man as neither beast nor machine. There is room in it for man at his heights, as well as his depths, his lights and his shadows, his creativity and his dreay sameness. Inherent in this scheme of interpretation is a genuine respect for the humanity of human beings. This, too, is a safeguard against the abuse of potential powers which social scientists might exercise.

Finally, and perhaps most important, the social sciences are conducted within and under the auspices of the great universities, which nearly everywhere in the West are the Gibraltars of a genuine humanism. It is on these forces that we rest our aspiration for a self-containing sense of responsibility which will guide intellectual curiosity and imagination amidst the dangerous opportunities which modern technique affords.

8 On the Ethics of Disguised Observation: an exchange between Norman Denzin and Kai Erikson*

Norman K. Denzin[1]

Four papers recently published in *Social Problems* on the ethics of social research point to an important and as yet unresolved aspect of the sociologist's work.[2] In brief the questions are: 'To whom is the sociologist responsible when he makes his observations?' 'Does he have the right to observe persons who are unaware of his presence?' And, 'What are the ethical consequences of those disguised observations that may disturb, alter, or cause discomfort to those observed?' In the previous chapter Shils argues that sociologists have no right to make observations on persons who have not consented to be observed.[3] In several senses the papers to which I make reference follow Shils' dictum; however, it is the paper by Erikson on the ethical consequences of disguised observations that most directly adheres to Shils' position and it is to this paper that I direct my comments.[4]

Erikson states that observations by the sociologist that either covertly or in some way deliberately disguise the role

---

* Reprinted from *Social Problems* 15, 1968, pp. 502–6 with the permission of the publishers and the authors. © The Society for the Study of Social Problems 1968.

or intent of the investigator pose significant ethical problems for the sociologist in his relationship to his subjects, his colleagues, his students, and his data. I turn to each of Erikson's arguments and present the counter-position which he submits is either unethical or ethically ambiguous.

First, a comment on my position.[5] I disagree with those who suggest the sociologist has no right to observe those who have not given their consent. I suggest the sociologist has the right to make observations on anyone in any setting to the extent that he does so with scentific intents and purposes in mind. The goal of any science is not willful harm to subjects, but the advancement of knowledge and explanation. Any method that moves us toward that goal, without unnecessary harm to subjects, is justifiable. The only qualification is that the method employed not in any deliberate fashion damage the credibility or reputation of the subject. The sociologist must take pains to maintain the integrity and anonymity of those studies — unless directed otherwise. This may require the deliberate withholding of certain findings from publication entirely, or until those observed have moved into positions where they could be done no harm.[6] My position holds that no areas of observation are in an a priori fashion closed to the sociologist, nor are any research methods in an a priori fashion defined as unethical. This position is clearly at odds with that of Shils' and Erikson's.

Erikson's first argument against disguised observation is that it represents an invasion of privacy of those studied. Such an interpretation, of course, assumes the sociologist can define beforehand what is a private and what is a public behavior setting. Cavan's recent findings suggest that any given behavior setting may, depending on the time of day and categories of participants present, be defined as either public or private in nature.[7] The implication is that the 'privateness' of a behavior setting becomes an empirical question. To categorically define settings as public or private potentially ignores the perspective of those studied and supplants the sociologist's definitions for those studied. Erikson continues his argument by suggesting that when sociologists gain entry into private settings via disguised roles they potentially cause discomfort to those observed. Because the sociologist lacks the means to assess this induced discomfort he has no right to disguise his intent or role in the research process.

If the research of Goffman is taken seriously, the statement that wearing masks, or disguising one's intents, raises ethical questions and causes discomfort during the research process may be challenged for the proper question becomes, not whether wearing a mask is unethical (since no mask is any more real than any other) but, rather, 'Which mask should be worn?'[8] There is no straightforward answer; for we, as sociologists, assume a variety of masks or selves depending on where we find ourselves (e.g., the classroom, the office, the field, etc.). Who is to say which of these are disguised and which are real? My position is that any mask not deliberately donned to injure the subject is acceptable. To assert that an assumed role during the research process is necessarily unethical and harmful is meaningless in this context.

Second, Erikson argues that the sociologist who assumes a disguised role jeopardises the broader professional community because in the event of exposure, he could simultaneously close doors to future research, while tainting the image of his profession. My position is that any research method poses potential threats to fellow colleagues.[9] The community surveyed twice annually for the past ten years can just as easily develop an unfavorable image of sociology and refuse to be studied as can a local Alcoholics Anonymous club studied by a disguised sociologist. Every time the sociologist ventures into the outside world for purposes of research he places the reputation of the profession on the line, and to argue that disguised observations threaten that reputation more than the survey or the experiment ignores the potential impact these methods can and often do have.

Third, Erikson argues that we, as sociologists, owe it to our students to not place them in situations where they might have to assume a disguised research role. The assumption of such roles, Erikson suggests, places moral and ethical problems on the investigator and students should not have this burden placed on them. My position, based on my own and the experiences related by other colleagues, is that this feeling of uncertainty and ethical ambiguity can just as easily arise from the circumstances surrounding the first interview with an irate housewife in a social survey. Certain persons feel more comfortable in the role of disguised observer than in the roles of survey interviewer, known participant observer, or laboratory observer for example. Therefore the belief — that encounters with subjects when in the role of disguised observer cause more investigator discomfort — may be questioned. I suggest there is nothing inherent in the role that produces ethical or personal problems for the investigator. Instead, it is hypothesised that this represents definitions brought into the role and not definitions inherent in the role itself.

Erikson's fourth argument is that data gathered via the disguised method are faulty because an observer lacks the means to assess his disruptive effects on the setting and those observed. I propose that sociologists sensitive to this problem of disruption employ the method of post-observational inquiry, recently adopted by psychologists, during which the investigator asks the subject what he thought the experiment entailed.[10] After completing observations in the disguised role our presence could be made public and those observed could then be questioned concerning our effect on them. Such a procedure would (1) provide empirical data on our perceived disruptive effect thereby allowing an assessment of this effect, and (2) it would allow us to empirically measure the amount of discomfort or harm our disguised presence created. Further, the investigator might make greater use of his day-to-day field notes to measure his own perceived impact.[11] Every time the sociologist asks a question of a subject, he potentially alters behavior and jeopardises the quality of subsequent data. It seems unreasonable to assume that public research methods (e.g., surveys) do not also disrupt the stream of events under analysis. To argue that disguised roles cause more disruption seems ill-founded and, at the very least, is an empirical question.

Erikson concludes by noting that sociologists never reveal everything when they enter the field. I suggest we not only never reveal everything, but frequently this is not possible because we ourselves are not fully aware of our actual intentions and purposes (e.g., long-term field studies).

Summarising his position, Erikson offers two ethical dictates: (1) it is unethical to deliberately misrepresent our identity to gain entry into private domains otherwise denied us; and (2) it is unethical to misrepresent the character of our research deliberately.

My reactions are perhaps in the minority among contemporary sociologists, but they indicate what I feel is a necessary uneasiness concerning the argument that sociologists are unethical when they investigate under disguise or without permission. To accept this position has the potential of making sociology a profession that only studies volunteer subjects. I suggest that such an argument misrepresents the very nature of the research process because sociologists have seldom stood above subjects and decided whom they had the right to study and whom they were obligated not to study. Instead, we have always established our domain during the process of research, largely on the basis of our own personal, moral, and ethical standards. In retrospect this can be seen to be so given the fact that such categories of persons as housewives, homosexuals, mental patients, prostitutes, and so on are now viewed as acceptable and legitimate persons for observation.

To conclude, I suggest that, in addition to these ethical questions, sociologists might also concern themselves with the fact that at this point in their scientific career they lack the automatic moral–legal license and mandate to gain entry into any research setting; nor do they have the power to withhold information from civil–legal authorities after their data have been obtained.[12] As Project Camelot recently demonstrated, sociology (as a profession and science) has little power in the eyes of the public and broader civil–legal order. To cast ourselves in a position which only sanctions research on what persons give us permission to study, continues and makes more manifest an uncomfortable public status. Certainly this need not be the case as the current examples of psychiatry, medicine, the clergy, and the law indicate.

That my position involves ethical issues of the highest order cannot be denied for I have placed the burden of ethical decision on the personal-scientific conscience of the individual investigator.[13] My value position should be clear for I feel sociologists who have assumed those research rules and strategies Erikson calls unethical have contributed more substantive knowledge to such areas as small group research than have those who have assumed more open roles. But again this is a matter of individual, as well as collective, scientific conscience and standards. The entry into any scientific enterprise potentially threatens someone's values — be it other sociologists or members of some society. We must always ask ourselves, 'Whose side are we on?'[14] Unfortunately I feel Erikson's position removes from the hands of the sociologist the right to make this decision. But, perhaps, rather than engaging in polemics and debate we might as a profession open these matters up to public discussion and empirical inquiry.[15]

A Reply to Denzin: Kai T. Erikson

I have been asked to make my remarks as brief as possible in the interests of preserving space, so I will respond to what I regard the more important of Professor Denzin's arguments in essentially the order that he presented them. Professor Denzin is certainly correct that his position is radically at odds with my own. He contends that any research method is justified so long as it is designed to advance scientific knowledge and does not willfully harm human subjects. This principle, I take it, would admit to the roster of legitimate research techniques not only such practices as disguised observation, but the use of wire-tapping and eaves-dropping devices of one sort or another, and all the rest of the contrivances that come from the new technology of espionage. I suspect that most sociologists — perhaps even Professor Denzin — would prefer to draw a line somewhere short of this. If so, the main point at issue here is not whether sociologists should respect some limits in their search for data but whether the deliberate use of masks falls inside or outside that line.

My objections to disguised observation are based on a broader set of considerations than are mentioned in Denzin's review. I feel that sociologists should not invade the privacy of other persons, no matter how genial their intentions or how impressive their scientific credentials, because the practice is damaging both to the climate of a free society and to the integrity of the profession that permits it. Now this is largely a personal reflection and I cannot see much point in arguing about it. But even if I agreed with Denzin that the case should rest with the subjects themselves, I would still have serious reservations about disguised observation. This is because I do not think that Denzin or I or anyone else really *knows* when we are harming other people; and, so long as this continues to be the case, it seems to me that we have no right to let others take the risks for projects that happen to mean something to us without first obtaining their informed consent. I am not at all sure that I know what 'informed consent' is, but it is evident that disguised observation does not fit under the heading.

I made four general points in my original article and Professor Denzin has discussed them in order. Regarding the first, I agree that it is sometimes difficult to distinguish between 'private' and 'public' settings in any objective fashion, but I propose the following rule of thumb: whenever an investigator goes to all the trouble of disguising his own identity and introducing himself as someone he knows he is not in order to enter a social sphere to which he is not otherwise eligible, then it is fair to infer (a) that *he*, at least, defines that sphere as private, and (b) that he expects others in that situation to define it similarly. Moreover, I think it is simply not true that 'no mask is any more real than any other', and in this assertion I would claim to be a student of Goffman's too. Every man plays many parts, to be sure; but every sane and moral man knows that certain roles in the repertory of his culture are proper for him to play while others are not, and it seems to me that we are completely forgetting what we know about the nature of human personality and the development of social selves if we view the matter as flatly as Denzin suggests. It is one thing for he and I to shift social gears as we move in a reasonably defined orbit from the office to the classroom and out into the field, but it is quite another thing for us to emulate those of our colleagues who join a group of alcoholics dressed in clothes picked out of a garbage can or who impersonate enlisted men while receiving the pay and privileges of officers. The elaborate disguises that most employers of the method have devised in order to 'pose' (their word) as someone they are not should be testimony enough to the fact that they are aware of the difference; and, if this is not persuasive, we need only consider what would happen if an unlicensed stranger were to appear in a professional gathering and present himself as an instructor of sociology. We might denounce it as a fraud, diagnose it as a delusion, or pass it off as a prank, but few of us would experience any difficulty determining whether the mask was real or not.

As for the second point, Professor Denzin offers a compelling argument and I will yield. It is of course true that other forms of sociological research have a potential for closing doors to future investigation. I happen to feel that the risks here are considerably greater, but Denzin is correct to suppose that this estimate is based as much on conviction as it is on information.

As for the third point, it may be that Denzin has me there, too. I have no particularly good reasons to insist that students are more compromised while engaged in undercover observation than they are, say, when confronting irate housewives during a door-to-door survey. Granting this, I am left the choice either of arguing that students should be protected from this latter practice as well, or of withdrawing as gracefully as possible. I think a strong case might be made for the first of these options, but instead I will retreat to the second — noting only that my original intention was to point out the incongruities one sees in the arguments of sociologists who discuss the moral ambiguities of disguised observation and then send students out to do the work.

The fourth point is in many ways the critical one, and here I suspect that Professor Denzin has confused the kind of undercover work I was discussing in my paper with other forms of small group research. He contends that we could measure the effect that disguised observation has on subjects by following up the attempt with such methods as post-observational inquiry and the like. Now I think it is reasonable to assume that researchers wear masks primarily when they cannot show their faces, and I cannot imagine why people who will not respond to a more open kind of investigation in the first instance should submit to a few cheerful rounds of interviewing in the second. People who have seen their trust violated, their privacy invaded, their personal worlds exposed, are not likely to be the most cooperative or reliable informants — unless, of course, Denzin is proposing that a second wave of observers should dress in costumes and follow the first, in which case all the objections I raised earlier are simply doubled. I agree that some empirical evidence would be valuable here: my problem is that no one to date has come up with any and I doubt very much that anyone ever will. The conditions that prompt investigators to wear disguises are almost always conditions that discourage any reasonable hope of measuring the disruptive influence of the observer.

The fact that the position I recommend limits our field of observation to volunteers is, I agree, something of an inconvenience; but any ethical stance is a limitation on one's freedom of movement and I cannot see that this is a reasonable objection. From a purely scientific point of view, after all, it is also an inconvenience that physicians cannot experiment on the persons of patients. The presumption in our society has always been that some things are more important than the needs of researchers.

In this connection, Denzin is concerned that sociologists do not enjoy the license to 'gain entry into any research setting' and proposes that this privilege be extended to us. What he fails to appreciate is that none of the professions he lists enjoy this license *when they are engaged in research*, but only when they are serving the interests of clients. If we were to find ourselves dealing only with volunteers, we would certainly be limiting our terrain; but we would then be in exactly the same position as those physicians and lawyers whose status Professor Denzin is so anxious for us to share. The only investigators I can think of who enjoy privileges when engaged in the business of gathering information for their own professional purposes are policemen and espionage agents, and I doubt very much that any of us would like to operate with the general level of trust and respect that they command.

In short, my main disagreement with Professor Denzin is his assumption — stated implicitly, at least — that what is good for sociology is inherently ethical. His 'value position', as he informs us near the end of his remarks, is that researchers 'who have assumed those research roles and strategies . . . have contributed more substantive knowledge . . . than have those who assumed more open roles'. I do not think that this is true by any means, but, even if it were, it would not strike me as the firmest moral ground on which to build a professional ethic. Surely the case should be decided on other merits.

I do not know whether Denzin is in the minority or not, as he seems to feel; but he has stated his case with refreshing candor and I admire his willingness to join the discussion in so straightforward a fashion.

9 The Protection of Human Subjects: a re-examination of the professional code of ethics*

John F. Galliher

The American Sociological Association Code of Ethics, as adopted several years ago, contains three rules dealing directly or indirectly with the subjects' right of privacy. Rule number 3 of the Code reads: 'Every person is entitled to the right of privacy and dignity of treatment. The sociologist must respect these rights.' Rule number 4 also has a bearing on the question of the subjects' right of privacy: 'All research should avoid causing personal harm to subjects used in research.' Rule number 5 begins as follows: 'Confidential information provided by a research subject must be treated as such by the sociologist.'[1]

Rule 3 implies that one must never conduct research without voluntary subject cooperation, while rule 5 indicates that the sociologist's use of data must not exceed the limits set by the subject. Rule 4, a more general mandate, proscribes causing personal harm and discomfort to research subjects, presumably including disclosure of any information about them against their wishes. These rules are not a dramatic departure for our discipline and probably reflect the long-

* Reprinted from *The American Sociologist* 8, 1973, pp. 93–100, with the permission of the publishers and the author. © American Sociological Association 1973.

standing values of most sociologists, and it has only recently become clear the extent to which such rules impose limitations on our profession.

These limitations have become increasingly evident, not because of developments within sociology, but due to events outside the discipline. Recently, several dramatic disclosures involving the operation of government and big business have been made by Jack Anderson, well-known investigative reporter and syndicated columnist, who relied on key informants in government and business to smuggle out highly-revealing information. No less notworthy was Daniel Ellsberg's decision to reveal the classified documents depicting the United States' entry into the war in Viet Nam. Many feel the efforts of Anderson and Ellsberg have made significant contributions to our understanding of the operation of government and big business, even though their techniques involve some duplicity. Certaintly those people and groups who were the objects of these disclosures were not aware of Anderson's and Ellsberg's activities nor would they have allowed the information to be disclosed had they been consulted.

There has been some precedent for similar duplicity in social science research since Bettelheim's well-known study of Jews in German concentration camps. In reading Bettelheim's study, one gets the impression that he obtained neither the permission of his fellow prisoners nor of the prison staff, and that the latter was most certainly not aware of his research.[2] Obviously, such secrecy was required. More recently, in a study of police behavior, Black and Reiss admit to 'systematic deception' of officers whose behavior they observed. They indicated to the officers that they were only interested in *citizen reaction toward the police* when, in fact, they were studying *police treatment of citizens.*[3] Black and Reiss apparently felt that this subterfuge was required since it is well-documented that there is a widespread concern among police to maintain secrecy from outsiders.[4]

Recently, Rainwater and Pittman issued a challenge to sociologists to increase the accountability of elites in business and government. They concluded that:

Sociologists have the right (and perhaps also the obligation) to study publicly accountable behavior. By publicly accountable behavior we do not simply mean the behavior of public officials (though there the case is clearest) but also the behavior of any individual as he goes about performing public or secondary roles for which he is socially accountable — this would include businessmen, college teachers, physicians, etc.; in short, all people as they carry out jobs for which they are in some sense publicly accountable. One of the functions of our discipline, along with those of political science, history, economics, journalism, and intellectual pursuits generally, is to further public accountability in a society whose complexity makes it easier for people to avoid their responsibilities.[5]

Presumably, Rainwater and Pittman would applaud the efforts of Anderson and Ellsberg, as well as those of Bettelheim and Black and Reiss, even though all engaged in forms of subterfuge required for their investigations and would applaud other similar research on conduct in accountable roles. Unfortunately, the ASA Code of Ethics, while somewhat vague, doesn't seem to specify any circumstances under which subterfuge or duplicity in dealing with persons in the course of our investigations might be permitted.

Commentary on the Code

Lofland has defended disguised participant observation as a legitimate research technique. He dismissed the idea of professional rules which would prohibit such techniques.

A professional rule to this effect would not only make for great past, present and future loss to the discipline, but would be an active violation of many people's moral standards who think that there are some groups, such as professional crime and fascist groups, that should be studied whether they are asked and give permission or not. In other words, in accepting this rule, we could not study 'bad' groups, which, as it happens, are also especially likely to be 'groups that do not want to be studied'.[6]

Roth also expressed opposition to a body of rules prohibiting secret research because: 'All research is secret in some ways and to some degree — we never tell the subjects "everything".' Moreover, he argued that:

If the possibility of disrespect for an organisation or group is at issue, we are faced with the question of just when a collection of people becomes a self-identifiable group that may have considered itself being researched on. Would this mean that groups which are consciously organised deserve more consideration than those which are not?[7]

During the initial consideration of the Code of Ethics, Becker expressed doubt about the usefulness of such a body of regulations. He astutely observed that on many issues such a code must be vague and equivocal because there is no consensus within the discipline on many critical problems unique to social science. It is especially interesting that the one example that Becker cited of such issues was the use of undercover research roles.[8]

A different opinion of subterranean research is found in Erikson's conclusions:

It is unethical for a sociologist to *deliberately misrepresent* his identity for the purpose of entering a private domain *to which he is not otherwise eligible*; and second, that it is unethical for a sociologist to *deliberately misrepresent* the character of the research in which he is engaged.

The only conceivable argument in favor of such experimentation is that the knowledge derived from it is worth the discomfort it may cause. And the difficulties here are that we do not know how to measure the value of the work we do or the methods we employ in this way . . . Sociologists cannot protect their freedom of inquiry if they owe the rest of the community (not to mention themselves) an accounting for the distress they may have inadvertently imposed on people who have not volunteered to take that risk.

Research of this sort is liable to damage the reputation of sociology in the larger society and close off promising areas of research for future investigators . . . any research tactic which attracts unfavorable notice may help diminish the general climate of trust toward sociology in the community as a whole.[9]

The NIH's social science grant review committee sponsored a conference on ethical issues involving the protection of subjects and, in contrast to Erikson's belief that the value of certain research can never be assessed, the participants generally agreed that the risks and potential harm of research must be balanced against the possible contributions to science and human welfare. Even so, problems created by deceptive experiments were a central theme of the discussions and ethical problems of participant observation and of gaining access to groups by the use of false credentials were also criticised. A number of participants felt that the involvement of the federal government in funding social science research introduced new responsibilities and constraint, in part because the use of public funds for research implied new responsibilities to the public.[10]

All participants, however, were not eager to generate new controls on social science research. Festinger reminded his colleagues that besides protecting subjects, they might want to remember 'the hard-won freedom of scientific inquiry and the social benefits of research in the social sciences'.[11] Also, at least one participant suggested that some important scientific discoveries have required flouting the norms of the time and place; the issue of illegal dissection of human corpses was used as an illustration.

Later, the report of the ASA Committee on Professional Ethics, which included the Code, was published. It recognised some areas of 'unfinished business' which were 'impossible to resolve', including the following questions:

To what extent can public figures claim the same rights of privacy as ordinary citizens? To what extent does the injunction about the confidentiality of research sites prevent legitimate criticism of organisations that have cooperated in the research? . . . Clearly, much more thought and analysis must be devoted to such questions, and others as well.[12]

However, since the Committee's report, such thought and analysis apparently have not developed; and, having heard of no opposition from other sociologists to the attempt to protect human subjects, through the Code, one may wonder if their silence indicates that they see these rules as reasonable, necessary, and perhaps moral and humane as well.[13]

The Empirical Consequences of Professional Morality

Perhaps the image that many sociologists conjure up when considering such categorical imperatives governing research is that of the ignorant and vulnerable ADC mother, the prison inmate, or the undergraduate student, all defenseless against the scheming sociologist armed with his one-way mirrors and trick questions. Kelman and Bonacich (comment on the need to protect student subjects,[14] while Rainwater and Pittman and Erikson discuss the problems of protecting the poor and relatively powerless segments of society.[15] This image is unquestionably well-founded, for only these types of people do, in fact, need protecting from sociologists and other social scientists as well. However, in studies dealing with the activities of the more powerful and affluent, the same quality and measure of protection is not required since, unlike ADC mothers and undergraduates, these people are often members of groups or organisations that have elaborate screening devices to insure that those sociologists who have contact with them operate in the research setting only as agreed to by prior arrangement. If one does not honor these arrangements, it is recognised that the host organisation, group, or individual will cease to cooperate. These groups also seek to filter out researchers and projects that are potentially embarrassing.[16] Moreover, Roth raises the possibility that, because these formal organisations are more easily identifiable than other groups, their interests may be more easily protected by the Code.[17]

Lowry observes that America is increasingly a closed society in which secrecy is a dominant concern of all types of organisations. Even so, he suggests that the myth of an open society where information is freely exchanged still prevails and that the hiatus between the myth and reality is not recognised by many social scientists.[18] Indeed, belief in an open society is reflected in the Code of Ethics which implies that much significant data are available for the asking.

The organisational affiliations of elites are often the avenues for the wielding of power. The Code, and the professional morality it reflects, ostensibly protect *individuals* but, in fact, serve to protect powerful *groups* as well. The individualistic orientation of the Code ignores the organisation as a unit of analysis and, as a consequence, makes no special provision for the study of social groups. Since it is impossible to betray the group without also betraying individuals, sociologists have failed to hold actors accountable in their organisational and occupational roles. Missing from the Code is some discussion of whether only people in their roles as private citizens are to be protected, or if this protection also extends to actors filling roles in government and business. Using this distinction, it appears that some social scientists have ignored the occupational and organisational roles of the more affluent in government and business and transgressed the private roles of the poor.

Since the relatively new formal Code of Ethics, as well as longstanding professional morality of most sociologists, seem to require the cooperation of our subjects, the only secret information obtainable is from individuals and groups who are too ignorant and/or powerless to demand the necessary limitations upon the researchers. Much more is known about the indiscretions and alleged pathologies of the ignorant, poor, and powerless than any other groups higher in the stratification system. Apparently the poor and powerless are least able to keep their private lives private from the social scientist. As a consequence of our professional ethics, therefore, the image we portray of American society is highly distorted. What the social scientist then describes is a great deal about the personal lives of the poor and powerless and little about the secrets of the more affluent. Even if only the aggregate characteristics of the poor are described, such information may still have adverse effects on the group. For example, a description of the work and sex habits or modes of family organisation of poor blacks may influence government social welfare policy, adversely affecting the subject group. The detailed view of the poor, together with the veneered image of the more affluent, can be used to legitimise a highly economically stratified and racist society. The imagery suggests that the poor are poor because they are the most pathological.

Our relatively detailed knowledge of the poor and powerless seems to indicate that the notion of consent may be inadequately developed to offer them adequate protection. It is likely that they do not as readily understand the aims of social science research as others and may not be as sensitive to the possible consequences of their participation in such research. Moreover, in our increasingly organisation-centered society, heads of organisation can frequently control the participation of subordinates in research on their organisations. In such settings, consent is usually not secured from each actor but rather is assumed if secured from the organisation's leader(s). This not only strips subordinates of the modicum of privacy provided by anonymity but also protects organisational elites.

In sum, the postulates reflected in our professional Code of Ethics that (1) all subjects require protection and (2) that our professional guidelines, in fact, offer adequate protection where needed, are open to serious question.

While all people may be worthy of the same respect as human beings, it does not necessarily follow that their activities merit the same degree of protection and respect. As indicated earlier, Lofland questioned possible prohibitions on the undercover study of fascist groups.[19] It is questionable whether the files of the American Nazi Party are deserving of the same respect as any other data source; must one secure the active cooperation of the Ku Klux Klan, or for that matter of the Pentagon, before conducting research in their organisations or with their personnel? While doing research in South Africa, van den Berghe concluded: 'From the outset, I decided that I should have no scruples in deceiving the government. . . .'[20] The question is, how much honor is proper for the sociologist in studying the membership and organisation of what he considers an essentiallydishonorable, morally outrageous, and destructive enterprise? Is not the failure of sociology to uncover corrupt, illegitimate, covert practices of government or industry because of the supposed prohibitions of professional ethics tantamount to supporting such practices?

Professional Morality and Methodology

The sociologist's professional ethics, which require the active cooperation of the subject, are reflected in the types of research problems developed in which power differentials are not, in effect, made problematic. These research problems have, in turn, influenced the types of methodologies employed. Young contends that:

> The dynamics of the greater part of contemporary methodology, based as that methodology is on tact, consensus, cooperation, persuasion, and establishment sponsorship, are compatible with a managed society — managed on behalf of the large-scale organisations of business, government, military, industry, finance, and education.[21]

These dominant sociological methods include widespread use of interviews and questionnaires and increasing reliance on statistical analysis.[22] Accordingly, in an unusually candid and enlightening statement, Fichter and Kolb suggest that statistical analysis is preferable for sociological research because it protects subjects, especially leading members of the group, by reporting only aggregate characteristics.[23] In any event, during the past thirty years, there has been a great elaboration of statistical techniques which are the creation of a social science which both emphasises the cooperation of subjects and the use of interview and questionnaire data. Since sociologists assume the cooperation of subjects, they have concentrated upon data that are easily observable, and have ultimately collected data that are easily enumerated. The use of data which can be readily counted encourages the search for large numbers and a burgeoning of statistical techniques.

On the other hand, techniques which don't require subject cooperation have not been developed and elaborated at least in part because they have not been considered professional. Many sociologists would probably argue that such techniques are not only unethical but can also involve the social scientist in 'politics' and, therefore, are the province of the political activist and the newspaperman but not the professional social scientist. Ironically, it is the sociologists themselves who have helped politicise their craft by treating methodological and empirical problems of data collection as political or ethical questions.

Concluding Discussion

The irony of the attempt to protect human subjects through a Code of Ethics is that this very Code encourages an approach to data that can be used to legitimise a highly stratified society. Far from protecting those who are vulnerable, the Code serves to aid those least in need of our concern. Becker and Horowitz observe that sociological research has generally serviced elites at the expense of the less powerful:

> Prison research has for the most part been oriented to problems of jailers rather than those of prisoners; industrial research, to the problems of managers rather than those of workers; military research, to the problems of generals rather than those of privates. . . . Wherever someone is oppressed, an 'establishment' sociologist seems to lurk in the background, providing the facts which make oppression more efficient and the theory which makes it ligitimate to a larger constituency.[24]

Becker and Horowitz then conclude:

> A sociology that is true to the world inevitably clarifies what has been confused, reveals the character of organisational secrets, upsets the interests of powerful people and groups.[25]

Alternative Rules

What is required to give a more balanced and accurate description of the workings of society are supplementary data from methodology not based on cooperation of subjects. To help facilitate such research, the following changes in rules 3, 4, and 5 of the Code are offered for consideration:

Rule 3.

From: Every person is entitled to the right of privacy and dignity of treatment. The sociologist must respect these rights.

To: Every person is entitled to equal privacy and dignity of treatment as a private citizen. However, equal protection may require unequal treatment of different types of subjects. More elaborate warnings and explanations may be required in dealing with economic and racial minorities and others who are poorly educated and likely to be ignorant of the research process than with other citizens. The sociologist must make the judgment regarding the amount of explanation required for adequate subject protection. When actors become involved in government and business or other organisations where they ara accountable to the public, no right of privacy applies to conduct in such roles.

Rule 4.

From: All research should avoid causing personal harm to subjects used in research.

To: All research should avoid causing personal harm to subjects used in research unless it is evident that the gain by society and/or science is such that it offsets the probable magnitude of the individual discomfort. The revelation of wrongdoing in positions of public trust shall not be deemed to cause 'personal harm' within the meaning of this rule.

Rule 5.

From: Confidential information provided by a research subject must be treated as such by the sociologist.[26]

To: Confidential information provided by a research subject must be treated as such by the sociologist unless it is evident that the gain by society and/or science is such that it offsets the probable magnitude of the individual discomfort. The revelation of wrongdoing in positions of public trust shall not be deemed to be 'confidential information' within the meaning of this rule.[27]

The latter two proposals reflect the balance of interests perspective regarding research risks agreed to at the NIH conference mentioned above. In these two cases, the professionals' judgment of 'the gain by society and/or science' will be directly related to the amount and significance of new information available. The significance of this information will in turn often be a function of how harmful the subject activity is viewed by the researcher.

Unlike the original rules, the suggested revisions are not vague categorical imperatives but rather explicitly require the use of professional judgments. That professional sociologists, in fact, do make such judgments is reflected in numerous and diverse types of research.[28]

Techniques which might be used under such a revised Code could include, but would not be limited to, the use of key informants, and confidential records, both of which are, of course, the stock in trade of the investigative reporter. Participant observation is a well-known sociological method which, when conducted in a clandestine manner, is also useful as a subterranean technique. Elsewhere, it has been suggested that sociologists set about analysing 'accidents' and even causing 'scandals', both of which can reveal the nature of societal elites.[29] The lawsuit involving cross-examination of subpoenaed witnesses is another research tool not requiring voluntary cooperation of subjects.[30]

However, it must be recognised that the use of these methodologies will very likely create problems for sociologists in a number of their environments. We can expect that some judges will place sociologists in jail who fail to reveal their informants as is increasingly true of newspaper reporters. One need only refer to the recent jailing of Samuel Popkin, the Harvard political scientist, who refused to tell a federal grand jury how he knew about details of the Pentagon papers before their public disclosure.[31] Social scientists are even more vulnerable than journalists because the former do not enjoy the constitutional guarantees of freedom of the press. Moreover, many universities are likely to become embarrassed and intolerant of such research activities under pressure from outraged leaders in business and government. In condemning the use of such techniques, Erikson has correctly observed that employing such methods will also probably change sociology's relations with the general public, including potential subjects, thereby altering the conditions and increasing the difficulty for traditional research.[32]

Research employing clandestine methodologies must not require vast expenditures of money since funding support will not likely develop for this type of research. Such techniques not only can challenge existing power arrangements but also violate the guidelines of most funding agencies. The Institutional Guide to Department of Health, Education, and Welfare Policy on Protection of Human Subjects, for example, requires 'informed consent' from all human subjects and clearly prohibits subterranean techniques.[33] If we are convinced by our methodologies that useful research, of necessity, requires vast sums of money, then our purview will be further narrowed by the partialities of financial sponsors. In any event, perhaps the use of such techniques will allow some sociological research to remain independent of the influence of government and private foundations over the development of ideas within our discipline. While it is not questioned that funding agencies have made possible much important research in sociology, it has nevertheless been established that only selected types of research are supported.[34]

Even after giving due weight to all the likely costs and risks to the profession, the unavoidable question sociologists must answer is whether a sociology that only poses approved questions in an approved fashion is either empirically or morally sound. Moreover, Erikson's warnings about risking our freedom of inquiry by using clandestine research methods may also be taken to suggest that freedom of inquiry exists only so long as no attempt is made to employ this 'freedom' by conducting research outside of approved and safe boundaries.[35] Erikson's foreboding may well represent a correct assessment of the situation, yet it seems wiser to recognise these problems as constraints on our research which require thoughtful consideration than to continue to believe in an academic freedom that does not exist.[36]

10 Freedom and Risk*

Sissela Bok

Free scientific inquiry and social stability are often at odds. Freedom of thought and inquiry threaten every form of authoritarian rigidity, every dogma by which men hold one another down. And when this freedom reaches into new areas — of acting upon people's minds, bodies, or environments, of using human beings as unwitting subjects, or of testing ever stronger means of destruction — a sense of alarm grows even in societies that have traditionally given free rein to research.

Communal self-defense and the protection of individual liberties then lead to demands for regulation of research with injurious or invasive potential. The freedom of scientists to pursue research unchecked must then be weighed against the freedom of those affected by the research. And the risk of hampering scientists and their work through regulation of scientific pursuits must, in turn, be weighed against the risk of harm in the absence of regulation.[1]

I would like to present some of the problems that arise in weighing such freedoms, such risks. These are *moral* problems: they concern choices by human beings of how to lead their lives and how to treat one another; of principles to

* Reprinted by permission of *Daedalus*, Journal of the American Academy of Arts and Sciences, Boston, Massachusetts, Spring 1978, *Limits of Scientific Inquiry*, pp. 115–27. © American Academy of Arts and Sciences 1978.

guide such choices; and of standards of integrity, accountability, and concern. They arise in most efforts to seek
knowledge experimentally: in the social sciences as well as in
the natural sciences; in individual as in large-scale institutional
or governmental experimentation; in basic as in applied
research.

I propose to consider first the views that moral problems
in science don't exist or don't matter or can be coped with
by scientists themselves. I shall then illustrate the nature of
the moral choices present in research, discuss the risks
involved, and the burden of proof regarding these risks.
Finally, I shall set forth three approaches to regulating
scientific investigations according to the seriousness and
complexity of the moral issues they raise.

Why Question Scientific Inquiry?

Many in the scientific community are disturbed that such
questions should be raised at all. Their response takes two
forms. 'What risks?' ask some. Others wonder why, if there
are risks, the traditional avenues of scientific self-regulation
cannot suffice to cope with them.

The first question is often a genuine one. A great many
scientists pursue tasks not even remotely capable of threatening anything or anyone. Many do observational studies,
administer questionnaires, or work with purely statistical
data. Others are engaged in basic scientific research from
which only very indirect harmful effects, if any, can be
imagined. To be sure, there is no clear dividing line between
basic and applied research; too many research activities
partake of both. Nor have risk and innocuousness ever fallen
neatly on either side even of such an artificial barrier.[2] It is
nevertheless safe to say that discernable direct risks arise
more rarely in basic than in applied research. When scientists
are engaged in inquiries they take to be harmless, they often
generalise from their own activities, and may come to regard
virtually all scientific investigations as fundamentally risk-free.

Others who do perceive some threats from certain kinds of
research may consider the potential benefits to humanity as
a sufficient compensation. Why, they ask, should our society

not accept certain risks in order to conquer its most debilitating illnesses or shortages? Such a question is legitimate, but the *distribution* of these risks raises profound issues of a moral nature.

Can scientists, for instance, place specific persons at risk in order to benefit others? Can they create randomly distributed risks to some for the potential benefit of many? Does our generation have the right to place future generations at risk through our experimentation? Is it right for scientists from a nation banning certain experiments as too dangerous to carry them out in societies without such restrictions? However beneficial the final results that are hoped for, it is by no means self-evident that these results justify the experimental means employed. Regulation, even where the highest benefits are expected, cannot merely be waved aside without inquiry into the legitimacy of the assignment of risk, and especially into the question of consent by those placed at risk.

Whether scientists see risks from research as nonexistent or as merely distant and unimportant, the placid connotations of the very term 'inquiry' fuels their puzzlement and their impatience with regulation. 'Inquiry' in science evokes the solitary scientist thinking and questioning. Freedom of such inquiry is freedom of limitless thought and unfettered speech.

Steven Weinberg conveys a splendid image of the world of such a scientist:

> In the Science Museum in Kensington there is an old picture of the Octagon Room of the Greenwich Observatory, which seems to me beautifully to express the mood of science at its best: the room laid out in a cool, uncluttered, early eighteenth-century style, the few scientific instruments standing ready for use, clocks of various sorts ticking on the walls, and, from the many windows, filling the room, the clear light of day.[3]

These solitary, reflective, almost passive connotations of 'scientific inquiry' do not in fact correspond, however, with many of the activities of today's scientists. These men and women are far from solitary in their interaction with others and in their use of vast public funds, far from passive in their use of powerful tools and machines and in the effect of their work on human welfare. They act upon nature and upon human beings in ways hitherto inconceivable. The freedom they ask to pursue their activities is, then, freedom of action, not merely freedom of thought and speech.

Even observational studies, in themselves seemingly least capable of having an effect of a harmful nature, can carry risks. These studies can hurt individuals through improper and intrusive observation, as where the subjects of research on private life are left in the dark about the fact that they are being observed. The means for such intrusive observations grow more ingenious each year; the research projects flourish.

Consider, for example, the social scientist who observed homosexual activities in men's rooms, then traced the participants, took notes on their homes and neighborhoods, and finally interviewed them without revealing his earlier observations upon them.[4] The harm from such studies can come from their instrusion alone; it can stem, also, from error or abuse of confidentiality in the communication of results.

Observational studies can also injure by taking the place of known therapy. When scientists who are also physicians merely observe patients to whom they have an obligation of assistance, their failure to act is unethical and in great need of regulation. Physician-scientists in the Tuskegee Syphilis Study 'observed' the progress of syphilis in a group of patients without asking their consent to being in a study, or discussing with them possible forms of treatment. Even when penicillin became generally available, the study was continued. To have withheld such treatment without telling the patients is profoundly unethical no matter how noble the intention to learn more about the disease may have been.[5]

In questionnaires, too, inquiry can be improper. The questioning can be intrusive and bruising; the information gained can be misused and exploited. Political surveys, questions asked of the vulnerable and the powerless: these can turn inquiries into inquisitions. School children, for instance, are currently subjected to research on sexuality that can only be described as inexcusable prying. It is no accident that much research of a questionable nature has been conducted on the most vulnerable and helpless: on children, the institutionalised, the sick and the poor.

When it comes to more active forms of experimentation, finally, we are clearly even farther from the image of the solitary inquiring scientist. It is easy to see how ill the placid term 'inquiry' fits much that seeks shelter under its umbrella. Research with dangerous drugs and ever more potent explosives can hardly be regarded as 'inquiry' pure and simple. Freedom to conduct such research goes far beyond freedom of thought and speech. At the very least, such research demonstrates that the question 'What risks?' is utterly inadequate to ward off all regulation of scientific inquiry.

The second question often raised by those wishing to protect scientific inquiry from the ravages of poorly planned or executed regulation is: if there is to be regulation, why not rely on *self-regulation*? Why should scientists not deal with abuses in research in the same way that they deal with plagiarism or the tampering with experimental results to expose them and render them harmless? Such internal policing seems the more necessary, the less likely it is that laymen will understand the complexities of modern research. Why not leave what regulation there has to be to those with long experience and the capacity to grasp what is at issue? George Ball, speaking about biological research, expressed strong support for such methods in his address to the 1977 annual meeting of the American Political Science Association:

> scientifically trained men and women are far better equipped to decide whether and how certain types of research should be conducted so as to safeguard to public interest than legislatures or administrative tribunals or courts. . . .
>
> [They] should be permitted maximum freedom to decide what research to undertake and how to undertake it, subject only to such safeguards as they might individually or collectively impose to prevent experiments being conducted in such a manner as to threaten the public health or welfare.[6]

Scientists argue, moreover, that the outside regulation which now looms — the committees, the commissions, the legislation, and the screening — will cut down both on the quality and on the quantity of research. Many, confronted by the bureaucracy and the paperwork already plaguing investigators, threaten to choose other lines of work. Freedom of inquiry is being stifled, they claim, because of nameless fears always directed to what is new and bold.

This discouragement is understandable. The growth of what has characteristically become an 'ethics business' in our society is so spectacular that the temptations of zealotry, demagoguery, and illicit uses of power are strong. The original concern for ethics can then become exploitative and unethical in its own right. The bureaucracy of regulation of research can weigh as heavily as all other bureaucracies, and impede legitimate activity as much. Paradoxically, it can then allow genuine abuses to slip by unnoticed in the flood of paperwork required and minute rules to be followed.

Scientists see risks from regulation, therefore, that laymen often ignore — risks to themselves and to their capacity to work in their chosen fields. And the very passion with which opponents of research sometimes conduct their polemic — the conjuring up of diabolical visions of a future ravaged by our Faustlike cravings for forbidden power and knowledge — encourage equally dramatic and far-reaching counter-arguments by defenders of research. They claim that the scientific undertaking as a whole is now in danger, that our capacity to survive is threatened once we shackle the exercise of curiosity, ingenuity, and reason. These capacities are brittle, they argue, and must be left to do their work in peace. Self-regulation by scientists is therefore in everyone's best interest; for its own sake, society ought not to try to interfere.

Such internal regulation is certainly indispensable in all professions. Yet is is far from sufficient for the protection of the public. Professionals have exhibited a pervasive inability to regulate themselves, whether in law, medicine, the military, or science. Severe abuses have been ignored; incompetents placing others at risk all too rarely expelled. In science, unethical research has seldom been combated by scientists themselves. The abuses of human subjects in biomedical research continued until the institution, in the last decade, of regulation. A recent UNESCO document on the status of scientific researchers, written in consultation with scientists, devotes much space to rights, but veils the subject of responsibilities in bland rhetoric.[7]

Self-regulation, then, does not suffice. What is needed is accountability not merely to colleagues, but to all who are at risk or their representatives. Neither the denial that research entails risk in the first place, nor the confidence in professional self-regulation obviate society's need to weigh freedom and risks for those conducting research as well as for those affected by it. The effort must be to refine, improve, and set just limits to the mechanisms of regulation, therefore, not to dismantle them.

Societies respond to the need for accountability in very different ways, if they respond at all; and different types of scientific inquiry are held accountable to different degrees. In the United States, biomedical research on human subjects has received increasingly strict inquiry and regulation.[8] Social science research, on the other hand, including large-scale social experimentation (on, for instance, education, housing, or income tax payments) is only beginning to receive outside attention of this kind.[9]

For all research, regulation is especially difficult whenever those at risk cannot be identified, or are very numerous. The difficulty is compounded when research is undertaken abroad — as when foreign scientists test contraceptive implants with unknown risks on women in Asia or Latin America, or when a nation tests nuclear devices far from its own shores and its major population centers. The risks may then be very differently understood and assessed on all sides; those who run the greatest risks may know least about them, or have insufficient power to impose regulation of any kind on the investigators.

The Freedom to Experiment

Freedom, risk, and benefit — these concepts have a long history of interaction in moral philosophy. How might we visualise their rules as we seek to evaluate scientific investigations? Are there, first of all, risky experiments where the freedom of the investigator should not be restricted?

Consider the research conducted by Anton Stoerck, a nineteen-year-old Viennese physician who wanted, in 1751, to demonstrate the safety of hemlock if used in the proper fashion, even though it was known as a poison since antiquity.[10] He had already applied hemlock solution externally, to his own skin and that of his patients, with no ill effects. He proceeded to drink increasingly large doses of the solution, once again with no mishaps. Only when he tried to taste the liquid extracted directly from the root of the hemlock plant did he experience great pain and swelling, fortunately temporary. He published these results, and claimed that further experiments showed that hemlock has 'extraordinary virtue and efficacy... in the Cure of Cancers, Ulcers, and Cataracts'.

Some of Stoerck's friends may well have thought him unwise to run such risks through experimenting on himself with a dangerous substance. Scientists might also think his experiment poorly designed for obtaining the knowledge he sought, and inadequate as a basis for the claims to curative powers. His method of preparing the hemlock solution may have been faulty; his dosage insufficient to prove his point. But it would be harder to argue that he should be *prevented* on moral grounds from performing such an experiment on himself, any more than that someone else should not risk mountain-climbing or childbirth.[11] It would be even more difficult to think of reasons why the government should regulate his autoexperimentation.

When, on the other hand, Stoerck went on to test his hemlock solution on his patients the moral aspects of his experiment altered drastically. At this point, it would have been perfectly proper to question the research on moral grounds. His freedom of inquiry could no longer be unlimited, as soon as he was placing other human beings at risk, no matter how important his aims, or how noble his intentions.

In such an experiment, it would have been appropriate (though unheard of on hospital wards until recent decades) to ask the investigator a number of questions before he could proceed: questions concerning what laboratory or other tests had preceded the use of human subjects; how well designed the experiment was for obtaining the desired knowledge (on the ground that *any* risk to others would be too great for an experiment doomed to failure); what risks the investigator foresaw for subjects and what safeguards he proposed in case of mishaps or untoward developments; what possible benefits to the patients themselves he envisaged from the experiment; how adequately he had informed the subjects of the purposes of the experiment, the procedures to be used, the risks attendant, alternative treatments available to them; and how free the subjects were to refuse to participate or to leave the experiment at any time.

Another way in which his experiment could have taken on moral dimensions is if he had undertaken it on himself alone but while he was responsible for the support of a family. Yet another moral concern would be present if he had acquired the funds to perform it from someone else; and a third, if he could foresee a direct and dangerous application of the knowledge he would gain. In each case, his research would affect others; in each, therefore, risks, alternatives, safeguards, advisability, and voluntary informed consent would matter to others besides himself.

Questions concerning these factors can be formulated and often answered. There is absolutely no reason why acknowledging that research has moral dimensions should lead to the familiar lapse into vague discourse about 'values', followed by the conclusion that since such talk leads nowhere, the moral dimensions of research must, regrettably, be set aside.

In the discussion that follows, I shall concentrate on risks of relatively *direct* harm to human beings from scientific investigations. These may be risks of actual physical harm, of psychological harm, of coercion through force or deceit, or of invasion of privacy. They may stem from the process itself of carrying out the investigation; they may also stem directly from applying the knowledge gained, as with the working out of blueprints for cheap and simple nuclear devices that could be used by almost anyone with a grievance and access to fissionable material.

It is not always easy to know whether, and to what extent,

research carries such direct risks. But the effort to see them clearly must be constant; for many invoke much more speculative, sometimes dogmatic reasons for restrictions on research. They may regard some forms of knowledge as threatening their own political or religious convictions. Perhaps they fear that the human spirit will be 'stifled', or that societies will lose all spontaneity or adaptability in the face of new knowledge: the knowledge, for instance, allowing the average life span to be prolonged; or that of beings more intelligent than ourselves on other planets; or of any fact that might precipitate ideological changes.

Questions may arise about how and when to fund such research; individuals may or may not wish to participate in it. But to forbid research on the basis of such nebulous worries is not only unwise, but doubly illegitimate: it interferes with the liberty of investigators without adequate grounds; and it thereby interferes with the public's right to know. As Laurence Tribe has noted, 'the Supreme Court has flatly rejected government measures "whose justification rests . . . on the advantages of [people] being kept in ignorance".'[12]

Nature of Risks

The *process* of carrying out scientific investigations can harm those, first, who participate: either the investigators themselves, their assistants, their human subjects, or bystanders. It can also harm persons at a greater distance, as when the process of research involves the spread of radiation or of toxic substances; at times it can also harm persons far from the site, as in the cancer deaths attributed to nuclear testing. The harm may be unforeseen, as when experimentation with the earth's atmosphere unleashes an unintended effect on the ozone layer, or on the contrary foreseen, as in the case of research with dangerous drugs in an effort to combat disease. Finally, the harmful effects directly attributable to an experiment sometimes only come to light long after the experiment is over. Unborn babies, for instance, may be exposed to drugs experimentally given to their mothers during pregnancy; but decades may elapse before the children manifest the symptoms caused by this exposure.

The *knowledge* that results directly from scientific experimentation can be equally dangerous. It can provide new, more easily accessible ways of harming people: blueprints for new weapons or for instruments to pry upon individuals and invade their privacy, or means for terrorising entire populations. The dangerous knowledge may be a completely unexpected by-product of research, or it may be foreseen as a possibility but not intended, as when a drug developed to remove the symptoms of a disease can also be misused at high doses as a poison; or when confidential data in a study of, for instance, abortion or alcohol abuse come to public attention. Finally, the danger may be foreseen and intended, as in research on biological warfare and on ever more lethal weaponry. The magnitude of such research is staggering: out of an estimated worldwide expenditure in 1972 of $60 billion for research and development, $25 billion was for military purposes.[13]

Concern about possible harm from different experiments depends on the estimated probability that the harm will come about; this, in turn, depends on the degree to which it is a direct result of the process of research or the knowledge obtained. The more the intervening steps multiply, the more opportunities there are for forestalling or alleviating the harm. Concern varies also with the degree of severity of the possible harm, its extent, its irreversibility, and its capacity to spread. For this reason people respond very differently to a self-limiting risk of minor pain, on the one hand, and, on the other hand, a risk, however unlikely, of severe harm, rapidly spreading to ever greater numbers of persons, and impossible to arrest or reverse.

It is no wonder that individuals and groups have widely divergent views of what they regard as tolerable levels of these factors — tolerable kinds and probabilities of injury, for example, or tolerable severity or extent. The divergent views are affected by the degree to which those concerned are informed about the risks in the first place, by the political climate which allows or prohibits discussion of these risks, and by the sense of power or powerlessness to influence the conduct of risky research. These views are also very differently affected by the hopes of benefit from the research in question. Some may regard the risk of disease and even death for a small number as more than counterbalanced by the development of a way to combat a disease such as yellow fever. A few may even be willing to risk their lives in such an endeavor. Others may regard the matter with indifference so long as they are not themselves at risk, but refuse to share the danger.

A fundamental disagreement arises here with respect to consent. Some are willing to countenance a risky experiment so long as it is outweighed by expected benefits; others insist on the additional prerequisite that those at risk should have given their consent. In biomedical experimentation on human beings, such consent is now required by law. Other forms of experimentation give greater freedom to investigators, sometimes because the risks are deemed slight, sometimes when those at risk are hard to pinpoint or so numerous that they cannot all be asked to consent.

Some experimentation carries such flagrantly unwarranted risks or is conducted with such inadequate subject consent as to be clearly unethical in the eyes of all objective observers. This is the case when incompetent investigators handle dangerous materials or perform experimental surgery. In this category, also, falls research on prisoners whose consent has been obtained by coercion, and the experimentation by physicians in German concentration camps on such questions as the action of poisons or the length of time human beings can survive in cold water.

No one should have the freedom of subjecting others to such 'inquiry' without the strictest procedures safeguarding the corresponding freedom of those at risk to know about the research and to refuse to participate. And there comes a level of risk to which not even consenting subjects or persons otherwise affected should be exposed. This level varies with the risks to these persons from alternative treatments. (Thus, a severely ill person may be willing to take chances with experimental surgery that someone with a milder form of illness would normally reject.)

Sometimes, on the contrary, the research is so innocuous that there can be no conceivable risk from it, either to any human subjects used or to others. Such processes as the gathering of data concerning the deceased, examining discarded fluids and organs of hospital patients in the laboratory, and a great deal of basic scientific research falls into this category. Other investigations may carry actual risks, but risks which are completely absorbed by the investigators themselves as in Stoerck's experiment.[14]

But in much research, there is neither such clear abuse nor such obvious innocuousness. The risks, their magnitude and probability, may be unknown or disputed. The benefits hoped for are often just as conjectural. The information itself on which the choice should be based is in dispute or uncertain. In the controversy concerning fetal research, for instance, one empirical factor in dispute is at what stage of development a human fetus responds to pain. In laboratory research, the number of persons at risk may be disputed; when investigators claim they alone run all the risks in a particular experiment, their research assistants, others in the vicinity, perhaps the inhabitants of an entire region may argue that the burden is shared and that safety precautions should therefore be jointly chosen. And in a great many cases, the past experience from which predictions of safety or risk are extrapolated is itself difficult to specify.

Burden of Proof

Given the widely divergent estimates of risk from controversial studies, we must ask: should proponents of a controversial investigation have to demonstrate why their low estimates of risk are correct? Or should the burden of proof fall on those who oppose the research?

In much of the discussion concerning controversial research, the disputants take sides on this issue; but they rarely state an argument for their choice nor provide arguments against the opposite position. Thus, Carl Cohen, in discussing limitations on research with a high probability of very injurious consequences, states:

> Our rational commitment to freedom of inquiry is such that, in judging any claim of highly probable disaster, the burden of proof clearly rests upon those who would

prohibit on that basis. They must present a convincing account of what concrete disasters are envisaged, what the methods are for determining the probability of such outcomes, and how those methods establish the high probability of the catastrophe pictured.[15]

If we used such high thresholds in other social decisions where there is some risk — regarding storm damage, for example, or war — we would take very few precautions indeed. Merely to avoid actions carrying a provable high probability of catastrophe is usually thought too careless an attitude for any society. Once again, the mesmerising image of 'scientific inquiry' has led some to adopt a double standard: they assign a recklessly high threshold of risk for action in the name of such inquiry but accept the normally more cautious threshold for nonexperimental action. They assume that scientists should have less of a burden of proof than others for the same level of risk.

Is this assumption reasonable? Should science be *exempt* to a greater extent than other undertakings from ordinary restrictions on action? Consider the exact same action — say, the drilling of holes in the crust of the earth — conducted by a scientific group seeking to learn how to control earthquakes, by a commercial establishment for financial gain, and by a government agency for defense purposes. Is there something special about the scientific purpose that lessens the burden of proof when the very same act is planned?

It would be unreasonable, I believe, to lessen the burden of proof for scientists alone at such times. Admittedly, scientific inquiry shares special protections when it comes to the freedom of thought and speech. But to the extent that scientific inquiry also involves action and direct risks, it has to be judged by standards common to other undertakings. If holes are to be drilled experimentally, therefore, we would expect those proposing such action to persuade us that the risks are worth taking — expect it as much from scientific investigators as from commercial or governmental entrepreneurs.

The burden of proof, then, rests on those proposing research carrying certain or possible risks. It rests, on the other hand, upon those wishing to interfere with research posing no apparent risk at all. And it can shift back and forth depending upon the cogency of the arguments offered in defense or in opposition of the proposed research.

In addition to asking where the burden of proof lies, we must also consider the degree of certainty of the proof of risk or harmlessness that is required. Even a catastrophe can sometimes be conclusively demonstrated only when it has already occurred. The same is true for assurances that nothing dangerous will take place. If total harmlessness were a prerequisite, little progress would be made in many areas where urgent needs must be met. Much will, therefore, depend on the standards of the decision-makers. An individual choosing whether or not to participate in experimentation as a subject can often allow himself to overlook or, on the contrary, to intensify the burden of proof to the point of lunacy; a committee or institution will have to adhere to standards that reasonable persons would regard as giving adequate protection.

Many despair of finding convincing solutions to these difficult problems of line-drawing, decision-making, and burden of proof. They may lapse into a facile relativism as a result, claiming that one solution is as good as the next, or that political clout will have to determine the outcome. Such a view can, however, be comfortably held only by those who will never themselves be the victims of an unjust policy; it does not make sense to hold it with respect to research policy, where each one of us may be among the victims should the wrong path be chosen.

We must, therefore, ask those who have taken sides on the issue of limiting controversial research to be very much clearer about how they formulate their arguments. We need to ask what they regard as a risk and as risk-free. We need to ask how carefully they have considered alternate forms of research leading to the knowledge sought. We need to know what kind of evidence underlies their estimates of risk; to what extent they rely on past experience, analogy, religious conviction; and where they locate the burden of proof. We need to ask what benefits they see as counterbalancing the risk, whose task they take it to be to weigh benefits and risk, and how informed consent will be sought from those whose decision it is.

Once the arguments are clearly set forth, it will at least be easier to determine where the disagreements lie, how cogent the arguments are, how acceptable the evidence, how suitable the decision-makers. The appeal of rhetoric and false analogies may diminish; and the substantive disagreements can be singled out for careful discussion.

Three Strategies

Three different strategies are needed in the face of moral problems posed by scientific investigations touching human lives. First of all, it is imperative that we become clear about the forms of research where no risks at all are posed to human beings, and that we work hard to remove the bureaucratic impediments from such innocuous research. (Decisions not to *fund* it may be made, of course, on many other grounds apart from moral ones.) Because of the growth of research activities and the confusion about what is and is not risky, there is now much needless harassment of investigators. It ought to be possible to set standards so clear that those who do harmless research can know from the outset that they will run into no roadblocks of an ethical nature.[16]

The second strategy addresses itself to the very opposite cases: those where all would agree that there is clear-cut abuse or recklessness. There is no need for complex moral reasoning to see that physicians should not deny treatment without consent to patients who suffer from curable illnesses merely in order to learn about the course of these illnesses; that social psychologists ought not to intrude surreptitiously upon sexual or political activities; or that dangerous substances ought not to be tested in unsafe laboratories. There is no need to have lengthy committee meetings or earnest soul-searching about whether or not to allow such research. What is needed, rather, is the mobilisation of public opinion and social change to combat such abuses perpetrated in the name of science. What is needed, here as for innocuous research, is to set clear standards, so that scientists can know beforehand when experimentation is too intrusive, or too dangerous to be undertaken. If these standards are clear and persuasive, they will in turn serve to reinforce individual standards of recoil by professionals from research that endangers or degrades human beings. Professional organisations may then come to take distance from such methods as sharply as they now condemn plagiarism or the falsification of data.

Experiments to be ruled out by such standards include the following:

— Experiments presenting some risk, yet so poorly designed that the results are worthless.[17] This common defect takes many forms, including inadequate sample, inadequate data-gathering, poorly formulated study aims, measurements not clearly defined, inconsistent research process from one instance to another, or inadequate links between expected findings and conclusions.

— Experiments presenting some risk performed by investigators lacking the requisite competence or skills.

— Experiments presenting some risk where the same knowledge can be obtained through comparable, but less dangerous studies.

— Experiments presenting some risk to human subjects whose informed consent has not been adequately ascertained. Deceptive experimentation, for instance, still pervasive in the social sciences, would thus be ruled out whenever it places subjects at risk.

— Experiments placing larger populations at substantial risk without thorough review and public accountability. Such public accountability is a surrogate for the individual consent that cannot be had from members of large groups.

These standards must be arrived at and enforced in the greater possible openness. Government regulation cannot itself be relied upon to provide wise and adequate, yet not excessive, safeguards. In the first place, there are by now so many different regulations from so many government agencies that changing and conflicting rules provide the very opposite of simple, well-structured regulation. Second, in spite of all such rules certain government agencies have allowed, indeed initiated, some of the most sinister research, as well as some of the most careless experiments, quite incapable of reaching any results at all. Complete accountability and openness serve to limit such permissiveness; it allows the oversight of experimentation by representatives of those with most at stake, the individuals whose lives may be affected for better or for worse by the research.[18]

The third strategy is reserved for the more complex problems, and those where great disagreement persists. We must press the limits of the clearly intolerable and the clearly innocuous so as to make this middle group as small as possible, in order to avoid as much unnecessary dispute as we can. This narrower group of experiments must then be carefully discussed *before* we even reach the point of considering definitive social policy. The constant effort should be to sort out the easier-to-resolve problems from the harder ones; this effort should include, also, deciding which aspects of the hard problems are capable of quicker solution.

The hard problems that remain will require efforts at defining what is tolerable risk in a particular scientific investigation, when informed consent is adequate, when investigators are competent to undertake potentially dangerous research, and what forms of public accountability are sufficient for different levels of risk.

Time is a major factor here. The deliberation, sorting out, and looking for alternatives cannot be instantaneous. The public consultation and accountability take time too. Many difficulties with proposed research can be eliminated beforehand. Poorly designed projects can be improved; alternatives can often be found to reduce risk and to guarantee adequate consent. If, on the other hand, the difficulties only become apparent once the research is under way, there is much to be said for the process of the moratorium:[19] of ceasing forward progress for a time, while techniques are improved, safer alternatives worked out, risks evaluated, safeguards built up. But the costs of moratoria should not be forgotten: the loss of momentum, the discouragement of scientists who cannot easily shift gears; the postponement of possible benefits from the research. For these reasons, the moratorium is only appropriate as a last resort for the narrowed middle category.

It ought never to be used as a weapon against politically unpopular research unless some demonstrable direct risk is at issue.

Time sufficient for deliberation and reasoned social choice is more important than ever when the damage feared is irreversible; and even more so when it may trigger irreversibly spreading harm. A moratorium can then allow an investigation of how reasonable the fears are, as well as the working out of ways to reverse possible damage and arrest its spread. It has the advantage of being reversible, unlike the damage itself.

The great obstacle to the taking of adequate time to consider risks and safeguards is the very natural individual drive to completion and achievement on the part of scientists, and the competition for priority, academic excellence, sometimes also for financial rewards and fame. The personal ambitions of individual scientists ought not, however, to be allowed to govern what is by now most often a joint undertaking, requiring joint safety and natural caution.

But in thinking about this third group of cases, there is no need to hesitate about the first two. Our society has every interest in speeding the efforts to eradicate clear-cut abuses in the name of research, and in lifting the many bureaucratic restrictions on innocuous scientific inquiry.

11 Moral Judgements: strategies for analysis with application to covert participant observation*

Paul Davidson Reynolds

Investigators hoping to develop unaffected, natural descriptions of the behaviour or perspectives of individuals, particularly those involved in atypical or controversial activities, often engage in covert participant observation. Acceptance as a social and cultural peer has a number of advantages for research. If successful, it increases confidence that the behaviour and comments of the participants have not been influenced by a concern for observation by outsiders, either by potential critics (for example, professors) or those legally obligated to report wrongdoing (for example, police). For some types of deviant or illegal behaviour, it may be the only way to develop accurate descriptions that are not affected by deliberate distortions, biased recollections or outright denial. In organisational settings (such as mental institutions or businesses), it can provide a conception of 'official' activities free from influences by members (to look good to their superiors) or the supervisors and managers (to look good to external authorities). For these and other reasons, it has been a common research procedure among criminologists, psychiatrists, psychologists, sociologists and

* Original material © Paul Davidson Reynolds 1982.

some anthropologists. However, all types of investigators, and particularly the latter, are restricted to applying covert participant observation to situations where they can be accepted as a social, racial, genetic and cultural peer, which excludes its use in dramatically different cultural groups.

Depending upon the circumstances, covert field observation may be seen as unethical because it is sneaky and deceptive (the participants are misled regarding the investigator's true purpose); may lead to an invasion of privacy (confidential thoughts or events may be recorded and publicly disclosed); harm may come to the participants (disclosure of illegal or embarrassing data may have negative impacts for individuals providing the information, details on deviant or atypical groups or subcultures may affect future activities); it infringes upon the 'right' of individuals to be 'let alone'; it denies the research participants the right to provide their informed consent; and general knowledge of this research practice may increase the level of suspicion and distrust in society (ordinary people may become more guarded in new friendships to avoid 'entrapment' in a research endeavour).[1] However, none of these effects would be unique to covert observations by a social scientist; the societal position of the observer is irrelevant. The freelance journalist, undercover police officer, private detective, and the like may engage in covert participant observation without elaborate formal training, credentials or institutional affiliations.

One response to such moral concerns (actions inconsistent with accepted notions of right and wrong) is to encourage the development of principles or standards to guide the implementation of covert participant observation; the establishment of a code of ethics (formally recognised standards of right and wrong) is one of the most common reactions of professional associations to moral controversy and member indignation.[2] Such a focus may reflect the hope that there are universal, yet specific, moral and ethical principles that — once explicated — will serve as a satisfactory guide for all time. However, the constant change in objectives and methods of social science investigators (as they study new phenomena and develop new research techniques) and the shifting standards of society (as the rights and privileges of its members are revised, usually expanded) makes it difficult to develop a set of principles that are specific, timely and appropriate to all future research activities.

An alternative to a code of ethics is the development of strategies for analysis of moral dilemmas, approaches that may be utilised as both research activities and societal norms change. The remainder of this chapter will review several alternatives for the moral analysis of covert participant observation; emphasis upon individual rights, utilisation of cost-benefit analysis, and attention to criteria for being a 'good' or 'moral' person. These are often the unacknowledged basis for the various principles in codes of ethics. Following a review of these forms of analysis, they will be applied to selected examples of covert participant observation. The final section reviews those factors that may affect the emphasis of the 'moral analyst' (whether investigator, participant or independent observer).

Strategies for Moral Analysis

Attempts to develop acceptable solutions to three issues have been the subject of religious, political, legal and philosophical analysis related to moral controversy for centuries.[3] These issues are:

(1) What is the justification for the establishment of a political state?
(2) How should public programmes and legislation be evaluated?
(3) What is the criteria for being a moral or good person?

The solutions developed to these issues form the basis for the strategies utilised in the ethical and moral analysis of all research involving human participants, including covert participant observation.

Individual rights

The evolution of the concept of individual rights closely follows the development of justifications for a political state (paralleled by the adoption of various political documents and state constitutions). While the advantages of an organised political state for the individual members have long been recognised (restriction upon violence and aggression from within and without society, regulation of commerce, efficient provision of public goods and services), a major problem has been to ensure that the individuals acting upon behalf of society did not abuse the ordinary citizens, either for personal advantage or to achieve some presumed social benefit. One solution (at least in political and legal thought) has been to emphasise the privileges or rights of ordinary members rather than a narrow specification of the authority of the rulers. It has been assumed that it is better for society if the rulers have broad authority and jurisdiction as long as they do not infringe upon the rights specified for individuals; many such rights were explicated in response to a history of specific abuses (as in the Magna Charta and the US Bill of Rights). Individual rights originally included the right to life, freedom from assault, unrestricted travel (movement), pursuit of happiness (economic wellbeing), freedom of speech, assembly, religion and the like; recent constitutions (and the UN Declaration of Human Rights) as well as reinterpretations or modifications of established constitutions have added the right to an education, medical care, productive employment, to form and raise a family, to share the benefits of scientific advancement, privacy, and so forth. The formal acceptance of these rights appears to be universal, regardless of the society's economic organisation (capitalistic, socialistic, mixed, and so on); although all may not be realised in practice.

Such a comprehensive list of individual rights leads to a variety of situations where conflicts may occur, either between the rights of different individuals or between individual rights and actions that may serve the common good. Examples of the first includes foregoing the right to property in return for economic advantage (a person may temporarily forgo the right to property to borrow money) or giving up the right to unrestricted personal relationships in exchange for intensely intimate relationships with one individual (as in a marriage 'contract'). The usual solution in such cases is to allow selected rights to be foregone if the person is a willing volunteer; assumed to exist when observers have confidence that they are (1) mentally competent, (2) fully informed regarding relevant details, and (3) under no coercion or duress to give up their rights. Examples of situations where the abridgement of rights without informed consent is assumed to serve the common good include the incarceration (loss of the right to movement) of those who violate the rights of others (such as a personal assault) or the commandeering of private property for the construction of public works (such as roads or dams) to benefit society. In order to ensure that the infringement of individual rights by the state is not capricious and unjustified, it is usually restricted to situations where there is equal treatment of all individuals and due process is adhered to (there is a procedure for ensuring that impartial observers review the action and consider it appropriate).

While the concept of individual rights was originally developed to provide protection for individuals against the capricious, self-serving actions of societal rulers, a much wider range of privileges than incorporated in legal standards are frequently proposed. These include the right not to be deceived by others; the right not to be treated as less than an autonomous, mature adult; the right to full knowledge and motives of all associates; the right not to be embarrassed; the right to a private personality; and the right to an opportunity to provide informed consent prior to contributing to any type of research activity. Considering the participation in an informed consent procedure as a basic right, when it was developed as one means for allowing individuals to forego important or fundamental rights, reflects an extreme emphasis upon one technique for demonstrating respect for the rights and welfare of individuals.

The initial legal specification of informed consent as applied to research was in the Nuremberg Code, standards explicated to provide a basis for judging physician-investigators accused of misuse of Nazi prisoners (Jews, political dissidents, mental defectives and so on) in biomedical research.[4] These experiments, where simulated high-altitude (low-pressure) environments were varied to study the limits of human tolerance (that is, when death occurred), where subjects for studies of frostbite treatments were stripped and forced outside until their body parts froze, and where healthy adults were infected with lethal diseases as a convenience for maintaining an inventory of the disease culture for future research, have several features in common. Knowledge of the research objectives and procedures would have little effect upon the biomedical phenomena under investigation; the negative effects for the participants were considerable, resulting in death for many; and there was substantial reason to assume that the prisoners were not free and autonomous in determining their degree of participation. Under such conditions, it is reasonable to assume that the utilisation of informed consent would provide substantial protection for the rights of participants.

However, informed consent, appropriate for a wide range of biomedical and behavioural research, is but one procedure for demonstrating respect for the rights and welfare of participants. In situations where the effects of research are minimal or indistinguishable from the influences of daily life, where knowledge of the research may have substantial, unpredictable effects on the research results, and where other procedures may be used to demonstrate respect for the rights and welfare of participants (maintenance of anonymity, full disclosure following the research, treatment with respect, amelioration of problems caused by the research, and so on), a full and formal informed consent procedure may provide a marginal contribution to protecting the rights of the participants. In this context, informed consent does not appear — by itself — as a fundamental right, comparable to life, liberty, property, and the like.

While most of the discussions of rights involved in research emphasise the participants, there has been acknowledgment of a right to benefit from scientific advancement (without scientific research, this right cannot be realised) and explication of the rights of scientific investigators.[5] In addition to those rights that derive from the status of investigators as ordinary individuals, the right to free speech is assumed to include the right to publish or discuss any issue, a meaningless right unless there was a right to engage in research on any topic as a basis for the discussions. The right to engage in research becomes a precursor to the right to engage in open discussion of ideas.

A focus upon individual rights shifts emphasis to conflicts between the rights of 'parties at interest' — the right of the general public to scientific advancement, the right of scientists to pursue ideas, and the rights of participants as members of society. While there are extreme cases where the resolution is obvious — it seems unlikely that anyone would argue that randomly selected individuals should be incarcerated to study the effects of confinement upon self-esteem; it is unlikely that research utilising public data (census records, photographs of crowds, and so on) would be seen as abuse of individual rights — the most challenging cases are those where the rights are more evenly balanced. Covert participant observation may be one research activity where this occurs and, hence, without an obvious, universally acceptable solution.

Utilitarian analysis

A major recurrent problem confronted by those administering societies is the selection of new programmes, legislation and public projects. The most common strategy for analysis is to systematically compare the costs and benefits of viable alternatives and adopt those where the benefits outweigh the costs and, implicitly, the rights of individuals are not violated. While this strategy is most applicable to problems where most costs and benefits are quantifiable, such as the economic effects of a new road, there are usually problems that preclude numerical estimates of all effects of any project and aggregation of costs and benefits to comparable numbers to facilitate computation of a cost/benefit ratio. (Estimates of the monetary value of a human life to assist the decisions regarding the 'value' of safety equipment implies that human life is not a basic, inalienable right and results in some controversy.)

More fundamental are the problems associated with the distribution of the costs and benefits; the analysis is least controversial when homogeneously distributed — equal effects, positive and negative, for all. A heterogeneous or unequal distribution is generally not seen as a problem when a few individuals benefit from solutions to problems they could not avoid; as when major, expensive medical treatment (kidney transplants) are supported by public funds. Controversy may develop when a small number bear great risks or substantial negative effects for the benefit of society or those in privileged situations (as when hazardous research is conducted with the disadvantaged). This had led to the suggestion that those in privileged situations (such as the upper class) should bear the risk of research to assure that an unequal distribution of any effects will always work to the disadvantage of those best able to cope with negative effects.[6]

Regardless of the problems associated with the full, complete implementation of cost–benefit analysis, it remains one of the most widely used framework for organising the analysis of activities considered for societal benefits. In most cases, the actual resolution is based on a subjective, intuitive comparison of effects before arriving at a decision. One way to assure that the final decision is not a reflection of individual idiosyncrasies is to have a group – usually representing society – make this decision. These are often legislators or, in the case of research involving human participants, committees composed to represent the general public as well as technical experts.[7]

An important feature of cost–benefit analysis is its development and application to societal endeavours; activities seen as affecting and benefiting society as a whole. From this orientation, it may be more appropriate to apply it to the scientific enterprise or major research programmes than specific projects. The benefits of specific projects, where participants come into contact with the research endeavour, may be indirect and obscure; the benefits from a research programme or the scientific enterprise may be more substantial and explicit. Further, such analysis emphasises the societal obligations of the investigator – to systematically explore new phenomena as best they can – as a source of new knowledge for the effective and efficient administration of society.

Personal morality

Social scientists are not immune from ambivalence about their personal moral worth. Standards or procedures for guiding personal behaviour would help them determine if they are morally good. At least three general strategies have been proposed for resolving this problem, one (deontological) is adherence to a set of rules of various types (such as the Golden Rule or the Ten Commandments) in which case the basis for the adoption of the rules becomes a major issue. The analysis of Kant[8] focused upon such rules and the procedure for selecting those to follow, emphasising the adoption of rules desirable as universal laws, that treat individuals as ends rather than means, and that would be acceptable to all members of the society (that is to say, rules they would have adopted on their own). An alternative strategy for adopting rules is to consider a cost—benefit analysis of any potential rules and adopt those principles that would consistently provide social benefits. Rigid adherence to rules is still advocated by some: 'We must do no wrong — even if by doing wrong, suffering would be reduced and the sum of happiness increased.'[9]

The major alternative (teleological) to a rigid adherence to a set of 'rules for life' emphasises analysis of the situation where a choice is required and consideration of the effects of alternative actions. In one form, this is an application of utilitarian cost—benefit analysis to the individual choices of daily life. In another form, this has been developed as 'situation ethics' (referred to by Holdaway in Chapter 4) and focuses upon a 'mature compassion for humanity' and considers the ends as 'justifying the means more than anything else'.[10] Perhaps a major drawback to this strategy is an emphasis upon a detailed, complete analysis of every personal choice; the desire to avoid such a time-consuming tactic may lead individuals to adopt rules, or habits of behaviour, for most routine activities.

A third strategy avoids the need for retaining a set of rules or completing an analysis of alternatives and effects by focusing upon the instinctual reaction to the situation; emphasising a response that will be intuitively satisfying.

Without a complete immersion in the situation with all the perceived constraints, alternatives and obligations, it is not possible to determine the morally appropriate choice — the one the choice-maker finds the most comfortable. While this strategy may be similar to that used by many individuals, it prevents others from verifying the decision to determine if it was appropriate.

Regardless of which strategy is involved in providing a solution to the problem of individual morality, the major emphasis is always the same — the individual, as an autonomous agent, is considered the major cause of effects upon others. For example, if one person helps another and contributes to their wellbeing, this is seen as a conscious act reflecting a personal choice that led to the benefits. There is some reason to question whether or not this is the most appropriate perspective for one representing an organisation or a profession — physician, lawyer, teacher and the like — routinely meeting occupational obligations designed to benefit others. Similarly, there are often individuals that conscientiously discharge responsibilities that may cause individual suffering — as executioners, prison guards or tax collectors. The incongruence between the accepted standards for individual morality and accepting an obligation to conduct societal procedures, designed to benefit society as a whole, is one of the more complex, recurrent problems in these analyses. It can also be a dilemma for scientific investigators.

In summary, these different strategies emphasise three different aspects of individuals as moral actors. The focus upon individual rights tends to emphasise the resolution of conflicting rights between those involved in the social science enterprise: members of society that support and encourage research, scientists that conduct investigations, and participants that are objects of study. The focus upon a utilitarian or cost—benefit analysis tends to emphasise the value of the research for the participants and society in relation to possible negative effects, including those experienced by the participants and society (financial cost, time of trained professionals, and so on); it is the only strategy that facilitates consideration of the value of scientific knowledge as a social asset. The focus upon individual behaviour tends to emphasise how one individual, regardless of societal roles or professional obligations, may affect the lives of others. Application of these strategies to examples of covert participant observation may help to make their distinctive features clear; each moral observer must develop their own judgements — this discussion can only review alternative strategies and relevant considerations.

Examples of Analysis

The relationship between gathering observations as a participant and using the information for research purposes can occur in at least two ways. There are numerous examples of individuals that participated in a series of activities and then, after the fact, decided to present an explicit description and formal analysis of a group they had joined for non-research purposes.[11] Graduate students (particularly in sociology) have frequently utilised part-time jobs (often of a menial nature) as a source of material for course papers, theses and dissertations.[12] In these cases, the research participants (colleagues and associates of the observer) have accepted and interacted with the 'investigator' under the assumption he or she had no ulterior motives, which may not have been present at the time. The alternatives are those situations where the investigator deliberately attempts to gain acceptance into a group, collection or aggregate of individuals as a social and cultural peer for predetermined research purposes; the true objectives of the participation is carefully concealed from the research participants. The following examples all involved such research; it minimises ambiguity over whether or not the observations are 'really research' and simplifies the moral analysis.

Male homosexuals and public deviance

Interested in the participants and patterns of behaviour associated with clandestine homosexual activity, a two-stage research project to gather information relevant to these issues was devised.[13] (D. P. Warwick in Chapter 3 provides an alternative description of this project and a criticism of its execution.) The first stage was to engage in covert participant observation in a physical location (public toilets (restrooms)) known for attracting individuals with a desire to participate in male homosexual acts (largely restricted to oral sex). In addition to frequenting these locations during the most popular times of the day (the noon break and immediately after 5 pm), the investigator also participated to the extent of acting as a lookout (a 'watchqueen' in the argot of the subculture) to ensure that the participants were not interrupted by teenage boys, the police or those that may be violently hostile to such behaviour. (Such a contribution to the sex life of the participants was technically illegal when the study was conducted.) The procedures for gathering information was apparently successful, for behaviour in public restrooms preceding, during and following fifty completed sexual acts involving over 100 men were observed.

Once the descriptions of the atypical sexual behaviour were obtained, the next stage was to develop descriptions of the participants that could be compared with a random sample of residents of the area. In order to gather such information without alerting these men that they had been observed in illegal, atypical sexual activity, the investigator obtained their licence numbers from the cars used to visit the locations of the rendezvous. (The 'tearooms' were public toilets (restrooms) in remote locations of a large public park, largely inaccessible by foot.) The names and addresses of the individual car owners were obtained from the police, but they were protected by misrepresenting the nature of the study; it was disguised as a project in market research. Utilising a questionnaire designed for a health status survey of men in the area, the investigator (with his appearance modified) and a research assistant interviewed the men eighteen months after they had been observed engaging in homosexual behaviour.

A major result of the study was a portrayal of homosexual behaviour in these remote public restrooms as predictable and routinised, conducted in almost total silence (less than ten interpretable utterances were heard during the completion of fifty sexual acts). There were infrequent interruptions by police or hostile teenagers. When the social characteristics of the participants were compared with that of typical males from the same urban area, there were no striking differences in terms of occupational status, marital status, socioeconomic characteristics, and so on. Aside from their participation in clandestine homosexual activity, there was little to distinguish them from typical adult males.

Attempts to analyse the rights of those associated with this project are complicated by the illegal nature of the sexual activity at the time of the study (late 1960s) in the jurisdiction where it was conducted. While there is now widespread agreement that consenting adults have the right to engage in sexual behaviour in private settings, whether or not the right extends to public settings is another matter. It can be argued by those participating in the homosexual behaviour that when they have accepted all participants (including the participant observer) into the subculture they have created a private setting, even though the physical location is public property. Otherwise the role of a lookout (normally fulfilled by a voyeur) would not have emerged; it takes 'three to tango', so to speak. On the other hand, the process of evaluating and accepting new participants into this distinctive, silent world is so casual that anyone (journalist, law officer, sociologist) is easily accepted as a member. It is difficult to argue that the right to privacy has been seriously infringed when the individuals concerned are so cavalier about their privacy — reflected in the casual screening of participants and utilisation of public settings.[14]

The rights of the participants as they were interviewed in the second part of the study are also mixed. On one hand, they were selected and interviewed because of their known involvement in atypical sexual behaviour; a truthful presentation regarding research objectives and procedures (the right to informed consent) was not fully honoured. To have provided them with the reason why they were chosen for the interview would have made it clear that their behaviour in the public toilets (restrooms), which they considered anonymous, was not only observed, but their identities had been determined. Any right to have anxiety over public disclosure and embarrassment minimised would be threatened by such revelations.[15]

Whether or not the rights of the police were given appropriate respect is another issue; they were deceived on two occasions. The first deception occurred when the observer was arrested for 'loitering' outside a restroom; the investigator was able to prevent the police from discovering his true identity and the purpose of his 'loitering', thus preventing the police from having a reason to seek access to his field notes to identify the homosexuals. Second, the police were misled regarding the true purpose for wanting the names and addresses of those registering automobiles; these were the license plates that had been recorded outside the public restrooms (the tearooms). It may be argued that the authorities have no right to a truthful presentation if they are so careless as to accept fabrications without independent attempts at verification. Further, if the illegal status of homosexual behaviour is controversial, it could be argued that the minor duplicity of the authorities in the attempt to study the 'true' nature of the activity and its participants is justifiable as a political act, one that may lead to a change in the political (legal) status of homosexual behaviour.

In sum, in exercising whatever rights might have been available to an investigator — unrestricted choice of research topics, unrestricted choice of research procedures — the potential for infringing upon the rights of the participants and other parties at interest, such as the police, were clearly present. That the investigator conducted the research in such a way that no participant was directly affected by information developed during the study and that no specific police officer was embarrassed would suggest that their rights and welfare received considerable respect. Other than a general degree of disrespect shown for the legal authorities, it is hard to argue that fundamental 'rights' have been violated.

A utilitarian analysis of this project would include a review of the positive and negative effects of research on atypical or deviant subgroups in the society. Aside from the intellectual curiosity about such aggregates, additional knowledge may help to determine the actual nature of the activities of such groups, whether or not they constitute a threat to the wellbeing of society, the types of individuals that become involved in atypical sexual activities, and the consequences of such involvement for the individuals themselves. While no one project can investigate all major issues, the study of the 'tearooms' and the participants provided new, and presumably accurate, information on some of these issues. It is quite possible, particularly considering the widespread knowledge of this research, that it had a major effect upon the shift in the legal status of male homosexuality in the United States during the decade following the publication of this research.

Pursuit of a utilitarian analysis to determine the direct effects for the participants is not very illuminating in this case, for the investigator went to great lengths to make sure they (the homosexuals) were not aware they were involved in research or were identified as specific individuals. There are no direct negative effects reported by the investigator (or the critics); a direct positive benefit for the participants was the observer's facilitation of a completed sexual act by perform-ing as a lookout. Few investigators can claim they assisted participants in achieving an orgasm.

Distribution of effects is a somewhat different issue. All members of society presumably gain from the additional knowledge developed by research, even though a small number of individuals were the source of the research data and bore any risks associated with the project. All members of the male homosexual subculture would bear the effects of changes in social orientations towards their sexual preferences — whether or not it is more repressive or more liberal. In this particular study, it is difficult to make a strong argument that the distribution of effects is dramatically unjust.

In terms of individual morality, it seems clear that the investigator's misrepresentations in interpersonal relation-ships — with both the participants and the police — was not that considered ideal for mature members of society. On the other hand, the investigator considered himself acting on behalf of society in the capacity of a social scientist, attempt-ing to gather information in such a way that the participants would not experience any negative effects and still allow the research objectives to be obtained. Had the investigator been open, above board and honest about the research goal and procedures it is unlikely that his felt obligation to develop useful information on a sensitive social issue could have been discharged.

The spaceman saviour sect: unconfirmed apocalypse

As several social psychologists were considering the effects of real events on the attitudes and beliefs of individuals, they became aware of a group of individuals that had concluded that the world was to be destroyed except for those 'true believers' to be saved by space persons; the date for the rescue was predicted with certainty and, eventually, the group assembled for this appointment. Expecting the world to persist and no rescue attempts, these investigators were interested in the reactions of the members with varying degrees of social support from other believers once they had developed a deep conviction in this belief, made a public commitment to the rescue, and received unequivocal disconfirmation of the key prediction (the space persons did not arrive). In order to be able to gather information regarding the nature of the beliefs and the reactions after the predictions were disconfirmed, a number of investigators and assistants joined the small group as covert participant observers to collect information preceding, during and after the disconfirmed event. They presented themselves as interested in flying saucers, space phenomena and responsive to the 'revelations' that 'came' to the group's leaders. They were apparently accepted as 'real believers' and welcomed into the group as equals.[16]

Major findings were an increased attachment to the beliefs after the initial disconfirmation (the believers were spared to assemble more individuals for a future rescue), especially for those that spent a great deal of time with the group. This zeal dissipated only after repeated disconfirmations of predictions and some harassment from officials (as a public nuisance). Those 'believers' not in frequent, prolonged contact with the main body and confronting the disconfirmation in isolation showed little attempt at proselytising and easily abandoned the belief system.

Reports of the procedures and techniques used to obtain interviews and participate in the group meetings reflect respect and courtesy for the believers.[17] There is no question but that the true purpose and identity of the five graduate students and three professors that engaged in observation and participated in the group activities was withheld. In order to provide credible rationales for interest in the group, some personal experiences and revelations were invented for presentation to the group leaders. These were often taken as evidence of support for the group's belief system, although the investigators could not predict which pseudo-revelations would be well received. On the other hand, there was a substantial attempt to ensure that the anonymity and privacy of the cult members was protected; it is very difficult for anyone (even those in the region where the research was conducted) to identify the individuals or communities where the events occurred.[18] The ability of the covert participant observers to gain access and acceptance into the group was largely due to the casual scrutiny of potential members; they tended to be accepted on the basis of the revelations they presented and recurrent appearances at group meetings. As there was no attempt to check the credentials or even verify their identity as individuals, elaborate, or even inelaborate, cover stories and false identities were unnecessary.

A utilitarian or cost—benefit analysis requires attention to the objectives of the research and its relationship to the development of systematic knowledge. While not public at the time of the research, this was an early study in a programme of research, relatively systematic, that focused upon the organisation of cognitions, how situational contexts affected them, and the relationship of cognitions to individual behaviours. The version developed by these investigators was referred to as 'cognitive dissonance'.[19] Several findings in this study were relevant to the research programme: including the effects of social support on the prevalence of the beliefs after disconfirmation (isolates more readily abandoned their beliefs), and the nature of the rationalisations utilised to justify continuation of the beliefs after the disconfirmed predictions (doomsday was postponed to allow the believers to convert and save more of the naive disbelievers). This exploratory study was related to a series of experimental studies that preceded and followed the field research, and the entire programme of research was seen for some time as a substantial contribution to the study of individual cognitive structures, group processes, and their interrelationship.

In terms of effects for the participants, it is not clear that there were any major positive or negative effects. While it is true that the observers became a substantial proportion of the group (five of fifteen awaiting rescue by flying saucers), the group was probably large and cohesive enough so that most of the activities and beliefs would have been pursued in the absence of the observers. The length of time between the collection of the data and the publication of the results in a professional monograph, combined with the careful attempts to conceal the location, participants or date of the study, was probably successful in concealing the identities of the participants and preventing embarrassment and ridicule. Whether or not the participants would recognise themselves and avoid personal chagrin may never be known: it is unlikely they ever saw the final report.

In terms of individual morality, it is clear that the covert participant observers were not truthful and honest in their personal presentations to the 'believers'. On the other hand, they appear to have been polite and co-operative in all their relations with the participants, making a substantial attempt to avoid hurting their feelings (or disclosing their true purpose); it was difficult for the observers to remain neutral in terms of their effects upon all activities — they would be asked to lead meditation in all-night prayer meetings. It is not clear how these participant observers could have discharged their dual responsibilities, to the social science enterprise as investigators and to the respondents as individuals, with more discretion and care.

In summary, despite the deception of the participants, there is little evidence that they were debased, injured or embarrassed by the conduct of this research; their rights of free speech, assembly and the like were certainly not abridged. The study was part of a research programme of some significance and there is no evidence of offsetting negative effects for the participants. The observers appear to have treated the participants with respect and attempted to be neutral in influencing group or individual beliefs.

Feigned insanity: institutional discovery of normals

Concerned with the ability of mental institutions to discriminate those that are sane (an operative test of the viability of considering sanity and insanity as dichotomous, discrete states), eight normal individuals feigned temporary hallucinations to gain admission to twelve mental hospitals,[20] described in Chapter 2. Following admission, they acted normally and responded truthfully to all questions (except those related to their actual identities and occupations) until released as part of the normal treatment and evaluation procedures followed in the mental institution, which took an average of nineteen days (range of seven to fifty-two days). While adopting the patient role, the covert participant observers systematically gathered descriptions of patient activities, treatment by the staff, and the extent to which there was an opportunity for them to be evaluated. Consider-able information was gathered to suggest that most contact between patients and professional staff was brief and infrequent and that the custodial staff (nurses and orderlies) tended to depersonalise and patronise the patients, initiating physical and verbal abuse at times (usually in response to being a perceived nuisance). The latter is consistent with a substantial amount of research on total institutions,[21] but the information on the 'time to release' of the pseudo-patients is difficult to interpret without a comparison with a time to release of 'real' patients.

The study was conducted as an investigation of the institutional response to patients not 'really' insane, although symptoms of insanity were presented to gain admission; it is difficult to determine what institutional rights may have been placed in jeopardy. Those that represented the institution – the psychiatrists, psychologists, nurses and orderlies – may have been deceived about the nature of the pseudo-patients, but their anonymity was protected and they were not directly affected by their inadvertent contribution to a research project. Those that served as participant observers underwent substantial hardships in some cases, not only incarceration in a rather bland and uninteresting environment (over seven weeks for at least one) but receiving verbal and physical abuse in several cases. However, most of the pseudo-patients were experienced, knowledgeable individuals (six of the eight with graduate training in medicine or social science) who could be presumed to be informed about the daily life of mental patients.

In terms of utilitarian analysis, there would seem to be some advantage in providing information regarding the treatment accorded those admitted to mental institutions with varying degrees or different types of mental deficiencies. Unfortunately, the study was designed without a clear measure of success or failure — how long should 'sane' individuals be incarcerated before their sanity is confirmed after feigned hallucinations? All the pseudo-patients were released with a diagnosis of 'in remission', none were adjudged sane after admitted and labelled 'insane'. Without any standard or a control group of individuals with 'standardised' mental problems, it is difficult to know how to interpret these outcomes. If the investigators had analysed the institutional or personal characteristics associated with varying lengths of pseudo-patient incarceration, there may have been some useful leads from this study, but this is not reported. (The sample is rather small for such an analysis.) The absence of such information prevents the development of any policy recommendations or the possibility of improved treatment for those with mental problems. The costs borne by the upper-class covert participant observers cannot lead to benefits for the disadvantaged, mental patients, society or anybody else.

In terms or individual morality, it would appear that aside from deceiving those responsible for accepting patients in the mental institutions, the participant observers acted as typical individuals with typical morality. Presumably they were polite and well-behaved towards the other patients and hospital staff during their incarceration and have not used their knowledge of other inmates to embarrass them after they had left the mental institutions.[22]

In summary, this example of covert participant observation

seems to have involved minimal infringement upon the rights of participants, primarily because the unit of analysis was the institutional practices and patient evaluations utilized by professional groups. There is little evidence that the participant observers were personally immoral and the major "unethical" aspect of the project was in its design, which failed to provide evidence related to the central issue: Does it take longer for a mental institution to discover pseudo-patients than rehabilitated, real patients? This problem is associated with the research strategy, rather than the actual treatment of participants, institutions, or their staff members.

*   *   *

Each of the three studies reviewed reflects important similarities and illustrates different problems. If the moral emphasis is upon the direct treatment of and influence upon individual participants, it is clear that the very nature of covert participant observation places major restrictions upon the potential for abuse. If the efforts to influence the thoughts and deeds of the participants go beyond those expected from social and cultural peers, they may become suspect and fail to be accepted and gain the confidence of the participants. This feature of the technique protects participants from direct or immediate abuse or influence attempts. On the other hand, there is no question that the participants are deceived about the true nature of the observers' interests and motives, and may reveal information that can be embarrassing, seriously affect their social prestige and personal relationships, or even lead to legal sanctions. In the most dramatic of the studies reviewed, the major potential for negative effects for participants was related to their willing involvement in illegal, atypical sexual behaviour that could lead to social stigmatisation or incarceration. No such effects were experienced due to the care and foresight of the investigator reflecting a substantial concern for the welfare of the participants. Whether or not their right to engage in illegal sexual behaviour in a public facility was infringed (or even infringeable) is a matter of controversy.

A second study involved the careful exploration of a group

with rather unusual beliefs by a team of covert participant observers; none of the legal rights of the group of participants appear to have been abused and their identities were disguised in the research reports, minimising the possibility that they would be embarrassed by its publication. The value of the research is enhanced by its relevance to an ongoing programme of research focusing on cognitive organisation of beliefs and their interrleationships to events and behaviours. A third study involved a 'test' of the efficiency with which mental institutions evaluated and adjudged 'pseudo' patients as sane. While there is little evidence that the rights of participants (institutional staff) were abused, the value of the research and its cost (in terms of the time of the investigators, covert participant observers and institutional resources expended upon the pseudo-patients) may not have been justified; deficiencies in the research design make it difficult to determine the significance of the major finding.

Emphasis in Moral Analysis

Most social scientists, regardless of their methodological preferences, are thoughtful individuals that tend to respect the rights of others (legally adopted and informal) and live up to most standards for individual morality in the conduct of their daily lives. Investigators conducting research that may infringe upon the rights and welfare of participants and subject them to a risk of negative effects are usually aware of their actions and the potential impact. But there is a wide range of opinions among social scientists, the intelligentsia and moral observers regarding the appropriateness of alternative research procedures, including covert participant observation. This variation in perspectives and emphasis in moral analyses may be systematically related to variations in other orientations and beliefs regarding the conduct of social science, its worth to society, and the appropriate relationship between the social science enterprise and society. The following discussion explores, in a tentative, speculative way, some possible interrelations between selected issues and the moral analysis of research.

Judgements related to numerous features of a research

project may affect its moral evaluation, including its relevance to different stages of the process of developing new knowledge, the conception of scientific understanding and the importance of the phenomena under investigation. When studies of social phenomena are initiated, there is often very little accurate, relevant descriptive information available; careful observation of the phenomena in natural (uncontrolled) settings may be the first step towards providing such a description. When there is no clear relationship of the research to the testing of hypotheses or aspects of an explicit theory, it may be more difficult to justify potential risks to the rights and welfare of the participants, although the social importance of the phenomena may be utilised in a utilitarian analysis. In the absence of clear advantages to be achieved from the research, the moral analysis may shift to an examination of the rights of the parties at interest – the right of investigators to pursue research versus the rights of participants to be treated with dignity and respect.

As a research programme progresses, the conception of the phenomena and the ambiguities to be resolved through empirical research may become explicit and the value of a specific research project to the overall endeavour becomes easier to estimate and defend; a utilitarian (cost–benefit) analysis may be applicable in such cases and used to justify risks to the rights and welfare of the participants, particularly if the research results have practical significance. The more universal the agreement among scientists, societal decision-makers and members of society (potential participants) that the research examines significant social phenomena – rather than issues of a personal interest to the investigators – the greater the confidence in using a cost–benefit analysis to justify the risks to the participants and the cost of the research.

Regardless of the stage of the research activity, there are a variety of different perspectives on the nature of an intellectual structure (or theory) that provides an understanding of phenomena. At least three different perspectives for understanding individual behaviour (the major focus of most observation) are emphasised among social scientists: some emphasise the effects of situational factors upon the individual, others emphasise the importance of enduring personal traits (or developmental patterns), and still others prefer a detailed knowledge of the person's (or actor's) own perceptions, analysis and judgement as a source of understanding. Those that emphasise the utilisation of situational characteristics or individual attributes may be more inclined to engage in research that tests hypotheses and to verify explicit theories involving concepts (attributes of situations or individuals) that are not well understood by the typical person. This would be consistent with an emphasis upon the development of an esoteric body of knowledge that may ultimately serve society and a predilection for a cost–benefit analysis of the value of research.

In contrast, those that emphasise an explication of the participant's world-view and personal rationalisations and analysis as the major source of understanding, may feel that the participant's co-operation is crucial before personal revelations will be made available. This may lead to a strong emphasis upon the rights of the participants and incorporating them into research projects as partners, perhaps facilitated when the investigators are morally good, compassionate, understanding individuals. This may lead to an identification with and concern for the welfare of disadvantaged participants (for example, minorities, deviants and so on).[23]

The emphasis upon the participant's world-view and analysis as the basis for scientific understanding may not always lead to a sympathetic identification with the participants and concern that they receive honest, forthright treatment from covert participant observers. Some investigators have concluded that participants are naturally deceptive and duplicitous, unwilling to provide others with honest and straightforward reports of their personal characteristics, attitudes, behaviours or social situations. Based on experience in the study of nudist beaches (where it is difficult to get participants to reveal anything but their physical attributes), massage parlours (used as covers for illegal sexual services; it is difficult to get accurate reports on behaviour therein from the masseuses) and television station newsrooms (where social scientists may be seen as naive academics or competitors), one investigator has concluded that 'our kind of society' (that is, southern California) poses problems for field researchers through 'evasiveness, secrecy, deceits, frontwork, and basic conflicts'. One solution has been to expand the scope and detail of data collected by using a team of field and covert participant observers (similar to that used in the study of the spaceman saviour sect) to trap the participants in any fabrications and extract the real truth (it took two years to get the real first name of one nude bather). It is not surprising that these investigators have concluded that there is no imperative for social scientists engaged in field research to act as moral examples for others.[24]

Two interrelated perspectives, the perceived importance of the results of social science research and the appropriate role of social scientists in society, appear to affect the type of moral analysis that may be pursued. Many are convinced, including some social scientists, that investigators should be restricted to those topics that would not be offensive to anyone, using techniques that are models of good moral behaviour.[25] The basic argument appears to assume two inconsistent positions: first, that social scientists could never study phenomena of such importance that any risks to individual rights, welfare or even embarrassment could be justified. Second, that the potential harm from participating in research is so great that investigators must be constrained. In short, social science is seen as trivial in its results and dangerous in its techniques — simultaneously impotent and threatening. Those with this perspective generally suggest that not only should investigators respect all the legal rights of participants but they should also serve as moral exemplars in their professional (and perhaps personal) lives. It would appear that this demonstrates a considerable lack of faith in both the value of social science research and the resistance and stability of individuals and social phenomena.

A less extreme, and perhaps the typical position, is to accept an obligation to respect the rights and welfare of participants (regardless of the research technique) but accept the presence of important phenomena, some with considerable import for practical problems, that can be illuminated through empirical research. Most research is considered to involve a balance between the value of the knowledge gained compared with the risks for the rights and welfare of the participants — emphasising a cost—benefit analysis. When the risks for the participants exceeds that found in daily life, the research may be justified only when there is a clear and substantial benefit to be gained, preferably for the amelioration of a social problem. (As covert participant observation rarely involves risks greater than that found in daily life, substantial benefits from such investigations may not be needed to justify its implementation.) Acceptance of the notion that all individuals are worthy of respect and that social scientists are subject to the same legal and moral standards that govern all members of society has led some to label this as a 'consensus methodology'.[26]

Perhaps the most distinctive position (represented by Galliher in Chapter 9) is to assume that the results of social science research will have a substantial impact upon the conduct of society and that social scientists have a special obligation to represent the interests of the disadvantaged, even at the expense of the more advantaged members of society.[27] Specifically, social scientists are seen as having a responsibility to study those institutions or government agencies that are in a position to mistreat the disadvantaged, and if evidence of wrongdoing is discovered on the part of government officials or administrators, it should be publicly disclosed in an effort to discourage future wrongdoing — regardless of any promises made to the public officials to respect confidential information, their anonymity or privacy. Because of the assumption that an adversary relationship should exist between social scientists and the 'establishment', this has been referred to as 'conflict methodology'. From this perspective, moral analysis tends to emphasise individual standards for morality, rather than those adopted for society (reflected in individual rights of members) or the effects for all affected parties (nothing is considered to justify the restraint of investigators, even promises of anonymity, when they discover establishment persons 'taking advantage' of the disadvantaged).

In summary, it would appear that an emphasis upon the rights of individuals (participants and investigators) is consistent with exploratory or unfocused research, scientific understanding defined in terms of individual interpretations, participants expected to be honest and straightforward, and little confidence that the results of social science research will be of practical significance. A stress upon a utilitarian (or cost—benefit) analysis is consistent with research with a well-defined purpose (tests of hypotheses or theories), attention to situational or personal attributes (scientifically defined and measured) as a basis for understanding phenomena, a perception of participants as honest and co-operative but frequently confused or unaware of major social or individual processes, a concern for producing useful knowledge that will benefit society, and confidence that social science research can provide societal benefits. A focus upon individual morality is consistent with understanding defined in terms of personal (participant) interpretation, pursuit of exploratory research, utilising the behaviour of typical individuals as a moral standard (rather than a conception of the ideal), adopting as an obligation the exposure of official wrongdoing, and low confidence that social science knowledge will be utilised to benefit the participants and society (either because the knowledge itself is of little value or will not be properly utilised by societal decision-makers). Nothing would preclude a specific social scientist from shifting orientations as they shift stages of research or phenomena for study. It is an empirical question, as yet unanswered, whether these orientations are found among moral observers as integrated belief systems.

Conclusions

While covert participant observations can be utilised at any stage of the research process, development of initial descriptions, a source of tentative theories, or as a test of explicit theories or hypotheses; it is most frequently associated with descriptive information, rather than systematic tests utilising an experimental design. It can also be used to provide information of value to those committed to various strategies for explaining individual behaviour and orientation: an emphasis upon situational or social factors, individual attributes, or the interpretations and perceptions of the actors themselves. Again, there is a tendency for field observation to be associated with the latter form of understanding, a focus upon the personal world of the individual.

The ability of social scientists to engage in unethical or morally questionable behaviour is considerably enhanced in settings where there is an asymmetrical influence relationship between investigator and participants (as in experimental and survey research). Such is not the case in covert participant observation: the very nature of the research endeavour precludes investigator actions that may go beyond that expected in normal social intercourse; extreme attempts to influence or interfere with the lives of the participants would prevent acceptance as a social and cultural peer. If the investigator is accepted and allowed access to private behaviours or confidential information, the major potential for negative effects for the participants is indirect, related to the public release of such information after it has been obtained. Moreover, the most dominant norm adopted by all social scientists, as well as journalists that utilise private sources for news stories, is that the anonymity and confidentiality of participants should be protected. This standard has been included in almost all codes of ethics adopted by professional associations representing social scientists, has some legal status in the United States (but not Germany), is a principle utilised in evaluating social science research by institutional review boards in the United States, and has resulted in the abandonment of research when there was low confidence that confidentiality could be protected.[28] In short, the major potential for causing harm to participants in covert participant observation is both well known and associated with substantial protective mechanisms.

Hence, the major basis for moral criticism of those engaged in covert participant observation would be the failure to meet accepted standards of individual morality, specifically the failure to present themselves to participants as investigators in an honest and straightforward fashion. Ignoring the problems associated with the extent to which any individuals are fully honest and explicit about their own motives and objectives when engaged in interpersonal interaction (it would be naive to ignore the impact of subconscious, unconscious or latent motives in such exchanges),[29] there is no question that some important and valued descriptions can only be obtained through covert participant observation. To conform to the highest standards of individual morality in temporary personal exchanges at the expense of examining important, critical scientific and societal problems may not be the choice preferred by a number of investigators. It is for each social scientist to decide how they wish to serve society: as a personal moral exemplar or as a source of useful and valued information.

Part Four

Conclusion

12 The Merits and Demerits of Covert Participant Observation

Martin Bulmer

The merits of covert participant observation, particularly when discussed in general terms, tend to be exaggerated by some of its proponents. This is not true of the sensitive discussion in earlier chapters by Holdaway, Fielding and Homan, but it is true of the increasingly strident general statements of Jack Douglas. Most recently, he has claimed that 'professional ethics are generally a deceit and a snare. . . . At the present time I believe it would be an irrational act of panic, possibly a form of scientific suicide to impose a professional ethics on ourselves.'[1] The first part of this concluding chapter will therefore re-state the view that the use of covert participant observation as a method of research is neither ethically justified, nor practically necessary, nor in the best interests of sociology as an academic pursuit. The second part will then examine the rather limited circumstances in which such a strategy may be used without damage to the subjects of research or to sociology. The position taken is not that secret participant observation is *never* justified, but that its use requires the most careful consideration in the light of ethical and practical considerations.

The Demerits of Covert Research

Informed consent

Covert participant observation is clearly a violation of the principle of informed consent. This principle, developed in the course of the Nuremberg trials of those charged with carrying out extreme medical experiments in Nazi Germany, states that in research:

> the voluntary consent of the human subject is absolutely essential. This means that the person involved should have legal capacity to give consent; should be so situated as to exercise free power of choice, without the intervention of any element of force, fraud, deceit, duress, over-reaching or any other ulterior form of constraint or coercion; and should have sufficient knowledge and comprehension of the elements of the subject matter involved as to enable him to make an understanding and enlightened decision.[2]

The responsibility for obtaining consent rests upon the researcher, whose duty it is to communicate the purposes of the research fully to the research subject.

In covert participant observation, the subjects of research have no opportunity to give their informed consent to being studied. By definition, they are kept in ignorance of the real purposes of the researcher, because they do not know he or she is doing research. They have no opportunity — as does the respondent in a social survey interview — to consider the purposes and content of the research and decide whether or not to participate.

Against this, it has been argued that the requirement of informed consent is not applicable to observational studies. A. J. Reiss maintains that 'a growing number of studies depend upon systematic observation of natural social phenomena where the informed consent of the observed is not regarded as problematical'.[3] Similarly, the shift in social psychology from deception in laboratory experiments to naturalistic observation in the real world (precisely to meet objections that deceptive experimentation violates informed consent) has not (it is argued) had deleterious consequences. 'If you watch people, record observations about them, and draw inferences from what you have seen and heard, without declaring yourself or asking permission, are you committing an ethical violation? If you do not affect their lives, and preserve their anonymity so that others cannot use your observations to affect them, most of us think not. But this is not informed consent.'[4]

There is clearly a distinction, however, between observational studies (perhaps in some cases not involving participation at all) carried out in public places, and participant observation studies where the researcher penetrates into a milieu by presenting himself in a particular role. In pursuing research in this way, he is quite clearly and explicitly ignoring the need to obtain the informed consent of those whom he is studying.

Invasion of privacy

Secret participant observation is also frequently an invasion of personal privacy. To insinuate oneself into a particular setting onfalse pretences, in order to gather material for research, violates the right of the individual to be let alone, to control his personal sphere and information about himself. Accounts of total institutions emphasise the degradation involved in admission and the standardised processes for the mortification of self. One aspect of these is the exposure of the individual to 'contamination'.

> On the outside, the individual can hold objects of self-feeling such as his body, his immediate actions, his thoughts and some of his possessions clear of contact with alien and contaminating things. But in total institutions these territories of the self are violated; the boundary that the individual places between his being and the environment is invaded and the embodiment of self profaned.[5]

The parallel with the inmates of total institutions is of course greatly exaggerated; covert participant observation never involves physical injury to the subjects of research. The point of the analogy is to make clear that the subjects of covert study may feel themselves treated by the social scientist in a demeaning way which contaminates private spheres of the self. The covert observation of a religious sect, for example, violates the personal privacy of those studied and exposes parts of themselves to observation in a way they would not necessarily wish. Those who undertake covert research must counter the criticism that what they do disregards the privacy of the individual, a point made earlier on page 110.

At the institutional level, they are quite clearly limits to the extent to which the social scientist can ignore the extent to which particular institutions are private and closed to outsiders. The police, as Holdaway argues, are less easily studied overtly than, say, a geographic community. Some would no doubt maintain that no sphere of social life is so private that it may not be observed. Certainly one would not want to avoid studying the police simply because they are relatively inaccessible (though even this, it will be argued later, can be exaggerated). But other cases suggest that determining what is permissible in the name of social science and what is not poses real problems. The outcome of the Wichita Jury research in the 1950s is referred to by Shils in Chapter 7. There, jury deliberations were secretly tape-recorded without the knowledge of the jurors. Although hedged around with extensive and watertight safeguards, the researchers came under very severe attack and Congress amended the law to prevent the recurrence of such research in the future. Although the outcry addressed many of the wrong issues, failed to consider the serious research purposes of the study, and used the researchers as whipping-boys,[6] there can be little doubt that the research intruded upon the privacy both of individual jurors and of the institution of the jury. How advisable was it to design research which so flagrantly violated both the privacy of individuals and of a 'sacred' social institution? What is different, logically, between secretly tape-recording jury deliberations and tapping telephones in the name of state security?

Of course, the intentions of those tape-recording juries and those tapping telephones are quite different, as are the objectives which they are pursuing and the uses to which the information which is gathered is put. These differences are exceedingly important and, in some people's view, would render the comparison inappropriate. As an invasion of privacy, however, seen from the point of view of those who are secretly observed, the covert behaviour of the observer is not very dissimilar.

Deception

A major criticism of covert methods is that they involve out-and-out deception. The researcher is pretending to be somebody whom he is not. This runs counter to the usual norm in empirical research — including observational studies — of building up relations of trust with those whom one is studying.

In certain very highly exceptional circumstances, deception may be justified by the context in which research is carried out. John F. Galliher, in Chapter 9, cites Bruno Bettelheim's study on the concentration camp (described in Chapter 1) as an example of a covert study which was justified. What he does not say — and what alters the perspective — is that Bettelheim was in the camp *under coercion*. Indeed, he embarked on the study in order to try to survive psychologically in an extreme situation which was not of his own choosing. This research may be justified ethically (if it needs such justification) on the grounds that Bettelheim was held in the camp under duress and not of his own choosing. He was not there out of voluntary choice, whereas in all the other research studies discussed in this book, the social scientist chose voluntarily to enter into a situation for research purposes, or to undertake such research voluntarily while employed in an organisation.

Thus, William Caudill's covert study of group processes in a psychiatric hospital, briefly described in Chapter 1, involved his being admitted as a pseudo-patient (a researcher masquerading as a patient). When, after the research was completed, Caudill and his supervisor, Fritz Redlich, revealed what had been going on, the medical personnel involved were angered.

There can be no doubt [Redlich later wrote] that the
effect of the clandestine observation on the professional
staff of the hospital was severe. They felt spied upon. They
were particularly angry over what they considered was the
betrayal of the psychotherapist [by Caudill]. This good
man himself actually never complained, but maintained
that he had learned something. . . . The nurses were
particularly angry, because they thought that Caudill was
not only deceitful but did not like them . . .[7]

A more notorious case is provided by Humphreys's study
of homosexual encounters in public lavatories, *Tearoom
Trade*, discussed by Warwick in Chapter 3. As part of his
observational data in this study, he collected the registration
numbers of cars parked outside the isolated public toilet
where the encounters took place. Subsequently he managed
to obtain from the police (by deception) the names and
addresses of the car owners. He then obtained the permission
of the research director of a 'social health survey' in which he
was involved to add these names and addresses to the list of
sample members in that survey. After altering his hairstyle
and dress and changing his car, Humphreys then himself
interviewed (after an interval of one year or more) in their
own homes men whose homosexual behaviour he had
previously observed in the public toilet. He did not reveal to
them that they had met previously, nor did any of the
respondents recognise Humphreys. The various deceptions
involved in this stage of the research have come in for
particularly sharp criticism, and even Humphreys himself has
expressed doubts about the wisdom of his methods. 'I now
think my reasoning was faulty and that my respondents were
placed in greater danger than seemed plausible at the time.'[8]
Apart from the direct ethical issues about the appropriateness of using deception, there is also the persuasive argument
that the use of deception may distort the quality of the data
collected. Caudill, as part of the study already referred to,
subsequently carried out in the same hospital a further period
of participant observation, but the second time using 'open'
methods (that is, he revealed to all those whom he studied
that he was a researcher). He concluded when writing up the

research that the second, 'open' study yielded a wider range of data over which it was possible to exercise a higher degree of control and with which he was more satisfied both intellectually and emotionally.[9]

Margaret Mead has made the same point in an attack on covert methods:

> When a human being is introduced who is conciously distorting his position, the material of the research is inevitably jeopardised, and the results always put in question as the 'participant' — introduced as a psychotic into a mental ward or a fanatic into a flying-saucer cult group — gives his subjects false clues of a nonverbal nature and produces distortions which cannot be traced in his results. Concealed instruments of observation may not distort the subjects' course of action, but the subsequent revelation of their presence — as in the jury room that was tapped for sociological purposes — damages the trust both of the original participants and of all others who come to know about it. The deception violates the conventions of privacy and human dignity and casts scientists in the role of spies, intelligence agents, Peeping Toms and versions of Big Brother. Furthermore, it damages science by cutting short attempts to construct methods of research that would responsibly enhance, rather than destroy, human trust.[10]

The analogy between the covert observer and the police informant or agent provovateur is also relevant at this point. G. T. Marx points out that although in theory a distinction may be made between the informant who merely gathers information and the agent provocateur who seeks to influence the actions taken by the group, empirically it is difficult to apply. 'There are pressures in the role that push the informant towards provocation. The most passive informant, of course, has some influence on the setting by his mere presence. His presence can make a movement seem stronger than it actually is. If nothing else, he may provoke the kind of information he is looking for. . . .'[11] Festinger and his colleagues, in studying the sect which believes that the end of the world was coming, faced this sort of problem. In order to be accepted, they had to support and reinforce the beliefs of the sect, thus influencing the behaviour which they were studying.[12] The process is lightly satirised in Alison Lurie's delightful novel, *Imaginary Friends*,[13] parts of which bear certain curious resemblances to the Festinger study.

A somewhat similar point is made by British sociologist James Patrick (a pseudonym), who made a covert observational study of a violent juvenile gang in Glasgow in the 1960s.[14] Patrick eventually was forced to withdraw from the field altogether because of the efforts of the gang to involve him in overt violence upon which they were engaged. He quotes a passage to the effect that 'social participation carries with it special dangers. Sometimes it becomes doubtful which side is doing the converting.'[15] To avoid becoming too complete a participant, he ended the research altogether, due to provocation of him by the gang.

Benefits and risks

A common defence of the use of covert methods of research is to argue that, although some criticisms of it have force, covert methods do not cause harm to those studied if the identities and location of individuals and places are concealed in published results, data collected are held in anonymised form, and all data are kept securely confidential. Thus Humphreys went to extreme lengths both to anonymise the data that he held and to keep it secure; it was stored in a safe deposit box 1000 miles from the location of the research and, when public criticism of the research was first expressed, he destroyed the data to prevent it ever falling into the wrong hands.[16] A. J. Reiss maintains that 'in much social observation, the only risk that ever exists is a risk arising from the failure of the society to grant legal protection for the information'.[17]

A typical justification for the use of covert methods (though it appears that as the study progressed the covert role was given up) is that provided by Ditton:

To present openly findings deceitfully gathered, to sell to one group the secrets of another, is to play the 'defrocked priest'. The end serves as the justification, and the ethical offence is mitigated in various ways. In the first case, I have sought to protect the identity of both the bakery and of those studied by omitting names and changing other irrelevant facts . . .[18]

Some would go so far as to claim that they can monitor the effects which their actions have and thus anticipate the consequences of engaging in deceitful or misleading behaviour. J. D. Douglas writes:

Every person in our studies, and most of the scenes, are carefully protected by the cloak of anonymity — except to ourselves. . . . We know of no single instance in which our research has injured anyone, but we know of scores of individuals we have helped to keep out of jail, to stay alive (by getting medical help), to try to understand their problems better, or simply to find a little more joy in their everyday lives.[19]

The argument then develops that the benefits from greater social scientific knowledge about society outweigh the risks that are run in collecting data using covert methods. In weighing up benefit and harm, the harm done by using deception is outweighed by the good that will flow from greater knowledge about the hidden parts of society. The risk—benefit balance is discussed in the chapters by Paul Reynolds and Sissela Bok, both of whom argue that the harm to subjects of research may, *in some circumstances*, be outweighed by the benefits flowing from the research. For example, the benefits to society from surreptitious monitoring of medical practices by pseudo-patients may outweigh the harm done to professional medical *armour propre*.[20] The argument is given a further twist by D. L. Rosenhan's re-study (pp. 21—2), a nice case in point of what can be achieved by telling professionals that they are going to be monitored and watching the results.

J. D. Douglas, as noted in Chapter 1, has gone a good deal

further. He has argued that the use of covert methods reflects the nature of social reality. Sneaky and deceptive methods are necessary to do good social science because social order rests on deceitfulness, evasiveness, secrecy, frontwork and basic social conflicts. Secrecy and deceit are particularly characteristic of the centres of power in society; in order to penetrate these, secrecy to outsiders must be matched by deception to get in.

There is clearly room for debate about the relative balance between good and harm arising from covert research. Some of the harmful consequences have already been mentioned. Three considerations in particular suggest that it is rather easy to exaggerate the benefits of covert research and play down the harm it may do. First, covert studies of power structures (assuming for the moment that one accepts Douglas's position) do not necessarily provide a model for the study of social milieux of any and every kind, whether juvenile gangs, geographic communities, mental hospitals or fundamentalist sects.

Then, the uses to which research is put, and the consequences of publication, are not within the control of the researcher. However well intentioned he or she may be, and however the research site is anonymised, consequences will follow. Ditton, for example, says in his Preface: 'I don't expect that many of the men at Wellbread's will look too kindly on the cut in real wages that this work may mean to them, and my bakery self would agree with them.'[21] At the group level, a work which takes every precaution to conceal the site and people studied may nevertheless have consequences for the group because their activities and attitudes are revealed for public gaze. Group resistance to certain types of research suggest that some social groups, at least, appreciate the damage which social research could do to them.[22]

Moreover, particular justifications for the use of covert methods evade the central issue in any risk/benefit equation: who is to draw up the balance sheet and determine whether particular methods are justified or not? Whose causes are the right causes in social research? This issue is obscured by the generally liberal or radical belief system of many social scientists and the relative absence of right-wing social scientists. It is attractive to claim that righteousness is on one's side but, if there were more varied social perspectives among sociologists, then claims made for the 'benefits' flowing from covert methods would seem less plausible.

Harm to sociologists and sociology

A further dimension to the problem, which is less often considered, is what effect does covert observation have on the social scientist who is doing the observing. In a very interesting recent discussion of his covert observational study of pentecostal sects, Roger Homan argues that the principal effect of covert research is upon the observer himself. There is support for this view in the experience of William Caudill. Redlich much later expressed the view: 'There can be no doubt that Caudill found the concealed study stressful. At the end for a short time I believe he lost his objectivity as a participant observer, and almost became a participant, a patient. Although Caudill felt there was too much fuss made over concealment in his own study . . . he suffered from it.'[23] George de Vos, who knew him at the time, comments in an obituary tribute that: 'The strain on Bill between his role as an objective observer and his human sensitivity to people who were deceived by his dissembling developed into a very severe personal and career crisis.[24] It is noteworthy that several scholars who have used covert methods have subsequently made statements against their use. Caudill did so in the monograph reporting his research. 'I have no wish to rationalise my actions in the earlier [covert] study. I did it, and learned much from it. I do not recommend others doing it because I believe the price is too high.'[25] John Lofland has subsequently stated that he no longer believes the methods used to study Alcoholics Anonymous were justified.[26] Homan has also expressed reservations about future use of covert methods.[27]

It has been argued more generally that covert methods produce hardened and cynical social scientists. Margaret Mead took the view that:

[e]ncouraging styles of research and intervention that

involve lying to other human beings . . . tends to establish a corps of professionally calloused individuals, insulated from self-criticism and increasingly available for clients who can become outspokenly cynical in their manipulation of other human beings, individually and in the mass.[28]

Whether or not covert research actually has these effects upon those who study collectivities and institutions using such methods, the use of them is likely to lead *others* to believe that sociologists develop such traits as a result of using such untrustworthy techniques. In other words, regardless of what actually happens, people come to believe that sociologists are (in the words of Donald Warwick) 'sly tricksters who are not to be trusted'. The more widespread such a view becomes, the more difficult it will be to carry out social research.[29]

This objection has been stated most lucidly by Kai Erikson:

> [R]esearch of this sort is liable to damage the reputation of sociology in the larger society and close off promising areas of research for future investigators . . . [W]e are increasingly reaching audiences whose confidence we cannot afford to jeopardise, and we have every right to be afraid that such people may close their doors to sociological research if they learn to become too suspicious of our methods and intentions . . . [A]ny research tactic which attracts unfavourable notice may help to diminish the general climate of trust toward sociology in the community as a whole.[30]

To be sure, what sociologists do is influenced by standards and behaviour in the wider society. The experience of Watergate, notably, has made the public more critical of the claims of political and business leaders to follow high standards in their public and private acts. Investigative journalists have appeared as a new breed claiming to uncover the 'real' workings of social institutions and political processes, without being too open or too particular about how they obtain information. And the use of undercover agents, decoys and entrapment by police authorities may give the use of deception a spurious legitimation. Indeed, G. T. Marx has suggested that as a result of these developments in American policing,

> general cultural standards regarding the ethical implications of deception may also be softening. Deception as a means of information gathering and social control seems to be increasingly used not only by police and private detectives but also by social reformers, investigative journalists and social scientists. There may be similar ethical issues, behaviour appearing as an artifact of intervention, and unintended consequences.[31]

Some of the cases which he describes are amusing, such as the FBI fencing operation in Washington, DC, and the New York undercover policeman working in gay bars who took a walk with a likely subject one evening, and when he said, 'I arrest you', received the reply, 'You can't, I was about to arrest you!', being another undercover cop.[32] How long will it be until some covert social scientist gets into a similar situation? How shocked sociologists would be if some famous ethnographic informant, enjoying an honoured status in the literature, turned out to have been another social scientist working under cover![33]

Changing ethical standards in the society do not, however, of themselves justify changes in the behaviour of social scientists. Just because investigative journalism and undercover police work have become more common does not mean that sociologists should follow. For the spread of such unethical practices leads to greater levels of distrust in the society. Who believes whom? Within social science, the effects of such cynicism are most apparent in experimental social psychology, where deception is widely practised. Subjects of experiments (the majority of whom are students) now routinely expect to be deceived and measures designed to counter this expectation have to be built into experimental designs.[34] Sociologists and sociology will only suffer in the long run if they adopt research strategies which lead others to believe, however mistakenly, that the word of the sociologist is not to be trusted and he or she becomes an object of suspicion.

Practical considerations

There are good grounds for believing that the need for covert research is frequently exaggerated and that settings which are studied by covert methods could also be studied by overt methods. There is not space to develop this point extensively but one or two factors point to this conclusion.

The first is the role played by the covert observer. In some settings – such as the Ku Klux Klan, or among professional criminals, for instance – it may be very difficult for the observer to convincingly adopt and maintain a covert role which persuades the members of the group that the researcher is genuine. Accounts of participant observation are replete with anecdotes indicating that the observed knew very well that the observer was a different sort of person from themselves. To quote one:

> I never approached you [for extra bread] down the bakery, you stood out, see? . . . and most people realised that you stood out, you weren't supposed to be there . . . and that was it, you didn't look like a bakery person.[35]

Simon Holdaway describes, in Chapter 4, two incidents where it was clear that fellow-policemen knew he was different from them. Even in Patrick's covert study of a Glasgow gang (in which one gang member knew his real identity), he appears to have eventually found the research role untenable. In other words, there remains a line, even in covert research, between observer and observed.

Polsky, indeed, goes so far as to suggest that in studying professional criminals, the sociologist should not spy or become one of them. His task is rather to become accepted while making clear that there is a distinction between himself and those whom he is studying.[36] G. J. McCall makes a similar point in discussing generally methodological problems of observing crime and criminals. 'Attempting to conduct field research by passing for a criminal is not only unnecessary but actually foolhardy. . . . First, aside from the standard risks . . ., the researcher will either be trapped into outright criminal acts or, more likely, be exposed as an imposter, destroying his field relations and perhaps incurring retribution. Second, his research activities will be sharply limited, in that he could not ask certain important questions of other criminals, for if he were indeed the criminal he pretends to be he would already know the answers.'[37]

In other words, sociologists are generally unconvincing when they try to pretend to be professional criminals. (One also imagines they would be unconvincing in a number of other covert roles, including cabinet minister, senior civil servant, industrial manager — to name them is to point to limits which there are to covert observation.) Successful studies of areas of criminal behaviour — Klockars's study of the fence, the Iannis's study of the Mafia, to name but two[38] — have been successfully carried out in an open fashion. Indeed, in Klockars's case, despite his most assiduous attempts to conceal the real identity of the subject of his book, the subject himself took a most lively interest in its promotion, sold copies openly in his shop, and only narrowly turned down an invitation to appear on national television to be interviewed about it. Apparently impenetrable and closed institutions have opened themselves up to researchers who did not conceal their real intentions. Heclo and Wildavsky's study of the British civil service is a good case in point.[39]

Is Covert Participant Observation Ever Justified?

The foregoing objections to the use of total concealment of one's role in participant observation constitute a powerful case. Some will object that these demerits are the preoccupation of 'ignorant and absolutist moralists who can only see black and white'.[40] Although such an objection is absurd — who would even *consider* justifying medical experimentation without regard to its human consequences and thus its ethics? — there are indeed shades of grey which somewhat modify the strength of the criticisms so far expressed. Many accounts of the ethical dilemmas in participant observation — from Melville Dalton[41] to Simon Holdaway — emphasise the complexities of the choices facing the investigator and the need to place the research in its context. Categorical moral statements — such as the principle of informed consent

— do less than justice to the realities facing a researcher when, for example, a relationship of trust with those being studied is impossible to achieve, or the researcher is deluded or lied to by his respondents. May certain types of research situation lead to the conclusion that in certain limited circumstances, covert methods are justifiable?

Retrospective participant observation

If poetry is 'emotion recollected in tranquillity', one mode of participant observation might be described as 'experience recollected in academia'. A number of distinguished observational studies have been conducted (at least partially) retrospectively, after the event. Howard Becker's study of dance musicians, for example, was begun in 1948–9 when he himself was working as a musician and also going through college.

> At the time I made the study I had played the piano professionally for several years and was active in musical circles in Chicago . . . I worked with many different orchestras and many different kinds of orchestras during that period and kept extensive notes on the events that occurred while I was with other musicians. Most of the people I observed did not know that I was making a study of musicians. I seldom did any formal interviewing, but concentrated rather on listening to and recording the ordinary kinds of conversation that occurred among musicians.[42]

Most of the observations were made on the job, even while playing, or in local 'job markets' where musicians found work.

Ned Polsky's study of poolroom hustling, though 'carried out' over eight months in 1962–3, was grounded in and inseparable from his own experience of poolrooms. He had frequented them for over twenty years, since billiard playing was his chief recreation. Prior to the time of the study, he had played pool (billiards) an average of six hours per week, mainly in the major pool-hall of New York. He knew and had played regularly with several of the hustlers who were the subject of the research.[43]

Simon Holdaway's research involved a retrospective element, in that he was a policeman before and after studying sociology as an undergraduate, and remained a policeman while conducting the postgraduate research discussed in Chapter 4. But the ethical issues raised by this type of continuing 'insider' research are rather different from the kind of retrospective participant observation done by Becker and Polsky.

The sociologist as citizen going about his business

The reservation expressed about retrospective participant observation also applies to the sociologist as a citizen. 'Sociologists live careers in which they occasionally become patients, occasionally take jobs as steel workers or taxi drivers, and frequently find themselves in social settings where their trained eye begins to look for data even though their presence in the situation was not engineered for that purpose.'[44] As Homan points out in Chapter 6, places of worship are public, and invite the public to participate. What distinguishes participation in a religious service as a (more or less) disinterested member of the public (that is, citizen) and participation in a research role? On one definition, even Humphrey's research was carried out in a public place ('public lavatory', 'public convenience'), albeit involving the observation of private behaviour in that public place.

Shils, in Chapter 7, discusses the dividing line between the public and private spheres, pointing out that it is not clear-cut and that in public settings some behaviour (for example, private conversations) can still be private. Non-participant observation in public settings — such as Lyn Lofland's studies of behaviour in urban public places — gives rise to fewest objections on ethical grounds, provided that the behaviour observed is really public, and not private. Studies of behaviour in public toilets clearly cross that barrier and are open to strong ethical criticism. Observation of public behaviour in public places is also only legitimate if it is non-interventionist. Psychological experiments such as the 'lost-letter' technique of Milgram[45] or the realistic faking of accidents to observe the reactions of passers-by[46] can have unethical or harmful consequences unpredicted by the investigator. It is even reported that at one American university, when a student murdered another student by shooting, passers-by took no notice because they believed it was a psychological experiment.[47]

This latter instance is a case of overdoing the distinction between researcher and citizen. But the two roles cannot easily be merged without conflict between ends. The observer cannot easily act at the same time as citizen, indeed the rare cases of participant observers 'going native' are examples of the difficulty of breaking down the distinction. Nor in some circumstances can the citizen–sociologist also act as observer–sociologist. For example, a sociologist called for jury service could only study the process of jury deliberations at the risk of jeopardising his effectiveness as a juror and breaking the confidentiality of the proceedings and trust among the twelve members of the jury.

The continuum from secrecy to openness

There is, as Roth pointed out,[48] a continuum from secrecy to openness. Dichotomies between 'open' and 'covert' research need to be modified to keep this in mind. Much 'open' research involves deception of one kind or another. Hart, for example, in studying the Australian aborigines, pretended that he was considerably older than he in fact was (twenty-three), in order to be taken seriously by the tribe that he was researching.[49] Other 'open' researchers may give misleading information about their marital status in order to facilitate access to one group or another.

Anne Sutherland faced particular and unusual problems of this kind in her research on Californian gipsies.

> The Rom often lie to each other about everyday matters, but they almost always lie to the *gaje* [non-gipsies]. There is no particular shame attached to lying to each other . . . but to lie to the *gaje* is certainly correct and acceptable behaviour. . . . Since being unpredictable and elusive is part

of the code of behaviour with *gaje*, it was not considered odd for me to act the same, and, of course, I was also not burdened with having to stick to the absolute truth. . . . [The Rom] rarely accepted a statement from me or any other Rom without some kind of corroboration from someone else. . . . Therefore, when I doubted their veracity, or tricked them into admitting something, or lied to them myself, they were just as cheerful about it as they would be with each other and respected me all the more for it.[50]

Nevertheless, this is something of a special case. Sutherland had revealed to at least some members of the community that she was writing a book about them. The mutual deception practised has something of the character of a game, or the mutual deception sometimes practised between doctor and a patient suffering from a terminal illness.[51]

A good example of the situational constraints faced by the researcher is provided by the question of how everyone whom he comes into contact can know that he is a researcher. Deception may be practised unintentionally or unavoidably in failing to make clear to those he meets that he is doing research. There is, in other words, an important distinction between disguised observation in transient situation and completely covert observation.

Most observers reveal their researcher identity to important informants, even though they may often 'hide behind' their field roles in many transient social situations.[52]

In many field situations, it is simply not practicable to make known to all those encountered that the social scientist is a social scientist. Those working as participant observers with the police or with medical students have usually done so overtly, their identities are known to those with whom they work while doing the research. But the members of the public or the patients whom they meet in the course of this research are likely simply to take them for another police-man or another medical student. Complete concealment of the research role — to which the earlier criticisms were directed — may rarely if ever be justified, but the converse —

that total openness is in all circumstances desirable or
possible — does not follow.

Another reason for using partial deception may be to gain
tactical advantage and access to data otherwise closed to the
researcher. A famous example of this in the literature is
W. F. Whyte's experience of 'repeating' (voting more than
once under different names at the same polling station in the
same election) in pursuing his study of the politics of
'Cornerville'. This involvement caused him both personal
anguish and a fear of exposure which would ruin the whole
research project. He was propelled into behaving in this way
by situational factors.[53]

Total versus partial secrecy

A more ambiguous situation arises where some participants
in a situation are told of the covert role of the researcher,
but others are deliberately kept in ignorance. In Caudill's
covert psychiatric research, only Redlich and one senior
psychiatrist at the hospital knew of his research role. Redlich
reports that 'the concealment study bothered the other
senior psychiatrist, who knew about the study and felt very
ambivalent over the whole matter. I believe she felt pressured
by me to take part in the plot, never liked it, but was loyal
enough not to let us down.'[54] Another case (discussed in
Chapter 6) where at least one participant knew of the
researcher's role, Ken Pryce's study *Endless Pressure*,[55]
involved the use by the minister of this secret knowledge to
'persuade' Pryce to undergo conversion.

Faraday and Plummer report that in their research on
certain aspects of human sexuality they have faced similar
problems in being drawn into covert observational roles by
their research subjects.

> Subjects have typically concealed their research roles from
> families and friends, who are often also unaware of the
> subject's sexual proclivities. This has meant that on many
> occasions subjects have allowed us entree into their groups
> by presenting us in such roles as 'journalist' or 'drinking
> partner', or by allowing us to assume whatever role would

be situationally appropriate without disclosing to others that we have met before. While this type of collusion has a potential for creating its own set of personal strains for both subject and researcher, we have found it necessary for the purpose of validating subject's accounts and to povide first-hand information about their everyday life.[56]

In Patrick's study of the Glasgow gang referred to earlier, Patrick (at the time an approved-school teacher) gained entree to the gang through one of its members who was at the time a pupil at the school, but going home at weekends. This gang member, Tim, knew Patrick's real identity and role, but kept it secret from the other gang members who were led to believe that Patrick was merely Tim's best friend at the approved school, out on leave at the same time. 'Tim and I came to an understanding that, whatever happened, nothing would be disclosed by either of us to other members of the staff or to anybody else. This was seen as a necessary precaution for our own protection.'[57]

Studies are thus not always completely covert or completely overt. Some of those with whom the researcher is in contact may be 'in the know', others may not. In pseudo-patient studies, it seems usual for at least one senior medical staff member to be informed both to facilitate discharge of the pseudo-patient at the end of their stay and to prevent adverse medical treatment during the stay if their feigning of symptoms was too realistic. From an ethical standpoint, however, such studies are not really very different from totally covert research. If the identity of the researcher becomes known, his cover is blown. One or more participants may share with him the secret that he is really a researcher, not a participant, but it is still a secret.

Role playing and role pretence

A further ambiguity is introduced by considering the insider/outsider distinction. Caudill as a patient, Patrick as a gang member, were playing the role of, and pretending to be, insiders. But it is misleading to simply contrast this role with that of the outsider in a *research* role. For the social scientist may play the role of outsider in a particular setting, but not the role of researcher. Indeed, the role that he or she plays may not just be different from that of social scientist, and the fact that he or she is a social scientist may be kept secret from some or all of those with whom the social scientist is in contact.

A good example of such a case is Cohen and Taylor's work on the experience of long-term imprisonment.[58] They visited 'E Wing' of Durham prison, where Category 'A' prisoners serving very long-term prison sentences were housed, as adult education lecturers, giving regular seminars to a small group of prisoners over a period of some months. Anne Sutherland was able to study a group of gipsies in California principally because she acted for nearly a year as Principal of a specially-established gypsy school, which was highly valued by the local Rom and brought her into close contact with them.[59] In both cases, acting as a teacher gave the researcher access to a group with otherwise would have been closed to them.

In Cohen and Taylor's case,

> the idea for the research came as much from the subjects as anyone else. We then took our proposals to the Assistant Governor who spoke on our behalf to the Governor [of the prison] who in turn commented favourably upon the research outline we submitted to the Home Office. . . . Eventually the Home Office rejected our ideas for research. Fortunately we were able to reply that most of the work had already been done.[60]

A non-research outsider role can therefore sometimes provide an opportunity to do research which would be denied to an outsider-who-is-a-researcher. Teaching is a role that comes naturally to an academic researcher, sometimes offering access where an overt research role would be denied or misunderstood. (Sutherland had great difficulty in persuading her subjects that 'social anthropologist' was any different from 'journalist' or 'detective', both categories of people they greatly distrusted.)[61]

The discussion so far has considered three of four alternatives:

(A) The overt outsider — the researcher looking in.
(B) The covert outsider — the researcher playing some other role (for example, teacher).
(C) The covert insider — the researcher as covert participant (for example, pseudo-patient, gang member).

	Insider	Outsider
Overt role	For example, Rubinstein (D)	For example, W. F. Whyte (A)
Covert role	(C) For example, Caudill	(B) For example, Cohen and Taylor

FIGURE 12.1   *A typology of research roles*

There is, however, an interesting fourth possibility (D), that of the overt insider, a social scientist who actually trains and adopts an entirely new insider role with the knowledge of those among whom he is working (Figure 12.1). Thus Jonathan Rubinstein,[62] after working for a year as a police reporter on a Philadelphia newspaper, then negotiated with the director of the Philadelphia Police Department that he actually work with policemen on the street. In September 1969, he entered the Philadelphia Police Academy, going through the full training of a police officer. On graduation, he joined a patrol unit, working with different units full-time for one year until September 1970 and at weekends for a further year until September 1971. He never spent less than two months with any unit.

He describes his role as follows:

Legal complications prevented me from becoming a sworn police officer, although I had fulfilled all the requirements at the academy. But I was permitted to go on the street as an armed observer (travelling in patrol cars). Since I worked mostly with uniformed policemen but had to wear plainclothes, I carefully chose some that would give me the appearance of a detective or superior officer. Many of the men I worked with knew that I was not a policeman (though some believed I was a federal agent or an undercover police operative), but policemen from other units and districts whom we encountered in the course of work did not. Only on a few occasions did my companions inform these men of my identity. On no occasion did any policeman I worked with inform a private citizen of my status in my presence, and only once did anyone question whether I was a police officer. . . . I worked only with those men who willingly accepted me as a worker and not just as a passenger. Everywhere I went there were men who granted me their company and introduced me to the police craft by allowing me to share their work.[63]

Yet this is written by a social science researcher, attached to the University of Pennsylvania and supervised by Erving Goffman, not by a policeman. In some respect, this research might be described as 'prospective' participant observation, the taking on of a new role specifically for research purposes. It was done with the full knowledge and co-operation of the police department. Rubinstein's immediate associates knew he was not a policeman, and most knew he was a researcher. But in the course of the research some other policemen, and all members of the public, were misled as to his identity. Was that unethical research behaviour? Is this not inevitable to some extent in any observational research? Does it not happen anyway when sociologists do observational studies in settings like schools and hospitals, that they are taken by some to be other than they are? The role played by the 'overt insider' indeed differs relatively little from the role played by someone just 'hanging around' in a particular setting doing research, except that the deliberate adoption of (and training for) the role gives the researcher access to settings from the which the 'hanger-around' might be excluded.

Holdaway's discussion of his research on the police is particularly relevant at this point. He was an 'insider' who played partly a covert and partly an overt role. His superiors apparently knew something of his analytic interest in police work, and his colleagues and those he supervised knew that he had a sociology degree and distinctive attitudes to some features of policing. The actual research, however, was done covertly and had to be kept concealed from those with whom he was working. His chapter illustrates well the potentialities not only of this type of research, but also the need to frame analysis of covert research ethics in terms of the career of the researcher.

The usual model over time is:

academic $\longrightarrow$ total participant $\longrightarrow$ academic
sociologist (sociologist) sociologist
again

In retrospective participant observation, the sequence is reversed:

total $\longrightarrow$ academic sociologist $\longrightarrow$ retrospective
participant observer
(non-sociologist) (sociologist)

In Holdaway's case, the sequence is more like:

total $\longrightarrow$ academic $\longrightarrow$ total $\longrightarrow$ academic
participant sociologist participant sociologist
(non-sociologist) (non-sociologist
and sociologist)

This discussion suggests that greater imagination is needed in designing observational studies. Instead of modelling themselves on secret agents or investigative journalists, more atten- attention might be paid to the potentialities of (B), the covert outsider, and (D), the overt insider, roles. Opportunities such as that enjoyed by Holdaway to be a working 'insider' will continue to be relatively rare, and sociologists need to think creatively about other ways in which access may be gained other than by outright deception.

Individual researchers and organisations

Covert research has been justified most plausibly in terms of its value in studying complex organisations. Hierarchically organised, formal bureaucratic structures lack the openness of informal associations or even geographical communities. Gatekeepers (literally and figuratively) exist to keep out those who do not belong or who are unwanted (including social scientists). The power which large organisations such as the police or industrial companies wield makes them a subject of legitimate scholarly and public interest, but possession of that power is equally likely to make them defensive about being studied by outsiders. Moreover, internal differentiation within organisations, competition and lack of communication between different parts, makes the task, even of the overt observer who has gained initial access, problematical. To find out what is going on within the organisation, he may have to adopt covert methods.

It is clear that organisations modify to some extent the context in which ethical decisions are made. An analogy from medicine may make this clearer. A general principle of medical practice is the absolute confidentially of communications between doctor and patient. A doctor cannot normally be required, for example, to reveal in a court of law what a patient has told him in a professional consultation. In certain contexts, however − notably the armed forces, prisons and at sea − these safeguards are modified by the overriding needs of the community. For example, 'the community may be put in danger if the captain of a ship is unaware that a member of a crew is incapable of carrying out his duties, or that a passenger is so ill as to constitute a risk to other passengers on board'.[64] So a doctor is justified in discussing particular patients with the captain, even though this breaches the normal rule of the absolute confidentiality of doctor−patient communications.

Sociologists in organisations, it is argued, face problems which justify departure from the normal standards of behaviour in research settings, even to the extent of concealing altogether that they are researchers. In order to penetrate behind fronts and gain access to information not available by overt means, deception and trickery are justified. In researching *Men Who Manage*, for example, Melville Dalton obtained secret data on the salaries of managers in one firm from a secretary who had access to the data. He reached a bargain with her whereby she fed him this data surreptitiously in return for information about the background and life of her boy-friend (a manager who worked elsewhere in the organisation), who Dalton reports she subsequently married despite Dalton's counselling.[65]

Dalton comments more generally on the sorts of ethical problems facing researchers in organisations that:

> the researcher who is obliged to get at all the relevant behaviour may obviously offend some persons in the organisation. If there is reason to believe that visible behaviour is minor and misleading, he must get at the unknowns essential to complete the picture without, of course, damaging the research, the persons studied and the profession. But in doing this, the researcher, and not a remote part-time ethicist who cannot say where his personal code comes from, must size up the moral issues peculiar to his problem and bear responsibility for reconciling the diverse moral commitments he assumes in and out of office. Naturally, he may involve himself and others in trouble, but the promise of his work may be worth the risk. Where would anatomy and surgery and dependent specialities be if Mondino, Leonardo, Vasalius and others had entirely honoured the absolutes of their day instead of haunting cemeteries and gibbets in search of their cadavers?[66]

Jack Douglas puts forward a justification couched in different terms which points to the same conclusion. Covert observation is justified particularly to study the centres of political and business power. Because those in power hide behind secrecy, manipulation of information and deceit, the sociologist has to adopt similar methods to penetrate into the milieu. Sjöberg and Miller recommend the adoption of some of the methods of investigative journalists for the study of bureaucracies, although they stop short of recommending some of the more dubious techniques of playing one informant off against another, collecting data under false pretences, or pilfering files.[67]

Even so, the force of these arguments is not tremendously

compelling, for the following reasons. In the first place, it rests on a view of the nature of power which is over-simplified. Another analogy may help to make this point. At the present time in Britain, there is a strong campaign for much greater freedom of official information, on the grounds of democratising the political process and making decision-makers more responsive. Though there are excellent arguments in favour of it, it is not clear that if there were greater freedom of official information, governmental decision-making would necessarily be improved. In some respects it might be made worse. What is certain is that many decisions would remain just as intractable, difficult and unlikely to command consensus as they do under the present system. In other words, freedom of information − as the American experience shows − is not the panacea it is held out to be. Similarly, the view is put forward that in order to discover what is really happening in organisations, one needs access to secret and hidden information which will help to uncover the underlying processes. Will it? Historical research on nineteenth- and twentieth-century government policy frequently suggests that the most significant, influential and awkward events, conversations, influences and so on are often *not* recorded precisely because of their significance, while memoirs written after the event are deliberately designed to present the author in the most favourable light and thereby cloud the truth of 'what actually happened'.

This is related to a second point, the misplaced admiration which some contemporary sociologists have for investigative journalism. There is a very good case to be argued for the view that sociological inquiry is quite unlike investigative journalism, and therefore the parallels which are made between Woodward and Bernstein and what sociological field researchers ought to be doing are quite misplaced. The task of sociological research upon organisations is less to expose the detailed workings of that organisation at one particular point in time than to understand and explain characteristics of the organisation which lead to it being the kind of organisation that it is. The British civil service is an excellent example. Many journalists would dearly love to be privy to the processes by which particular major government decisions are reached, such as the invasion of Suez in 1956, or devaluation in 1967, or whatever. Investigative journalists with sufficient persistence might in some cases get some way behind the scenes to do this. Yet what the sociologist of organisations is interested in looking at in the civil service is less the facts about particular events and much more the character of the organisation, its patterns of recruitment and occupational socialisation, and the ways in which the structure of the organisation influences particular outcomes. This a book like Heclo and Wildavsky's *The Private Government of Public Money* does in exemplary fashion, even though the research was done overtly and does not contain any of the juicy titbits of information about individual decisions so sought after by journalists.[68] The focus and frame of reference is different, and the methods to be used accordingly different also.

A third point, particularly relating to government, has been made by John Barnes. Most discussions of covert research relate to situations in which the citizen could, if he wanted, take the scientist fully into his confidence and tell him everything he wanted to know. 'But in some situations citizens are not free to open their hearts to even the most persuasive and trustworthy scientist. Yet these same situations may be of particular theoretical interest and of major practical importance. . . . Meetings of the British Cabinet fall into this category . . .'[69] In some cases, first-hand account by participants — such as Richard Crossman's *Diaries* — may provide evidence which would not otherwise be available, though the account of any one individual, however gifted, is likely to be disputed and contradicted by others involved.

Fourth, exaggerated attention to the need for subterfuge and trickery in the study of organisations directs attention away from much more important ethical issues in organisational research such as: to whom does the sociologists' responsibility primarily lie? For whom is the research being produced? What negotiations have been entered into with organisational members, what bargains struck? Who is sponsoring the research? What is the likely audience of the research? What can the sociologist do about the problem that

once the research is published it is public property, no longer
within his control, and may be used for purposes that he did
not anticipate and of which he does not approve? A case
study of these issues is provided in Kynaston-Reeves and
Harper's work on employee survey research.[70] Those who do
social surveys within organisations into industrial relations
problems face particular difficulties in maintaining their
autonomy and impartiality, and in the fact that information
that the researcher discovers may be made use of by persons
or groups in that organisation in their dealings with other
groups or persons. This difficulty is well-recognised at the
individual level, in terms of anonymising and maintaining the
confidentiality of data, but it is much broader than this.

Research on organisations poses many more methodological and ethical problems than can be solved by the adoption
of covert methods. The problem raised on page 226 of whose
causes are the right causes is one that needs more attention,
as are the practical possibilities of doing overt research in
settings where access is difficult. Did Rosenhan, for example,
really need to do his pseudo-patient research covertly? To
what extent can research on the police be done overtly?
American studies summarised by McCall suggest that it can.[71]
The merits of covert observation can easily be considerably
exaggerated as well as displacing attention from more
significant matters.

Ethical Decision-Making in Practice

A work such as this invites the criticism that it engages in
abstract moralism. Dilemmas and choices will continue to
face the field researcher that dogmatic statements of 'should'
and 'must' will not eliminate. The complexity of practical
ethical decision-making will continue to dog the steps of the
sociologist using observational methods. The object of the
present work, however, is not primarily to lay down moral
principles for the conduct of social research. Although the
editor inclines to be critical, for the reasons stated earlier
in the chapter, of the use of covert or secret methods, he also
recognises that there are situations in which their use may be
justified. The primary purpose of the present work, however,

is to set out some of the different views on the subject and hopefully thereby to provide some guidance for those who may contemplate the use of covert methods in the future. The matter can hardly be left there, for having read the previous twelve chapters, the reader may still wonder what to do in a particular case.

Several different kinds of answer may be given to further questions as to what to do. One, clearly stated by Norman Denzin in Chapter 8, is that it is a matter for the conscience of the individual and his own ethical judgement what is possible and permissible in the field. This kind of moral perspective has a sound pedigree in ascetic protestantism, one reflected in many reflective accounts about the ethics of research using covert observational methods. Ultimately, it is unsatisfactory, for it neglects the extent to which sociologists or social scientists form a professional community whose actions have repercussions for others among them. They exist, too, in a society which will take cognisance of the ethics of the activities which they undertake.

A different sort of answer, reflected in Donald Warwick's critique of *Tearoom Trade* in Chapter 3, is to appeal to general ethical principles which should govern the conduct of research. Many such principles are appealing and just, such as informed consent. Yet critics of appeals to such principles point to the ethical absolutism which can be involved and the difficulties which putting principles into practice can entail for social research. If informed consent was interpreted strictly, for example, much research in social science — experimental, survey-based or observational — would become well-nigh impossible. Those who defend such principles reply that if one does not adopt them, then ethical decision-making in research becomes a relative matter, in which departures from principle can be justified on pragmatic grounds and lead to what they regard as quite unethical behaviour.

One kind of compromise between these two views is for professional associations to develop their own code of ethics. Both the American and British Sociological Associations, for example, have their own codes of ethics, which are binding upon their members.[72] Each has an Ethics Committee whose job it is to consider possible infringements of the code which are brought to their attention. The BSA Code of Ethics, for example, states:

> . . . the sociologist should subscribe to the doctrine of 'informed consent' on the part of subjects and accordingly take pains to explain fully the object and implications of his research to individual subjects. . . . He should be aware of the ethical issues involved in observation or experimental manipulation of subjects without their knowledge, a form of research inquiry which should be resorted to only where it is not possible to use other methods to obtain essential data. These methods should only be used where it is possible to safeguard completely the interests and anonymity of the subjects.[73]

John Galliher, in Chapter 9, criticises such codes as a basis for deciding how sociologists should act, with particular reference to the ASA Code published in 1968. A further criticism of such codes is that they tend to be so general that only the most flagrant departures from normal research practice are likely to infringe them. Moreover, unlike medicine or the law, sociologists have no monopoly of professional practice and no licensing body. To work as a sociologist in the United States or Britain, it is not necessary to be a member of the ASA or BSA. Hence, even expulsion for unethical behaviour is not a very effective sanction, and codes of ethics for sociologists lack teeth as a result. Sociologists have also shown themselves quite reluctant to become more professionalised, so that a solution to the problem on the medical model of state licensing to practice linked to a legally-enforceable ethical code seems unlikely in the near future.

A more imminent means of control is government regulation of research through institutional self-policing. The setting up of Institutional Review Boards in the United States as a means of achieving the 'protection of human subjects' is referred to by Galliher, and has gone considerably further since he wrote. More recently, both Wax and Cassell[74] and Duster, Matza and Wellman[75] have expressed concern about the likely impact of such federal regulations upon field research using observational methods. One may be fairly certain, too, that Institutional Review Boards, on which a majority of members are non-sociologists, are unlikely to be impressed by some of the finer points made in justification of covert methods by those who advocate them. This has led to some sociologists to launch a head-on attack on the idea of federal regulation as such, seeing it as an attempt by government to impose constraints upon freedom of scientific thought.

Certainly, federal regulation can have adverse effects on sociological research which were not intended originally. The situation is a rapidly changing one and, to some extent, peculiar to the United States. Some references to the current debate appear on page 258. Critics of such regulations, however, fail to perceive that they are a necessary and worthwhile attempt to bring home to social scientists that they have responsibility for their actions, and that ends do not override means. The 'protection of human subjects' means what it says and developed in response to some flagrant instances of the neglect of the interests of the research subjects in bio-medical research. The subjects of *social* research have interests too, and social science research can indeed do harm, though not over matters of life and death as in medicine. Social scientists need to be aware of their wider social responsibilities. Though social science is driven by its search for truth,

at the same time, this search for social truths must itself operate within constraints. Its limits arise when inquiry infringes on the rights of individuals to be treated as persons, to be considered — in the renewable phrase — as ends and not means. Just as sociologists must not distort or manipulate truth to serve untruthful ends, so too they must not manipulate persons to serve their quest for truth. The study of society, being the study of human beings, imposes the responsibility of respecting the integrity, promoting the dignity and maintaining the autonomy of these persons.[76]

Conclusion

'There will always remain many areas of social life that would be interesting to investigate but which are inaccessible to open inquiry. The moral problem of whether or not these should be tackled by covert inquiry will still be with us.'[77] The controversy will continue, with fresh empirical research to charge the ethical debate.

The most compelling argument in favour of covert observation is that it has produced good social science which, moreover, would not have been possible without covert means. Rosenhan's study of the labeling of psychiatric patients is a distinguished instance. Festinger *et al.*'s *When Prophecy Fails* is another. The benefits which flow from the use of the method are enhancement of our knowledge of society. It would be churlish to end a collection such as this without recognising that the use of covert methods has advanced our understanding of society.

There are areas of grey between the black and the white, but there are also powerful arguments against covert research. Perhaps the following summary points can draw together the theme of this chapter:

(1) The rights of subjects override the rights of science. Human personality should not be sacrificed in the name of 'science'.

(2) This means that some research which might be desirable may not be possible. This is an inevitable consequence of (1).

(3) Anonymity and confidentiality are necessary but not sufficient safeguards for the subjects of research. Identification of individuals may still be possible, and such safeguards do nothing to protect a group from publication of information about them. Social scientists cannot predict the consequences which will follow from their publications.

(4) Covert observation is in general harmful not only to the subjects of research but to the sociologist(s) doing the research and to sociology as an activity.

(5) The need for covert methods is considerably exaggerated. Open entry may more often be negotiated than is commonly supposed.

(6) More attention should be paid to the 'overt insider' role being adopted. Sociologists' distrust of many agencies of social control is more evidence of their political proclivities than of their capacity for scientific detachment. Yet becoming a recognised insider may provide good research access.

(7) To be a covert outsider, present in a research setting in some role other than that of researcher, while engaged in covert observation, is less reprehensible than playing the role of 'covert insider' and masquerading as a true participant.

(8) Sociologists have responsibilities to the subjects of their research, and when embarking on research, particularly observational research within organisations, need to clarify for their own benefit where those responsibilities lie.

(9) Sociologists themselves are not the only judges of what constitutes ethical behaviour. Although attempts to limit free inquiry are to be resisted, constructive criticism and advice from non-sociologists are worth listening to.

(10) The sociologist contemplating covert participant observation is well advised to seek guidance from the ethical codes of professional associations, from the published reflections of other sociologists and from colleagues before embarking upon the use of a research method which may be both unethical and unnecessary.

Select Bibliography

This *short* and *selective* guide to further reading on the ethics of covert participant observation is arranged *chronologically* within sections, in order to show the development of the debate in social science. It makes no claim to be comprehensive and includes a variety of materials: monographs and journal articles reporting research done using (mainly) covert or semi-covert observational methods; articles and books discussing more generally the ethics of social research, including covert observational research; in recent years, several discussions of government regulation of social research; and examples of professional codes of ethics.

Empirical Research (not all using covert participant observation)

B. BETTELHEIM (1943) 'Individual and Mass Behaviour in Extreme Situations', *Journal of Abnormal and Social Psychology* 38, 417—52.

W. CAUDILL, F. REDLICH, H. GILMORE and E. BRODY (1952) 'Social Structures and Interaction Process on a Psychiatric Ward', *American Journal of Orthopsychiatry* 22, 314—34.

A. H. STANTON and M. S. SCHWARZ (1954) *The Mental Hospital* (New York: Basic Books) pp. 426—48.

W. F. WHYTE (1955) *Street Corner Society*, 2nd ed. (University of Chicago Press).

L. FESTINGER *et al.* (1956) *When Prophecy Fails* (Minneapolis: University of Minnesota Press) (Harper Paperback 1964).

W. CAUDILL (1958) *The Psychiatric Hospital as a Small Society* (Cambridge, Mass.. Harvard U.P.).

M. A. SULLIVAN *et al.* (1958) 'Participant Observation as Employed in the Study of a Military Training Program', *American Sociological Review* 23, 660—7.

M. DALTON (1959) *Men Who Manage* (New York: Free Press).

J. F. LOFLAND and R. A. LE JEUNE (1960) 'Initial Interaction of Newcomers in Alcoholics Anonymous: a field experiment in class symbols and socialisation', *Social Problems* 8, 102—11.

J. H. GRIFFIN (1961) *Black Like Me* (Boston: Houghton Mifflin).

H. S. BECKER (1963) *Outsiders* (Glencoe, Ill.: Free Press).

M. DALTON (1964) 'Preconceptions and Methods in *Men Who Manage*', in P. Hammond (ed.), *Sociologists at Work* (New York: Basic Books) pp. 50—95.

A. DANIELS (1967) 'The Low Caste Stranger in Social Research', in G. Sjöberg (ed.), *Ethics, Politics and Social Research* (London, Routledge & Kegan Paul) pp. 267—96.

N. POLSKY (1967) *Hustlers, Beats and Others* (Chicago: Aldine).

A. J. VIDICH and J. BENSMAN (1968) *Small Town in Mass Society*, revised ed. (Princeton U.P.) esp. appendices.

J. D. DOUGLAS (ed.) (1970) *Observations on Deviance* (New York: Random House).

L. HUMPHREYS (1970 and 1975) *Tearoom Trade: impersonal sex in public places* (Chicago: Aldine); revised ed. with new appendices, 1975.

G. D. SPINDLER (ed.) (1970) *Being an Anthropologist* (New York: Holt, Rinehart & Winston).

W. CHAMBLISS (1971) 'Vice, Corruption, Bureaucracy and Power', *Wisconsin Law Review* 17, 1150—73.

S. COHEN and L. TAYLOR (1972) *Psychological Survival: the effects of long-term imprisonment* (Harmondsworth: Penguin Books).

F. and E. IANNI (1972) *A Family Business: kinship and social control in organised crime* (London: Routledge & Kegan Paul).

J. PATRICK (1973) *A Glasgow Gang Observed* (London: Eyre Methuen).

D. L. ROSENHAN (1973) 'On Being Sane in Insane Places', *Science* 179, 350—8.

J. RUBINSTEIN (1973) *City Police* (New York: Farrar, Straus & Giroux).

G. SPENCER (1973) 'Methodological Issues in the Study of Bureaucratic Elites: a case of West Point', *Social Problems* 21, 90—102.

W. CHAMBLISS (1975) 'On the Paucity of Original Research on Organised Crime', *American Sociologist* 10, 36—9.

G. L. KIRKHAM (1975) 'Doc Cop', *Human Behaviour* 4, 16—23.

A. SUTHERLAND (1975) *Gypsies: the hidden Americans* (London: Tavistock).

R. W. BUCKINGHAM *et al.* (1976) 'Living with the Dying', *Canadian Medical Association Journal*, 18 December, vol. 115, pp. 1211–15.

M. A. RYNKIEWICH and J. SPRADLEY (eds) (1976) *Ethics and Anthropology: dilemmas in fieldwork* (New York: Wiley).

R. WALLIS (1976) *The Road to Total Freedom: a sociological analysis of scientology* (London: Heinemann).

J. DITTON (1977) *Part Time Crime* (London: Macmillan).

J. D. DOUGLAS *et al.* (1977) *The Nude Beach* (London: Sage).

C. KLOCKARS (1977) 'Field Ethics for the Life History', in R. S. Weppner (ed.), *Street Ethnography* (London: Sage Annual Review of Drug and Alcohol Abuse) vol. 1, pp. 201–6.

R. WALLIS, (1977) 'The Moral Career of a Research Project', in C. Bell and H. Newby (eds), *Doing Sociological Research* (London: Allen & Unwin).

J. BALDWIN and M. McCONVILLE (1978) 'Plea Bargaining: legal carve-up and legal cover-up', *British Journal of Law and Society* 5, 228–34.

W. CHAMBLISS (1978) *On the Take: from petty crooks to Presidents* (Bloomington, Indiana U.P.).

R. HOMAN (1978) 'Interpersonal Communication in Pentecostal Meetings', *Sociological Review* 26, 499–518.

K. PRYCE (1979) *Endless Pressure: a study of West Indian lifestyles in Bristol* (Harmondsworth: Penguin Books).

N. FIELDING (1981) *The National Front* (London: Routledge & Kegan Paul).

General Discussions of Covert Observation and/or Research Ethics Generally

F. BOAS (1919) 'Scientists as Spies', *Nation* 109, 797 (reprinted in T. Weaver (ed.), *To See Ourselves* (Glenview, III.: Scott Foresman, 1973) pp. 51–2).

J. H. FICHTER and W. L. KOLB (1953) 'Ethical Limitations on Sociological Reporting', *American Sociological Review* 18, 544–50.

L. A. COSER *et al.* (1959) 'Participant Observation and the Military: an exchange', *American Sociological Review* 24, 397–400.

E. SHILS (1959) 'Social Research and the Autonomy of the Individual', in D. Lerner (ed.), *The Human Meaning of the Social Sciences* (New York: Meridian) pp. 114–57.

F. DAVIS (1961) 'Comment on "Initial Interactions of Newcomers in Alcoholics Anonymous" ', *Social Problems* 8, 364–5.

J. LOFLAND (1961) 'Comment on "Initial Interactions of Newcomers in AA" ', *Social Problems* 8, 365–7.

M. MEAD (1961) 'The Human Study of Human Beings', *Science* 133, 163–5.

J. ROTH (1962) 'Comments on "Secret Observations"', *Social Problems* 9, 283—4.

J. A. BARNES (1963) 'Some Ethical Problems in Modern Fieldwork', *British Journal of Sociology* 14, 118—34.

H. S. BECKER (1964) 'Problems in the Publications of Field Studies', in A. Vidich *et al.* (eds), *Reflections on Community Studies* (New York: Wiley) pp. 267—84.

H. S. BECKER (1967) 'Whose Side Are We On?', *Social Problems* 14, 239—47.

K. T. ERIKSON (1967) 'A Comment on Disguised Observation in Sociology', *Social Problems* 14, 366—73.

H. KELMAN (1967) 'The Human Use of Human Subjects: the problem of deception in social psychological experiments', *Psychological Bulletin* 67, 1—11.

A. LURIE (1967) *Imaginary Friends* (London: Heinemann) (novel).

L. RAINWATER and D. J. PITTMAN (1967) 'Ethical Problems in Studying a Politically Sensitive and Deviant Community', *Social Problems* 14, 357—66.

N. DENZIN (1968) 'On the Ethics of Disguised Observation', *Social Problems* 15, 502—4.

K. T. ERIKSON (1968) 'A Reply to Denzin', *Social Problems* 15, 505—6.

A. W. GOULDNER (1968) 'The Sociologist as Partisan; Sociology and the Welfare State', *American Sociologist* 3, pp. 103—16.

H. C. KELMAN (1968) *A Time to Speak* (San Francisco: Jossey Bass).

G. SJOBERG (ed.) (1968) *Ethics, Politics and Social Research* (London, Routledge & Kegan Paul).

I. C. JARVIE (1969) 'The Problem of Ethical Integrity in Participant Observation', *Current Antropology* 10, 505—23.

M. MEAD (1969) 'Research with Human Beings: a model derived from anthropological field practice', *Daedalus* 98, 361—86.

R. A. BERK and J. M. ADAMS (1970) 'Establishing Rapport with Deviant Groups', *Social Problems* 18, 102—17.

P. BONACHICH (1970) 'Deceiving Subjects: the pollution of our environment', *American Sociologist* 5, 45.

J. JORGENSON (1971) 'On Ethics and Anthropology', *Current Anthropology* 12, 321—34.

J. D. DOUGLAS (ed.) (1972) *Research on Deviance* (New York: Random House).

M. GLAZER (1972) *The Research Adventure* (New York: Random House).

J. KATZ (1972) *Experimentation with Human Beings* (New York: Russell Sage).

H. KELMAN (1972) 'The Rights of the Subject in Social Research', *American Psychologist* 27, 989—1016.

P. D. REYNOLDS (1972) 'On the Protection of Human Subjects and Social Science', *International Social Science Journal* 24, 693—719.

B. BARBER (1973) 'Experimentation on Human Beings: another problem for civil rights', *Minerva* 11, 1973, 415—19.

J. F. GALLIHER (1973) 'The Protection of Human Subjects: a reexamination of the professional code of ethics', *American Sociologist* 8, 93—100.

F. REDLICH (1973) 'Ethical Aspects of Clinical Observation of Behaviour', *Journal of Nervous and Mental Disease* 157, November, 313—19.

Social Problems (1973), special issue on 'The Social Control of Social Research' 21, 1, including: G. Sjöberg and P. J. Miller, 'Social Research on Bureaucracy: limitations and opportunities', 129—43; and E. Sagarin, 'The Research Setting and the Right Not to be Researched', 52—64.

D. P. WARWICK (1973) 'Tearoom Trade: means and ends in social research', *Hastings Center Studies* 1, 27—38.

D. MIXON (1974) 'If You Won't Deceive, What Can You Do?', in Nigel Armistead (ed.), *Reconstructing Social Psychology* (Harmondsworth: Penguin Books) pp. 72—85.

W. B. SANDERS (1974) *The Sociologist as Detective: an introduction to research methods* (New York: Praeger).

D. C. GIBBONS (1975) 'Unidentified Research Sites and Fictitious Names', *American Sociologist* 10, 32—6.

D. C. GIBBONS and F. F. JONES (1975) *The Study of Deviance: perspectives and problems* (Engelwood Cliffs, N.J.: Prentice-Hall) chapter 9.

R. L. GORDEN (1975) *Interviewing* (Homewood, Illinois: Dorsey) chapter 7 on the ethics of interviewing.

P. D. REYNOLDS (1975) 'Value Dilemmas in the Professional Conduct of Social Science', *International Social Science Journal* 27, 563—611.

I. WADDINGTON (1975) 'The Development of Medical Ethics: a sociological analysis', *Medical History* 19, 36—51.

D. P. WARWICK (1975) 'Social Scientists Ought to Stop Lying', *Psychology Today* (US) vol. 8, February, pp. 38—49 and 105—6.

R. S. BROADHEAD and R. C. RIST (1976) 'Gatekeepers and the Social Control of Social Research', *Social Problems* 23, 325—36.

J. D. DOUGLAS (1976) *Investigative Social Research* (London: Sage).

W. B. MURRAY and R. W. BUCKINGHAM (1976) 'Implications of Participant Observation in Medical Studies', *Canadian Medical Association Journal* 115, 1187—90.

P. NEJELSKI (ed.) (1976) *Social Research in Conflict with Law and Ethics* (Cambridge, Mass.: Ballinger).

J. A. BARNES (1977) *The Ethics of Inquiry in Social Science* (Delhi: O.U.P.).

S. BOK (1978) 'Freedom and Risk', *Daedalus* 107, 115—28.

R. T. BOWER and P. DE GASPARIS (1978) *Ethics in Social Research* (New York: Praeger).

E. DIENER and R. CRANDALL (1978) *Ethics in Social and Behavioral Research* (University of Chicago Press).

G. J. McCALL (1978) *Observing the Law: field methods in the study of crime and criminal justice systems* (New York: Free Press).

H. KELMAN (1978) 'Research, Behavioural', entry in W. Reich (ed.), *Encyclopedia of Bioethics* (New York: Macmillan Co.).

J. A. BARNES (1979) *Who Should Know What? Social science, privacy and ethics* (Harmondsworth: Penguin Books).

S. BOK (1979) *Lying: moral choice in public and private life* (Hassocks: Harvester Press).

P. D. REYNOLDS (1979) *Ethical Dilemmas and Social Science Research* (San Francisco: Jossey Bass).

W. F. WHYTE (1979) 'On Making the Most of Participant Observation', *American Sociologist* 14, 56—66.

M. BULMER (1980) 'The Impact of Ethical Concerns upon Sociological Research', *Sociology* 14, 125—30.

R. HOMAN (1980) 'The Ethics of Covert Methods', followed by M. Bulmer, 'A Comment', *British Journal of Sociology* 31, 46—65.

C. B. KLOCKARS and F. W. O'CONNOR (1980) *Deviance and Decency: the ethics of research with human subjects* (Beverley Hills: Sage).

G. T. MARX (1980) 'Police Undercover Work', *Urban Life* vol. 8, January, pp. 399—446.

E. SHILS (1980) *The Calling of Sociology and Other Essays on the Pursuit of Learning* (University of Chicago Press) part 4, 'The Ethics of Sociology'.

Social Problems (1980) 27, 3, special issue on 'Ethical problems in fieldwork', edited by J. Cassell and M. L. Wax.

M. USEEM and G. T. MARX (1980) 'Ethical Dilemmas and Political Considerations in Social Research', in R. B. Smith (ed.), *A Handbook of Social Science Methods: Qualitative Methods* (New York: Irvington Press).

R. DINGWALL (1980) 'Ethics and Ethnography', *Sociological Review* 28, 871—91.

Regulation of Research

B. BARBER *et al.* (1973) *Research on Human Subjects: problems of social control in medical experimentation* (New York: Russell Sage).

B. H. GRAY (1975) *Human Subjects in Medical Experimentation* (New York: Wiley).

258 Select Bibliography

B. H. GRAY (1975) 'An Assessment of Institutional Review Committees in Human Experimentation', *Medical Care* 13, 318—28.

M. L. WAX (1977) 'On Fieldworkers and Those Exposed to Fieldwork', *Human Organisation* 36, 321—8.

American Sociologist (1978) 13, 3. Special issue on the regulation of research, including articles by R. Stephenson, J. Cassell and R. Bond and responses by thirteen leading field researchers.

Daedalus (1978) *Limits of Scientific Inquiry*, Spring issue.

K. M. WULFF (1978) *Regulation of Scientific Inquiry: societal concerns with research* (Boulder: Westview Press, for AAAS). Contains chapter by A. J. Reiss Jr, Eliot Friedson and Hans O. Mauksch.

T. DUSTER *et al.* (1979) 'Fieldwork and the Protection of Human Subjects', *American Sociologist* 14, 136—42.

M. WAX and J. CASSELL (eds) (1979) *Federal Regulations: ethical issues and social research* (Boulder: Westview Press, for AAAS).

C. B. KLOCKARS and F. W. O'CONNOR (1980) *Deviance and Decency: the ethics of research with human subjects* (Beverley Hills: Sage) chapters 1—4.

Code of Ethics: examples

American Anthropological Association (1971) 'Principles of Professional Responsibility'.

American Sociological Association (1971) 'Code of Ethics'.

British Sociological Association (1973) 'Statement of Ethical Principles and Their Application to Sociological Research'.

Notes and References

Chapter 1

1. Two useful general discussions are J. A. Barnes, *Who Should Know What?* (Harmondsworth: Penguin Books, 1979) and E. Diener and R. Crandall, *Ethics in Social and Behavioral Science* (University of Chicago Press, 1978).

2. Sherri Cavan, *American Journal of Sociology* 83, 1977, p. 810.

3. For a selection of the extensive literature, see the Select Bibliography following page 252. Several of the most significant articles up to 1970 are usefully collected in W. J. Filstead (ed.), *Qualitative Methodology* (Chicago: Markham, 1970).

4. On biomedical research, see S. J. Reiser *et al.* (eds), *Ethics in Medicine* (Cambridge, Mass.: M.I.T. Press, 1977), and the *Encyclopedia of Bioethics* (New York: Free Press, 1978) 4 vols. On psychological research ethics, see Barnes, op. cit. and Diener and Crandall, op. cit. and H. Kelman, *A Time to Speak* (San Francisco: Jossey Bass, 1968).

5. Cf. G. J. McCall and J. L. Simmons (eds), *Issues in Participant Observation: a text and a reader* (Boston: Addison-Wesley, 1969).

6. News story in *The Guardian* (London), 'How Spy was Blown', 23 January 1980, p. 5.

7. J. Conrad, *Secret Agent* (New York: Doubleday, 1975).

8. G. T. Marx, 'Thoughts on a Neglected Category of Social Movement Participant: the agent provocateur and informant', *American Journal of Sociology* 80, 1974, pp. 402–42, and G. T. Marx, 'Police Undercover Work', *Urban Life* 8, January 1980, pp. 399–446.

9. R. L. Gold, 'Roles in Sociological Field Observations', *Social*

Forces **36**, 1958, pp. 217—23, reprinted in McCall and Simmons, op. cit. pp. 30—9.

10. J. Roth, 'Comments on "Secret Observation"', *Social Problems* **9**, 1961, pp. 283—4.

11. Cf. S. Bok, *Lying: moral choice in public and private life* (Hassocks: Harvester Press, 1978).

12. F. Boas, 'Correspondence: Scientists as Spies', *The Nation* (New York) vol. 109, 1919, reprinted in T. Weaver (ed.), *To See Ourselves: anthropology and modern social issues* (Glenview, Ill.: Scott Foresman, 1973) pp. 51—2.

13. G. W. Stocking, Jr, *Race, Culture and Evolution* (New York: Free Press, 1968) pp. 270 ff.

14. B. Bettelheim, 'Individual and Mass Behaviour in Extreme Situations', *Journal of Abnormal and Social Psychology* **38**, 1943, pp. 417—52, reprinted in B. Bettelheim, *Surviving & Other Essays* (London: Thames & Hudson, 1979) pp. 48—83. Its rejection by other journals is discussed in *Surviving*, pp. 13—18.

15. B. Bettelheim, *The Informed Heart* (New York: Free Press, 1960).

16. M. A. Sullivan, S. A. Queen and R. C. Patrick, 'Participant Observation as Employed in the Study of a Military Training Program', *American Sociological Review* **23**, 1958, pp. 660—7 (reprinted in Filstead, op. cit.).

17. Ibid. p. 664.

18. W. Caudill, F. Redlich, H. Gilmore and E. Brody, 'Social Structure and Interaction Processes on a Psychiatric Ward', *American Journal of Orthopsychiatry* **22**, 1952, pp. 314—34, at p. 315.

19. Ibid. p. 315.

20. See the Select Bibliography following page 252 for a partial guide to this literature.

21. K. T. Erikson, 'A Comment on Disguised Observation in Sociology', *Social Problems* **14**, 1967, pp. 366—73 (reprinted in Filstead, op. cit.) at pp. 367—8.

22. Ibid. p. 373.

23. J. D. Douglas *Investigative Social Research* (Beverley Hills: Sage, 1976).

24. Ibid. p. xiv.

25. Ibid. p. 55.

26. Ibid. p. 56.

27. C. Bernstein and B. Woodward, *All the President's Men* (New York: Simon & Schuster, 1974).

28. Cf. *The Handbook of Medical Ethics* (London: British Medical Association, 1980); S. J. Reiser *et al.*, *Ethics in Medicine*, op. cit.; A. Duncan *et al.*, *Dictionary of Medical Ethics* (London: Darton, Longman & Todd, 1977).

Chapter 2

1. P. Ash, *J. Abnorm. Soc. Psychol.* 44, 1949, p. 272; A. T. Beck, *Amer. J. Psychiat.* 119, 1962, p. 210; A. T. Boisen, *Psychiatry* 2, 1938, p. 233; N. Kreitman, *J. Ment. Sci.* 107, 1961, p. 876; N. Kreitman, P. Sainsbury, J. Morrisey, J. Towers and J. Scrivener, ibid. p. 887; H. O. Schmitt and C. P. Fonda, *J. Abnorm. Soc. Psychol.* 52, 1956, p. 262; W. Seeman, *J. Nerv. Ment. Dis.* 118, 1953, p. 541. For an analysis of these artefacts and summaries of the disputes, see J. Zubin, *Ann. Rev. Psychol.* 18, 1967, p. 373; L. Phillips and J. G. Draguns, ibid. 22, 1971, p. 447.

2. R. Benedict, *J. Gen. Psychol.* 10, 1934, p. 59.

3. See in this regard H. Becker, *Outsiders: Studies in the Sociology of Deviance* (New York: Free Press, 1963); B. M. Braginsky, D. D. Braginsky and K. Ring, *Methods of Madness: The Mental Hospital as a Last Resort* (New York: Holt, Rinehart & Winston, 1969); G. M. Crocetti and P. V. Lemkau, *Amer. Sociol. Rev.* 30, 1965, p. 577; E. Goffman, *Behavior in Public Places* (New York: Free Press, 1964); R. D. Laing, *The Divided Self: A Study of Sanity and Madness* (Chicago: Quadrangle, 1960); D. L. Phillips, *Amer. Sociol. Rev.* 28, 1963, p. 963; T. R. Sabin, *Psychol. Today* 6, 1972, p. 18; E. Schur, *Amer J. Sociol.* 75, 1969, p. 309; T. Szasz, *Law, Liberty and Psychiatry* (New York: Macmillan, 1963); *The Myth of Mental Illness: Foundations of a Theory of Mental Illness* (New York: Hoeber-Harper, 1963). For a critique of some of these views, see W. R. Gove, *Amer. Sociol. Rev.* 35, 1970, p. 873.

4. E. Goffman, *Asylums* (Garden City, New York: Doubleday, 1961).

5. T. J. Scheff, *Being Mentally Ill: A Sociological Theory* (Chicago: Aldine, 1966).

6. Data from a ninth pseudo-patient are not incorporated in this report because, although his sanity went undetected, he falsified aspects of his personal history, including his marital status and parental relationships. His experimental behaviors therefore were not identical to those of the other pseudo-patients.

7. A. Barry, *Bellevue is a State of Mind* (New York: Harcourt Brace Jovanovich, 1971); I. Belknap, *Human Problems of a State Mental Hospital* (New York: McGraw-Hill, 1956); W. Caudill, F. C. Redlich, H. R. Gilmore and E. B. Brody, *Amer. J. Orthopsychiat.* 22, 1952, p. 314; A. R. Goldman, R. H. Bohr and T. A. Steinberg, *Prof. Psychol.* 1, 1970, p. 427; unauthored, Roche Report, vol. 1, no. 13, 1971, p. 8.

8. Beyond the personal difficulties that the pseudo-patient is likely to experience in the hospital, there are legal and social ones that, combined, require considerable attention before entry. For example,

once admitted to a psychiatric institution, it is difficult, if not impossible, to be discharged on short notice, state law to the contrary notwithstanding. I was not sensitive to these difficulties at the outset of the project, nor to the personal and situational emergencies that can arise, but later a writ of habeas corpus was prepared for each of the entering pseudo-patients and an attorney was kept 'on call' during every hospitalisation. I am grateful to John Kaplan and Robert Bartels for legal advice and assistance in these matters.

9. However distasteful such concealment is, it was a necessary first step to examining these questions. Without concealment, there would have been no way to know how valid these experiences were; nor was there any way of knowing whether whatever detections occurred were a tribute to the diagnostic acumen of the staff or to the hospital's rumour network. Obviously, since my concerns are general ones that cut across individual hospitals and staffs, I have respected their anonymity and have eliminated clues that might lead to their identification.

10. Interestingly, of the twelve admissions, eleven were diagnosed as schizophrenic and one, with the identical symptomatology, as manic-depressive psychosis. This diagnosis has a more favourable prognosis, and it was given by the only private hospital in our sample. On the relations between social class and psychiatric diagnosis, see A. de B. Hollingshead and F. C. Redlich, *Social Class and Mental Illness: A Community Study* (New York: Wiley, 1958).

11. It is possible, of course, that patients have quite broad latitudes in diaanosis and therefore are inclined to call many people sane, even those whose behaviour is patently aberrant. However, although we have no hard data on this matter, it was our distinct impression that this was not the case. In many instances, patients not only singled us out for attention, but came to imitate our behaviours and styles.

12. J. Cumming and E. Cumming, *Community Ment. Health* 1, 1965, p. 135; A. Farina and K. Ring, *J. Abnorm. Psychol.* 70, 1965, p. 47; H. E. Freeman and O. G. Simmons, *The Mental Patient Comes Home* (New York: Wiley, 1963); W. J. Johannsen, *Ment. Hygiene* 53, 1969, p. 218; A. S. Linsky, *Soc. Psychiat.* 5, 1970, p. 166.

13. S. E. Asch, *J. Abnorm. Soc. Psychol.* 41, 1946, p. 258; *Social Psychology* (New York: Prentice-Hall, 1952).

14. See also I. N. Mensh and J. Wishner, *J. Personality* 16, 1947, p. 188; J. Wishner, *Psychol. Rev.* 67, 1960, p. 96; J. S. Bruner and R. Tagiuri, in G. Lindzey (ed.), *Handbook of Social Psychology* (Cambridge, Mass.: Addison-Wesley, 1954) vol. 2, pp. 634—54; J. S. Bruner, D. Shapiro and R. Tagiuri, in R. Tagiuri and L. Petrullo (eds), *Person Perception and Interpersonal Behavior* (Stanford University Press, 1958) pp. 277—88.

15. For an example of a similar self-fulfilling prophecy, in this instance dealing with the 'central' trait of intelligence, see R. Rosenthal and L. Jacobson, *Pygmalion in the Classroom* (New York: Holt, Rinehart & Winston, 1968).

16. E. Zigler and L. Phillips, *J. Abnorm. Soc. Psychol.* 63, 1961, p. 69. See also R. K. Freudenberg and J. P. Robertson, *A.M.A. Arch. Neurol. Psychiatr.* 76, 1956, p. 14.

17. W. Mischel, *Personality and Assessment* (New York: Wiley, 1968).

18. The most recent and unfortunate instance of this tenet is that of Senator Thomas Eagleton.

19. T. R. Sarbin and J. C. Mancuso, *J. Clin. Consult. Psychol.* 35, 1970, p. 159; T. R. Sarbin, ibid. 31, 1967, p. 447; J. C. Nunnally, Jr, *Popular Conceptions of Mental Health* (New York: Holt, Rinehart & Winston, 1961).

20. A. H. Stanton and M. S. Schwartz, *The Mental Hospital: A Study of Institutional Participation in Psychiatric Illness and Treatment* (New York: Basic Books, 1954).

21. D. B. Wexler and S. E. Scoville, *Ariz. Law Rev.* 13, 1971, p. 1.

22. I thank W. Mischel, E. Orne and M. S. Rosenhan for comments on an earlier draft of this manuscript.

Chapter 3

1. This paper has profited from the suggestions and criticisms of numerous colleagues and friends, including Robert Michels of Columbia University; Michael Horowitz, New York City; Herbert Kelman, Ann Orlov, Bruce Smith and Mary Thomas, Harvard University; Paul Rosencrantz, College of the Holy Cross; C. Michael Lanphier of York University, Toronto; Leon Kass and Daniel Callahan. Lee Rainwater of Harvard University was especially helpful in commenting on the factual accuracy of my interpretations of the research in question. The manuscript was also sent to Laud Humphreys of the State University of New York for his comments.

2. Laud Humphreys, 'The Sociologist as Voyeur', *Trans-Action* 7, p. 15.

3. Humphreys, *Tearoom Trade* (Chicago: Aldine, 1970 and 1975) p. 38.

4. Humphreys, 'The Sociologists as Voyeur', p. 15.

5. Ibid.

6. Humphreys, *Tearoom Trade*, p. 172.

7. Cf. Herbert C. Kelman, *A Time to Speak: On Human Values and Social Research* (San Fransisco: Jossey-Bass, 1968).

8. Cf. Donald P. Warwick, 'Human Freedom and National Development', *Cross Currents* 18, 1968, pp. 495—517.

9. Ted R. Vaughan, 'Governmental Intervention in Social Research: Political and Ethical Dimensions in the Wichita Jury Recordings', in Gideon Sjöberg (ed.), *Ethics, Politics and Social Research* (Cambridge, Mass.: Schenkman Publishing Co., 1967) p. 71.

10. Humphreys, *Tearoom Trade*, p. 25.

11. Ibid. pp. 170—1.

12. Ibid. p. 171.

13. Ibid. pp. 169—70.

14. James Gustafson, 'Basic Ethical Issues in the Bio-Medical Fields', *Soundings* 53, 1970, pp. 151—80.

15. Horowitz and Rainwater, 'Sociological Snoopers and Journalistic Moralizers', *Trans-Action* 7, May 1970.

16. Ibid.

17. Ibid.

18. Ibid.

19. Arthur R. Miller, 'Personal Privacy in the Computer Age: the Challenge of a New Technology in an Information Oriented Society', *Michigan Law Review* 67, 1969, p. 1150.

20. Humphreys, *Tearoom Trade*, p. 168.

21. Rome G. Arnold, 'The Interview in Jeopardy: a Problem in Public Relations', *Public Opinion Quarterly* 38, 1964, p. 120.

22. Humphreys, *Tearoom Trade*, p. 167.

23. Ibid. p. 169.

Chapter 4

1. For a discussion of situation ethics, see Joseph Fletcher, *Situation Ethics* (London: S.C.M. Press, 1966). I accept J. A. Barnes's *Who Should Know What? Social Science, Privacy and Ethics* (London: Penguin Books, 1979) p. 16 definition of an ethical problem, 'When we try to decide between one course of action and another by reference to standards of what is morally right or wrong'. This begs a definition of 'the moral' which, very broadly, should be understood as human physical and mental well being.

2. See Ken Plummer, 'Misunderstanding Labelling Perspectives', in David Downes and Paul Rock (eds), *Deviant Interpretations* (London: Martin Robertson, 1979).

3. Respectively, Ian Taylor, Paul Watson and Jock Young, *The New Criminology* (London: Routledge & Kegan Paul, 1973) and Michael Phillipson and Maurice Roche, 'Phenomenology, Sociology and the Study of Deviance', in P. Rock and M. McIntosh (eds), *Deviance and Social Control* (London: Tavistock, 1971).

4. Michael Banton, *The Policeman in the Community* (London:

Tavistock, 1964) and Maureen Cain, *Society and the Policeman's Role* (London: Routledge & Kegan Paul, 1975).

5. W. A. Westley, *Violence and the Police* (Cambridge, Mass.: M.I.T. Press, 1970); Jerome Skolnick, *Justice Without Trial* (New York: Wiley, 1966).

6. See Lee Rainwater and David J. Pittman, 'Ethical Problems in Studying a Politically Sensitive and Deviant Community', *Social Problems*, vol. 14, no. 4, 1967, pp. 357—66; Leon Festinger *et al.*, *When Prophecy Fails* (Minneapolis: University of Minnesota Press, 1956); Laud Humphreys, *Tearoom Trade: Impersonal Sex in Public Places* (Chicago: Aldine, 1970); John Lofland, 'Comment on "Initial Interactions with Newcomers in AA" ', *Social Problems* **8**, 1961, pp. 365—7; D. L. Rosenhan, 'On Being Sane in Insane Places', *Science* **179**, 1973, pp. 250—8 (also Chapter 2 in this volume).

7. Work conducted in Britain suggests a similar conclusion. Michael Chatterton, *Organisational Processes and Relationships: A Case Study of Urban Policing*, unpublished Ph.D. thesis, University of Manchester, 1975; Peter Manning, *Police Work* (London: M.I.T. Press, 1977); Robert Reiner, *The Bluecoated Worker* (London: Cambridge U.P., 1977) esp. Methodological Appendix: and 'Assisting with Inquiries: problems of research on the police', *Quantitative Sociology Newsletter* 22, Summer 1979, pp. 37—67. Also see Maurice Punch, *Policing the Inner City* (London: Macmillan, 1979) for the Dutch context.

8. R. N. Harris, *The Police Academy: An Inside View* (New York: Wiley, 1973). George L. Kirkham, 'From Professor to Patrolman: a fresh perspective on the police', *Journal of Police Science and Administration*, vol. 2, no. 2, 1974, pp. 127—37. Jonathan Rubinstein, *City Police* (Boston: Ballantine Books, 1973). John Van Maanen, 'On Watching the Watcher', in Peter K. Manning and John Van Maanen, *Policing: A View From The Streets* (Santa Monica, 1978) pp. 309—50. H. Taylor Buckner's Ph.D. thesis: 'The Police: The Culture of a Social Control Agency' (Univ. of California, Berkeley, 1967) remains unpublished. G. J. McCall, *Observing the Law: field methods for the study of crime and the criminal justice system* (New York: Free Press, 1978) chapter 6, 'Observing the Police' is a general discussion which refers to some of these studies.

9. William Foote Whyte, *Street Corner Society* (London: University of Chicago Press, 1955) p. 317.

10. Raymond L. Gold, 'Roles in Sociological Field Observations', *Social Forces* **36**, March 1958, pp. 217—33.

11. Norman K. Denzin, 'On the Ethics of Disguised Observation', this volume, pp. 142—7, replies to Kai T. Erikson, 'A Comment on Disguised Observation in Sociology', *Social Problems*, vol. 14, no. 4, 1967, pp. 366—73.

12. Michael Clark, 'Survival in the Field: Implications of Personal Experience in Field Work', *Theory and Society* 2, 1978, pp. 63—94.

13. Bruno Bettelheim, 'Individual and Mass Behaviour in Extreme Situations', *Journal of Abnormal and Social Psychology* 38, 1943, pp. 417—52.

14. Alfred Schutz, *Collected Papers*, vol. I (The Hague: Nijhoff, 1962).

15. Roy Wallis, 'The Moral Career of a Research Project', in Colin Bell and Howard Newby, *Doing Sociological Research* (London: Allen & Unwin, 1977) pp. 149—69.

16. Simon Holdaway, 'Changes in Urban Policing', *British Journal of Sociology* 28 (2), 1977, pp. 119—37.

17. Simon Holdaway, 'The Reality of Police Race Relations: towards an effective community relations policy', *New Community*, vol. VI, no. 3, Summer 1978, pp. 258—67.

Chapter 5

1. N. Fielding, *The National Front* (London: Routledge & Kegan Paul, 1981).

2. J. Douglas, *Investigative Social Research* (London: Sage, 1976) pp. 28—9.

3. J. Lofland, *Analysing Social Settings* (Belmont, Calif.: Wadsworth, 1971), p. 13.

4. S. Bruyn, *The Human Perspective in Sociology* (Englewood Cliffs, N.J.: Prentice-Hall, 1968).

5. N. Polsky, *Hustlers, Beats and Others* (Harmondsworth: Penguin Books, 1969).

6. W. Chambliss, 'On the Paucity of Original Research on Organised Crime', *American Sociologist* 10, 1975, pp. 36—9.

7. J. Douglas, op. cit. p. 29.

8. R. Gorden, *Interviewing: strategy, techniques and tactics* (Homewood, Ill.: Dorsey, 1975) p. 172.

9. F. Bonilla and M. Glazer, 'Note on Methodology: fieldwork in a hostile environment', in *Student Politics in Chile* (New York: Basic, 1970) pp. 313—33.

10. J. Barnes, *Who Should Know What* (Harmondsworth: Penguin Books, 1979) p. 116.

11. Ibid. p. 126. See W. Murray and R. Buckingham, 'Implications of Participant Observation in Medical Studies', *Canadian Medical Association Journal*, 1976, pp. 1187—90.

12. A. Daniels, 'The Low Caste Stranger in Social Research', in G. Sjöberg (ed.), *Ethics, Politics and Social Research* (London: Routledge & Kegan Paul, 1967) p. 267.

13. Ibid. p. 273.

14. See G. Sjoberg and J. Miller, 'Social Research on Bureaucracy', *Social Problems*, vol. 21, no. 1, Summer 1973.

15. S. Bruyn, op. cit.

16. *Observation*, 25 June 1974.

17. 7 June 1974.

18. J. Barnes, op. cit. p. 142.

19. D. Douglas, 'Managing Fronts in Observing Deviants', in J. Douglas (ed.), *Research on Deviance* (New York: Random House, 1972) p. 113.

20. F. Davis, 'Comment on "Initial Interactions of Newcomers in Alcoholics Anonymous"', *Social Problems* 8, 1961, pp. 364—5.

21. H. Riecken, 'The Unidentified Interviewer', *American Journal of Sociology* 62, 1956, pp. 210—2.

22. J. Douglas, op. cit. p. 47.

23. Ibid.

24. His view that too sharp a distinction has generally been made between 'sympathy' and 'empathy' accounts for this confusion. See ibid. p. 106.

25. Ibid. pp. 48—9.

26. J. Roth, 'Comments on "Secret Observation"', *Social Problems* 9, 1962, pp. 283—4.

27. J. Robb, *Working Class Anti-Semite* (London: Tavistock, 1954) p. 74.

28. J. Douglas, op. cit. p. 139.

29. H. Becker, 'Problems in the Publication of Field Studies', in A. Vidich *et al.* (eds), *Reflections on Community Studies* (New York: Wiley, 1964) pp. 267—84.

30. E. Sagarin, 'The Research Setting and the Right Not to be Researched', *Social Problems*, vol. 21, no. 1, Summer 1973.

31. J. Galliher, 'The Protection of Human Subjects: a re-examination of the professional code of ethics', Chapter 9.

32. J. Fichter and W. Kolb, 'Ethical Limitations on Sociological Reporting', *American Sociological Review* 18, 1953, pp. 544—50.

33. H. Becker, op. cit. p. 275.

34. American Sociological Association, *Footnotes*, August 1979, p. 20.

35. G. Spencer, 'Methodological Issues in the Study of Bureaucratic Elites', *Social Problems*, vol. 21, no. 1, Summer 1973.

36. P. van den Berghe, 'Research in South Africa', in G. Sjöberg, *Ethics, Politics and Social Research*, op. cit. p. 185.

37. H. Becker, op. cit. p. 267.

38. T. Duster, D. Matza and D. Wellman, 'Fieldwork and the Protection of Human Subjects', *American Sociologist* 14, 1979, p. 138.

39. See R. Lowry, 'Towards a Sociology of Secrecy and Security systems', *Social Problems* 19, Spring 1972; J. F. Galliher, op. cit.

40. J. Douglas, op. cit. p. xiv.

41. See L. Rainwater and D. Pittman, 'Ethical Problems in Studying a Politically Sensitive and Deviant Community', *Social Problems* 14, 1967, pp. 357—66.

42. R. Evans, 'The Behavioural Scientist as a Public Informant', *Journal of Social Issues* 19, April 1963, p. 108.

43. J. Douglas, op. cit. p. 106.

44. Ibid. p. 113.

45. F. Goldner, 'Role Emergence and the Ethics of Ambiguity', in G. Sjöberg, *Ethics, Politics and Social Research*, op. cit. p. 258.

46. K. Erikson, 'A Comment on Disguised Observation in Sociology', *Social Problems* 14, 1967, pp. 366—73.

47. G. Condominas, *We Have Eaten the Forest* (London: Allen Lane, 1977).

48. T. Duster *et al.*, op. cit. p. 141.

49. G. Sjöberg and J. Miller, 'Social Research on Bureaucracy', op. cit.

50. Ibid. p. 99.

51. J. Lofland, op. cit. p. 2.

52. Ibid.

53. Ibid. p. 7.

54. P. Rock, *The Making of Symbolic Interactionism* (London: Macmillan, 1979) p. 191.

55. Barnes doubts that 'a social scientist who is a pacifist could establish empathic relations with an active military group'. (J. Barnes, *The Ethics of Inquiry in Social Science* (Delhi, Oxford University Press, 1977) p. 32.) I am loathe to conclude that those who establish rapport with racists are themselves racists.

56. R. Gorden, op. cit. pp. 161—3.

57. J. Douglas, op. cit.

58. P. Rock, op. cit. pp. 19—20.

59. J. Barnes, *Who Should Know What*, op. cit. p. 22.

60. J. Douglas, op. cit. p. 3.

61. Ibid. p. xi.

62. Ibid. p. 4.

63. Ibid. p. 8.

64. F. Burton, *The Politics of Legitimacy* (London: Routledge & Kegan Paul, 1979).

65. P. Willis, *Learning to Labour* (Farnborough: Saxon House, 1977).

66. J. Patrick, *A Glasgow Gang Observed* (London: Eyre Methuen, 1973).

67. M. Punch, *Policing the Inner City* (London: Macmillan, 1979).

68. J. Douglas, op. cit. pp. 42—3.

69. K. Erikson, op. cit. p. 371.

70. J. Douglas, op. cit. p. 76.

71. P. Manning, 'Observing the Police', in J. Douglas (ed.), *Research on Deviance* (New York: Random House, 1972) p. 248.

72. See also G. D. Berreman, *Hindus of the Himalayas: ethnography and change*, 2nd ed. (Berkeley: University of California Press, 1972) p. xxiv.

73. K. Erikson, op. cit. p. 367.

74. M. Sullivan *et al.*, 'Participant Observation as Employed in the Study of a Military Training Program', *American Sociological Review* 23, 1958, p. 664.

75. J. Douglas, *Investigative Social Research*, op. cit. p. 31.

76. J. Barnes, 'Some Ethical Problems in Modern Fieldwork', *British Journal of Sociology*, vol. 13, no. 2, 1963, p. 127.

77. P. Rock, op. cit. p. 205.

78. M. Phillipson, *Sociological Aspects of Crime and Delinquency* (London: Routledge & Kegan Paul, 1971) p. 169.

79. H. Becker, *Sociological Work* (London: Allen Lane, 1971) p. 5.

80. H. Becker, 'Whose Side Are We On?', *Social Problems*, vol. 14, no. 3, 1967, p. 245.

81. H. Becker, 'Problems in the Publication of Field Studies', op. cit. p. 269.

82. Ibid. pp. 273—4.

Chapter 6

1. B. R. Wilson, *Sects and Society: a Sociological Study of Three Religious Groups in Britain* (London: Heinemann, 1961) p. 87.

2. R. L. Gold, 'Roles in Sociological Field Observations', in G. J. McCall and J. L. Simmons, *Issues in Participant Observation: a Text and Reader* (Reading, Mass.: Addison-Wesley, 1969) p. 38.

3. K. Pryce, *Endless Pressure: a Study of West Indian Lifestyles in Bristol* (Harmondsworth: Penguin Books, 1979).

4. R. Homan, 'Interpersonal Communication in Pentecostal Meetings', *The Sociological Review* 26, 1978, pp. 499—518.

5. Extracts from the correspondence between Dingwall and Frankenberg were published in *Network: Newsletter of the British Sociological Association*, May 1979, p. 7.

6. R. Barbour, 'The Ethics of Covert Research', *Network*, September 1979, p. 9.

7. R. Homan, 'The Ethics of Covert Research: Homan defends his methods', *Network*, January 1980, p. 4.

8. R. Homan, 'The Ethics of Covert Methods', *British Journal of Sociology* 31, 1980, pp. 46—59, with a comment following by M. Bulmer.

9. Cf. 'The Nuremberg Code (1949)', reprinted in S. J. Reiser *et al.*, *Ethics in Medicine* (Cambridge, Mass.: M.I.T. Press, 1977) pp. 272—3.

10. Cf. *The American Sociologist* 13, 1978, pp. 134—72; and M. L. Wax and J. Cassell (eds), *Federal Regulations: ethical issues and social research* (Boulder: Westview Press, for AAAS, 1979).

11. Cf. E. Singer, 'Informed Consent', *American Sociological Review* 43, 1978, pp. 144—62; M. Bulmer (ed.), *Censuses, Surveys and Privacy* (London: Macmillan, 1979) esp. chapter 5.

12. R. Homan, op. cit. 1980, p. 55.

13. E. Shils, 'Privacy and Power', in *Center and Periphery* (University of Chicago Press, 1975) p. 344.

14. Cf. G. T. Marx, 'Thoughts on a Neglected Category of Social Movement Participant: the Agent Provocateur and Informant', *American Journal of Sociology* 80, 1974, pp. 402—42.

15. N. von Hoffman and S. W. Cassidy, 'Interviewing Negro Pentecostals', *American Journal of Sociology* 52, 1956, pp. 195—7.

16. R. Homan, op. cit. 1980, p. 56.

17. K. Pryce, op. cit. 1979, esp. pp. 282—7.

18. Cf. D. C. Gibbons, 'Unidentified Research Sites and Fictitious Names', *The American Sociologist* 10, 1975, pp. 32—6.

19. Cf. J. A. Barnes, *Who Should Know What?* (Harmondsworth, Penguin Books, 1979) pp. 156—7.

20. L. Humphreys, *Tearoom Trade: a Study of Homosexual Encounters in Public Places* (London, Duckworth, 1970).

21. M. Henle and M. B. Hubble, ' "Egocentricity" in Adult Conversation', *Journal of Social Psychology* 9, 1938, pp. 227—34.

22. L. Festinger *et al.*, *When Prophecy Fails* (Minneapolis: University of Minnesota Press, 1956).

23. R. Homan, op. cit. 1978.

24. D. P. Warwick, Chapter 3 above, p. 58.

25. British Sociological Association, 'Statement of Ethical Principles and their Application to Sociological Practice', 1973, p. 3.

26. W. J. Hollenweger, *The Pentecostals* (London: S.C.M. Press, 1972) p. 199.

27. Parts of Martin Bulmer's contribution to this chapter previously appeared in the *British Journal of Sociology* 31, 1980, pp. 59—65.

28. British Sociological Association, op. cit. 1973, p. 2.

Chapter 7

1. There are situations in which such unadmitted observations are necessary, for example, in the pursuit of criminals, spies, etc. Their necessity on behalf of social order does not diminish their morally objectionable character; it simply outweighs it.

2. It is not entirely proper when only one of them does so without the consent of the other or others, but that is always happening in normal life.

3. I do not mean to imply here that the police should be perfectly free to use these devices to observe the conduct and conversation of any suspected criminal or any person suspected of espionage. On the contrary, in these instances, too, the use of these instruments must be subjected to the strict control of the courts and the highest levels of political officialdom.

4. A confidentiality which is not, however, always strictly adhered to by jury members and the press, once the deliberations are completed.

5. Naturally, the knowledge that their tentatively expressed opinions were being recorded might inhibit the free play of imagination and intelligence and thus prevent the final decision from being as good as it might be if such inhibitions were not created. The same holds true for the deliberations of any committee or the action of any person who knows that his conduct is being observed and his statements recorded, even if he has no reason to suspect hostile intentions in connection with the observation. This is one of the liabilities of properly conducted observation, but it is not inevitably injurious to the research. In fact, it is quite likely that consciousness of being recorded would not play a significant part in the course or content of the deliberations.

6. The fact that there are so many 'leaks' of secret information, utterly unconnected with espionage, is no argument against the interpretation given in the text. The eagerness to penetrate and disclose secrets is not motivated only by professional journalistic pride and democratic concern for the common good, but rather by an urge to be in contact with the sacred zones of authority and to give public evidence of that contact. Likewise, the readiness in the United States of officials and congressmen to 'leak' the proceedings of secret meetings is in part a product of political tactical considerations and an act of conciliation toward powerful journalists. Yet it is also the product of a desire simultaneously to give evidence of being in contact with a sacred zone and to degrade it by disclosure to the uninitiated. The populistic ethos is made up of such elements as these.

7. Such is the ambivalent nature of the human being that the need

for secrecy is often accompanied by the equal and concurrent need for publicity about what is secret.

8. I might in this instance mention the work of C. Wright Mills, *The Power Elite*, a work deeply permeated with the sense of the potency of the powerful. The author did not seek even a single interview with those whose deeds so engage his thoughts and sentiments.

9. Many would be more widely read if they were 'classified' as secret or as confidential. Sometimes the best way to assure that something is left unknown is to publish it.

10. Yet, by and large and for the most part, social scientists hold themselves aloof. They hold themselves aloof partly because they themselves fear the reaction of the public, which might take umbrage at the sacrilegious character of detached direct observation of the seats of power, however much it delights in reading and retelling gossip about those who sit or have sat in those seats.

Chapter 8

1. A revised and lengthened version of this communication was presented at the 63rd Annual Meeting of the American Sociological Association, 1968. I am grateful to Steven Cox, Daniel Glaser and John P. Clark for their comments on an earlier version of this note.

2. *Social Problems* 14 Spring 1967. See the papers by Rainwater and Pittman, Erikson, Mills, and Seeley.

3. Edward Shils, Chapter 7 in this volume.

4. Kai T. Erikson, 'A Comment on Disguised Observation in Sociology', *Social Problems* 14, 1967, pp. 366—73.

5. See my *The Research Act* (Chicago: Aldine, 1970) chapter 13, where this is more fully elaborated.

6. This draws from Howard S. Becker, 'Problems in the Publication of Field Studies', in Arthur J. Vidich, Joseph Bensman and Maurice R. Stein (eds), *Reflections on Community Studies* (New York: Wiley, 1964).

7. Sheri Cavan, *Liquor License: An Ethnography of Bar Behavior* (Chicago: Aldine, 1966).

8. Erving Goffman, *The Presentation of Self in Everyday Life* (New York: Doubleday, 1959).

9. Quite obviously, discovery in the disguised role, of the publication of findings from a study in which the research role was not clearly established, can have damaging effects as the 'Springdale' incident indicated. See Arthur J. Vidich and Joseph Bensman, 'The Springdale Case: Academic Bureaucrats and Sensitive Townspeople', in Vidich, Bensman and Stein, op. cit. pp. 313—49, for a review of the circumstances surrounding this incident. This is not the point at issue, however.

10. See Martin T. Orne, 'On the Social Psychology of the Psychological Experiment: With Particular Reference to Demand Characteristics and Their Implications', in Carl A. Backman and Paul F. Secord (eds), *Problems in Social Psychology* (New York: McGraw-Hill, 1966) pp. 14–21.

11. Benjamin D. Paul, 'Interview Techniques and Field Relationships', in A. L. Kroeber (ed.), *Anthropology Today* (University of Chicago Press, 1953) pp. 430–541, presents strategies for this use of the field notes.

12. Ned Polsky also points to this issue in his *Hustlers, Beats and Others* (Chicago, Aldine, 1967) pp. 117–49.

13. This is also Becker's conclusion. See Becker, op cit.

14. Howard S. Becker, 'Whose Side Are We On?', *Social Problems* 14 Winter 1967, pp. 239–48.

15. I am currently engaged upon a series of studies with Rita James Simon of the University of Illinois which will provide empirical data for a number of issues that to this point can only be taken at face value, or be resolved by personal choice. An issue not treated in this note is the efficacy and ethicality of unobtrusive measures of observation in sociology. My position would sanction their use but, as I interpret Erikson, he would not. See Eugene J. Webb *et al.*, *Unobtrusive Measures: Nonreactive Research in the Social Sciences* (Chicago: Rand McNally, 1966) where a catalogue of these measures is presented.

Chapter 9

1. 'Toward a Code of Ethics for Sociologists', *American Sociologist* 3, 1968, pp. 316–18.

2. B. Bettelheim, 'Individual and Mass Behaviour in Extreme Situations', *Journal of Abnormal and Social Psychology* 38, 1943, pp. 417–52, reprinted in B. Bettelheim, *Surviving* (London: Thames & Hudson, 1979) pp. 48–83, and briefly outlined in Chapter 1 above.

3. D. J. Black and A. J. Reiss Jr, 'Police Control of Juveniles', *American Sociological Review* 35, 1970, pp. 63–77, at p. 65.

4. Cf. W. A. Westley, 'Secrecy and the Police', *Social Forces* 34, 1956, pp. 254–7; E. R. Stoddard, 'The Informal Cost of Police Deviancy', *Journal of Criminal Law, Criminology and Police Science* 59, 1968, pp. 201–13; L. Savitz, 'The Dimensions of Police Loyalty', *American Behavioral Scientist* 13, 1970, pp. 693–704; A. J. Reiss Jr, 'Police Brutality — answers to key questions', *Trans-Action* 5, 1968, pp. 10–19.

5. L. Rainwater and D. J. Pittman, 'Ethical Problems in Studying a

Politically Sensitive and Deviant Community', *Social Problems* 14, 1967, pp. 357—66, at pp. 365—6.

6. J. Lofland, 'Comment on "Initial Interaction of Newcomers in Alcoholics Anonymous"', *Social Problems* 8, 1961, pp. 365—7, at p. 366.

7. J. A. Roth, 'Comments on "Secret Observation"', *Social Problems* 9, 1962, pp. 283, 284.

8. H. S. Becker, 'Against the Code of Ethics', *American Sociological Review* 29, 1964, pp. 409—10.

9. K. T. Erikson, 'A Comment on Disguised Observation in Sociology', *Social Problems* 14, 1967, pp. 366—73, at pp. 368, 369, 373.

10. G. M. Sykes, 'Feeling Our Way: a report on a conference on ethical issues in the social sciences', *American Behavioral Scientist* 10, 1967, pp. 8—11.

11. Ibid. p. 9.

12. 'Toward a Code of Ethics . . .', op cit. p. 316.

13. More general questions about the utility of the Code of Ethics have, however, been raised by J. A. Roth, 'A Codification of Current Prejudices', *American Sociologist* 4, 1969, p. 159, and by R. W. Friedrichs, 'Epistemological Foundations of a Sociological Ethic', *American Sociologist* 5, 1970, pp. 138—40.

14. H. C. Kelman, 'Human Use of Human Subjects: the problem of deception in social psychological experiments', *Psychological Bulletin* 67, 1967, pp. 1—11; P. Bonacich, 'Deceiving Subjects: the pollution of our environment', *American Sociologist* 5, 1970. p. 45.

15. Rainwater and Pittman, op cit., and Erikson, op cit. p. 371.

16. For examples of such self-protective reactions, see J. C. Record, 'The Research Institute and the Pressure Group'; F. H. Coldner, 'Role Emergence and the Ethics of Ambiguity'; and A. K. Daniel, 'The Low Caste Stranger in Social Research'; all in G. Sjöberg (ed.), *Ethics, Politics and Social Research* (London, Routledge & Kegan Paul, 1968) respectively pp. 25—49; pp. 245—66; and pp. 267—96.

17. J. Roth, 'Comments on "Secret Observation"', *Social Problems* 9, 1962, pp. 283—4.

18. R. P. Lowry, 'Towards a Sociology of Secrecy and Security Systems', *Social Problems* 19, 1972, pp. 437—50, at p. 437.

19. J. Lofland, op. cit. p. 366.

20. P. van den Berghe, 'Research in South Africa', in G. Sjöberg (ed.), op. cit. pp. 183—97, at p. 185.

21. T. R. Young, 'The Politics of Sociology: Gouldner, Goffman and Garfinkel', *American Sociologist* 6, 1971, pp. 276—81, at p. 279.

22. J. S. Brown and B. G. Gilmartin, 'Sociology Today: lacunae, emphases and surfeits', *American Sociologist* 4, 1969, pp. 283—91.

23. J. H. Fichter and W. L. Kolb, 'Ethical Limitations in Sociological Reporting', *American Sociological Review* 18, 1953, pp. 544—50.

24. H. S. Becker and I. L. Horowitz, 'Radical Politics and Sociological Research', *American Journal of Sociology* 78, 1972, pp. 48—66, at p. 48.

25. Ibid. p. 55.

26. The remaining sections of rule 5 can be deleted. They are:

Even though research information is not a privileged communication under the law, the sociologist must, as far as possible, protect subjects and informants. Any promises made to such persons must be honored. However, provided that he respects the assurance he has given his subjects, the sociologist has no obligation to withhold information of misconduct of individuals or organisations.

If an informant or other subject should wish, however, he can formally release the researcher of a promise of confidentiality. The provisions of this section apply to all members of research organisations (i.e. interviewers, coders, clerical staff, etc.), and it is the responsibility of the chief investigators to see that they are instructed in the necessity and importance of maintaining the confidentiality of the data. The obligation of the sociologist includes the use and storage of original data to which a subject's name is attached. When requested, the identity of an organisation or subject must be adequately disguised in publication.

27. Other sections of the code, such as the rules concerning disclosure of the sources of financial support and acknowledgement of research collaboration and assistance, are not problematic. Moreover, the existence of a Code of Ethics for sociology is useful, if for no other reason than furtherance of public relations, since it keeps sociology professionally abreast of other social sciences, including psychology and anthropology, which have such bodies of rules.

28. M. Glazer, *The Research Adventure* (New York: Random House, 1972).

29. H. Molditch and M. Lester, 'Accidents, Scandals and Routines', paper presented at the 67th Meeting of the ASA, New Orleans, 1972.

30. T. R. Young, op. cit. pp. 279—80.

31. B. Kovach, 'Harvard Professor Jailed in Pentagon Papers Case', *New York Times*, 22 November 1972, pp. 1, 40.

32. Erikson, op. cit. pp. 368—9.

33. National Institutes of Health, *Institutional Guide to DHEW Policy on Protection of Human Subjects* (Washington, D.C.: DHEW Publication No. (NIH) 72—102, 1971) pp. 7—8.

34. J. L. McCartney, 'On Being Scientific', *American Sociologist* 5, 1970, pp. 30—5; J. F. Galliher and J. L. McCartney, 'The Effects of Funding on Juvenile Delinquency Research', *Social Problems* 21,

1973, pp. 77–90; H. G. Tibbits, 'Research in the Development of Sociology', *American Sociological Review* 27, 1962, pp. 892–901; L. A. Coser, 'The Functions of Small-Group Research', *Social Problems* 3, 1955, pp. 1–6, at pp. 5–6.

35. Erikson, op. cit. pp. 368–9.

36. I am grateful to my colleagues in the Department of Sociology at the University of Missouri at Columbia who have helped me with this paper, and I am especially indebted to James L. McCartney who initially suggested that I put these ideas in writing and who made many helpful comments on earlier drafts of the paper.

Chapter 10

1. For a discussion of the expressions 'freedom to' and 'freedom from', see Isaiah Berlin, *Two Concepts of Liberty* (Oxford: Clarendon Press, 1958); and Gerald C. MacCallum Jr, 'Negative and Positive Freedom', *The Philosophical Review* 76, 1967, pp. 312–34.

2. See Hans Jonas, 'Freedom of Scientific Inquiry and the Public Interest', *The Hastings Center Report*, 6, August 1976, pp. 15–17.

3. Steven Weinberg, 'Reflections of a Working Scientist', *Daedalus* 103, Summer 1974, p. 45.

4. Laud Humphreys, 'Tearoom Trade – Impersonal Sex in Public Places', *Trans-Action* 15, January 1970.

5. See 'Final Report of the Tuskegee Syphilis Study Ad Hoc Advisory Panel' (Washington, D.C.: US Public Health Service, 1973).

6. George W. Ball, 'Biology and Politics', Address to the Annual Meeting of the American Political Science Association, September 1977, pp. 13–14.

7. UNESCO Recommendation on the Status of Research Scientists, adopted by the General Conference, 20 November, 1974.

8. See 'Protection of Human Subjects', *Code of Federal Regulations* title 45 CFR part 36, 6 November 1975, and the Reports of the National Commission for the Protection of Human Subjects of Biomedical and Behavioral Research.

9. See Alice M. Rivlin and P. Michael Timpane (eds), *Ethical and Legal Issues of Social Experimentation* (Washington, D.C.: The Brookings Institution, 1975).

10. See Anton Stoerck, *An Essay on the Medicinal Nature of Hemlock* (London: J. Nourse, 1760); and Lawrence K. Altman, 'Autoexperimentation. An Unappreciated Tradition in Medical Science', *New England Journal of Medicine* 286, 1972, pp. 346–52.

11. A perennial question in ethics is whether it covers not only what human beings do to one another, but what they do to themselves. 'Duties to oneself' are discussed under this heading. Yet, whatever the

resolution of this jurisdictional dispute, such duties are clearly of a very different nature for any discussion of outside limitation or regulation.

12. Laurence H. Tribe, *American Constitutional Law* (Mineola, N.Y.: Foundation Press, 1978) pp. 904—5.

13. *Disarmament and Development: Report of the Group of Experts on the Economic and Social Consequences of Disarmament* (United Nations, 1972). See also Alva Myrdal, *The Game of Disarmament* (New York: Pantheon, 1976) pp. 11—14, 155—6.

14. See Henry K. Beecher, 'Ethics and Clinical Research'. *The New England Journal of Medicine* 274, 1966, pp. 1354—60; and Jay Katz, *Experimentation on Human Beings* (New York: Russell Sage Foundation, 1972).

15. Cf. p. 1207 in Carl Cohen, 'When May Research Be Stopped?', *New England Journal of Medicine* 296, 1977, 1203—10.

16. Periodic review could be required to ensure that unforeseen dangers, should they arise, do not go unnoticed.

17. See David D. Rutstein, 'The Ethical Design of Human Experiments', *Daedalus*, Spring 1969, pp. 523—41.

18. I discuss problems of accountability and risk in connection with deceptive experimentation in S. Bok, *Lying: Moral Choice in Public and Private Life* (New York: Pantheon Press, 1978).

19. See Judith Swazey and Renée Fox, 'The Clinical Moratorium: A Case Study of Mitral Valve Surgery' in Paul A. Freund (ed.), *Experimentation with Human Subjects* (New York: George Braziller, 1970) pp. 315—37.

Chapter 11

1. See Diana Baumrind, 'Snooping and Duping', paper presented at the meeting of the Society for Applied Anthropology, San Diego, Calif., April 1977 for a critical review of field investigation.

2. A survey of such codes is discussed in Paul D. Reynolds, 'Ethics and Status: Value Dilemmas in the Professional Conduct of Social Science', *International Social Science Journal*, 27 (4), 1975, pp. 563—611.

3. This section is a summary of chapter 2 of Paul D. Reynolds, *Ethical Dilemmas in Social Science Research* (San Francisco, Calif.: Jossey-Bass, 1979) pp. 8—37.

4. A thorough treatment of this issue is found in G. J. Annas *et al.*, *Informed Consent to Human Experimentation: The Subject's Dilemma* (Cambridge, Mass.: Ballinger, 1977). A discussion of the research, from the trial of the physician-investigators, is presented in J. Katz, *Experimentation with Human Beings* (New York: Russell Sage) pp. 292—306.

5. Article 27 of the Universal Declaration of Human Rights (adopted by the United Nations Educational, Scientific, and Cultural Organisation on 10 December 1948) states that: 'Everyone has the right freely to . . . share in scientific advancement and its benefits.' John Robertson, 'The Scientist's Right to Research: A Constitutional Analysis', *Southern California Law Review*, 51(6), 1978, pp. 1203–80, discusses the potential legal rights of scientists to engage in research, speculating upon their constitutional status (in the United States).

6. John Rawls, *A Theory of Justice* (Cambridge, Mass.: Harvard U.P., 1971) has argued that the rights of the disadvantaged require more 'protection' or 'consideration' than those of the advantaged. H. Jonas, 'Philosophical Reflections on Experimenting with Human Subjects', *Daedalus* 89(2), 1969, pp. 219–47, has suggested that only those in the upper middle class (the advantaged) can understand what it means to do research and give truly informed consent.

7. The federally required Institutional Review Boards in the United States must be composed of individuals possessing the 'professional competence necessary to review specific activities, . . .' and ascertain the acceptability of proposals in terms of '. . . community attitudes' and 'must therefore include persons whose concerns are in these areas'. (Title 45, Part 46.6 (b)(1) of the United States Code of Federal Regulations.)

8. I. Kant, *The Fundamental Principles of the Metaphysic of Ethics*, trans. O. Manthey-Zorn (New York: Appleton-Century-Crofts, 1928) (originally published 1785).

9. Charles Fried, *Right and Wrong* (Cambridge, Mass.: Harvard U.P., 1978) p. 2.

10. John Fletcher, *Situation Ethics* (Philadelphia: Westminster Press, 1966) and *Moral Responsibility: Situation Ethics at Work* (Philadelphia: Westminster Press, 1967).

11. See S. Dornbusch, 'The Military Academy as an Assimilating Institution', *Social Forces* 33, 1955, pp. 316–21 and G. Homans, 'The Small Warship', *American Sociological Review* 11, 1946, pp. 294–300.

12. J. A. Roth, 'Dangerous and Difficult Enterprise?', *American Sociological Review* 24(3), 1959, p. 398.

13. Based on reports in Laud Humphreys, *Tearoom Trade: Impersonal Sex in Public Places* (Chicago: Aldine, 1970).

14. As, for example, when prostitutes service their clients in cars, doorways and parking lots in full public view were filmed covertly and presented on national television ('Weekend', 4 September 1976) in the United States. Needless to say, the identities of the individuals involved were not explicit, although they could have been if the producers had not been conscientious about protecting identities.

15. S. Bok, 'The Ethics of Giving Placebos', *Scientific American* 231,

1974, (5), pp. 17–23, reviews some of the advantages for patients' physical wellbeing when they are deceived by physicians about their 'true' status.

16. Based on L. Festinger, H. W. Riecken and S. Schachter, *When Prophecy Fails* (Minneapolis: University of Minnesota Press, 1956). See M. Brewster Smith, 'Of Prophecy and Privacy', *Contemporary Psychology* 2 (4), 1957, pp. 89–92 for a useful review of this study.

17. See the Methodological Appendix (pp. 237–52) of L. Festinger *et al.*, op cit., for a review of their observation procedures.

18. It would be possible, of course, to check the regional newspapers at the approximate time of the study to determine the exact location and identities of the individuals involved; both newspaper and television reporters were sought and welcomed by the group members on many occasions. This capacity to identify the sect and the individual members was neither facilitated nor preventable by the participant observer investigators.

19. See the theoretical development related to group processes in Leon Festinger, 'A Theory of Social Comparison Processes', *Human Relations* 7, 1954, pp. 117–40, and to cognitive (mental) structures in Leon Festinger, *A Theory of Cognitive Dissonance* (Stanford U.P., 1957).

20. D. L. Rosenhan, 'On Being Sane in Insane Places' Chapter 2.

21. E. Goffman, *Asylums* (Garden City, N.Y.: Doubleday & Co., 1961).

22. A more complete evaluation of the staff of a hospital to a single 'bogus' mental patient is presented by F. Redlich, 'The Anthropologist as Observer; Ethical Aspects of Clinical Observations of Behavior', *The Journal of Nervous and Mental Disease* 157(5) 1973, pp. 313–19; there was a rather substantial negative reaction by the psychiatrists and nurses who felt that they had been deceived and tricked and that their noble motives had not been given appropriate consideration; one analysis (footnote 2, p. 318) even suggested that the covert participant investigator misused his power to reduce the choices available to the unsuspecting staff. Most of the 'ethical complaints' appeared to de-emphasise the dependent helplessness of the true patients and their situation: subordinates that could, prior to this study, be taken for granted.

23. M. Mead, 'Research with Human Beings: A Model Derived from Anthropological Field Practice', *Daedalus* 98 (2), 1969, pp. 361–86.

24. Jack D. Douglas, *Investigative Social Research* (Beverley Hills, Calif.: Sage Publications, 1976).

25. This is often associated with an emphasis upon the 'morality' of the research techniques utilised by social scientists and the subsequent effect upon public support for the social science enterprise; such

discussions usually give little or no attention to the societal reaction to or public support for the results of social science investigations. Examples include D. Baumrind, op. cit.; H. S. Conrad, 'Clearance of Questionnaires with Respect to "Invasion of Privacy, Public Sensitivities, Ethical Standards, etc." ', *American Psychologist* 22, 1967, pp. 356—9; K. T. Erikson, 'A Comment on Disguised Observation in Sociology', *Social Problems* 14 (4), 1967, pp. 366—73; and D. P. Warwick, Chapter 3.

26. See R. J. Lundman and P. T. McFarlane, 'Conflict Methodology: An Introduction and Preliminary Assessment', *Sociological Quarterly* 17, 1976, pp. 502—12, and the response from R. M. Christie, 'Comment on Conflict Methodology: A Protagonist Position', *Sociological Quarterly* 17, 1976, pp. 513—19.

27. J. F. Galliher, 'The Protection of Human Subjects: A re-examination of the professional code of ethics' (Chapter 9), suggests that the code of ethics for the American Sociological Association be revised to encourage members not to honour promises of confidentiality given to those in positions of authority.

28. See P. D. Reynolds, 1975, op. cit. for a review of statements in codes of ethics; P. D. Reynolds, 1979, op. cit. pp. 304—21 for a review of the legal status of an 'investigator's privilege' in the United States; P. Nejelski, 'Researchers in West Germany Survey Report Difficulty in Obtaining or Protecting Confidential Data', *ASA Footnotes* 1 (8), 1973, p. 2, discusses problems in West Germany for field investigators; the major issues that appear to confront Institutional Review Boards in evaluation of social science projects are the nature of the informed consent procedure and procedures for maintaining anonymity of the participants or confidentiality of the data; E. Sagarin, 'The Research Setting and the Right Not to be Researched', *Social Problems* 21 (1), 1973, pp. 52—64, reviews examples of research abandoned because of problems with maintaining anonymity for participants.

29. S. Bok, *Lying: Moral Choice in Public and Private Life* (New York: Pantheon, 1978) reviews many of the complications associated with trying to distuinguish truth from falsehood; she concludes with a series of recommendations regarding changes in the context for most individuals that would reward truthfulness and punish lying.

Chapter 12

1. J. Douglas, 'Living Morality versus Bureaucratic Fiat', in C. B. Klockars and F. W. O'Connor, *Deviance and Decency: the ethics of research with human subjects* (London: Sage, 1979) pp. 13, 32.

2. The Nuremberg Code 1949, reprinted in S. J. Reiser *et al.*, *Ethics in Medicine* (Cambridge: M.I.T. Press, 1977) pp. 272—3.

3. A. J. Reiss, 'Conditions and Consequences of Consent in Human

Subject Research', in K. M. Wulff (ed.), *Regulation of Scientific Inquiry* (Boulder, Colorado: Westview Press, for the American Association for the Advancement of Science, 1978) p. 163.

4. M. Brewster Smith, 'Some Perspectives on Ethical/Political Issues in Social Science Research', in M. L. Wax and J. Cassell (eds), *Federal Regulations: Ethical Issues and Social Research* (Boulder, Colorado: Westview Press, for the American Association for the Advancement of Science, 1979), p. 14.

5. E. Goffman, *Asylums* (Harmondsworth: Penguin Books, 1968) pp. 31—2.

6. Cf. T. R. Vaughan, 'Governmental Intervention in Social Research', in G. Sjöberg (ed.), *Ethics, Politics and Social Research* (London: Routledge & Kegan Paul, 1967) pp. 50—77.

7. F. Redlich, 'Ethical Aspects of Clinical Observation of Behaviour', *Journal of Nervous and Mental Disease*, vol. 157, no. 5, November 1973, p. 316.

8. Laud Humphreys, *Tearoom Trade* (Chicago: Aldine, 1975) (2nd ed. with appendices discussing ethical issues) p. 230.

9. W. Caudill, *The Psychiatric Hospital as a Small Society* (Cambridge, Mass.: Harvard U.P., 1958) pp. xiv-xvi.

10. M. Mead, 'The Human Study of Human Beings', *Science* vol. 133, no. 3447, 20 January 1961, leading article reproduced with permission of the publisher.

11. G. T. Marx, 'Thoughts on a Neglected Category of Social Movement Participant: the agent provocateur and informant', *American Journal of Sociology* 80, 1974, pp. 404—5.

12. L. Festinger *et al.*, *When Prophecy Fails* (Minneapolis: University of Minnesota Press, 1956) pp. 234—49.

13. A Lurie, *Imaginary Friends* (London: Heinemann, 1967).

14. J. Patrick, *A Glasgow Gang Observed* (London: Eyre-Methuen, 1973).

15. Ibid. p. 142, quoting D. J. West, *The Young Offender* (Harmondsworth: Penguin Books, 1967) p. 249.

16. Laud Humphreys, op. cit. p. 215.

17. Reiss, op. cit. p. 175.

18. J. Ditton, *Part Time Crime* (London: Macmillan, 1977) p. 9.

19. J. Douglas, *Investigative Social Research* (London: Sage, 1976) pp. xiv—xv.

20. Cf. S. Bok, *Lying* (Hassocks: Harvester Press, 1978) pp. 197—202.

21. J. Ditton, op. cit. p. vii.

22. Cf. M. Bulmer, *Censuses, Surveys and Privacy* (London: Macmillan, 1979) esp. chapter 7; E. Sagarin, 'The Research Setting and the Right Not to be Researched', *Social Problems* 21, 1973, pp. 52—64.

23. Redlich, op. cit. p. 315.

24. G. de Vos, 'William Caudill', *Journal of Nervous and Mental Disease* vol. 157, no. 4, 1973, p. 234.

25. Caudill, op. cit. p. xiv.

26. Cf. J. Lofland, 'Reply to Davis's Comment', from *Social Problems* 8, 1960, pp. 365—7, reprinted in W. J. Filstead (ed.), *Qualitative Methodology* (Chicago: Markham, 1970) where it is stated in a footnote: 'John Lofland no longer subscribes to the argument he presents here. His current position is in essential accord with the views developed by Kai T. Erikson in "A Comment on Disguised Observation in Sociology" ' (cited in footnote 30, below) (Filstead, p. 275).

27. R. Homan, 'The Ethics of Covert Methods', *British Journal of Sociology* 31, 1980, pp. 46—59. See also M. Clark, 'Survival in the field', *Theory and Society* 2, 1978, pp. 63—94.

28. M. Mead, 'Research with Human Beings: a Model Derived from Anthropological Field Practice', *Daedalus*, 1969, p. 376.

29. D. P. Warwick, p. 58 above.

30. K. T. Erikson, 'A Comment on Disguised Observation in Sociology', *Social Problems* 14, 1967, pp. 366—73, at p. 369.

31. G. T. Marx, 'Police Undercover Work', *Urban Life* 8, January 1980, pp. 399—446, at pp. 431—2.

32. Ibid.

33. For a different though related discussion, see S. O. Murray, 'The Scientific Reception of Castaneda', *Contemporary Sociology* 8, 1979, pp. 189—96.

34. Cf. E. Diener and R. Crandall, *Ethics in Social and Behavioral Research* (University of Chicago Press, 1978) chap. 5 *passim*.

35. J. Ditton, op. cit. p. 11. For a more general discussion, see R. Wax, *Doing Fieldwork* (University of Chicago Press, 1971) pp. 47—55.

36. N. Polsky, *Hustlers, Beats and Others* (Harmondsworth: Penguin Books, 1969) pp. 124 ff.

37. G. J. McCall, *Observing the Law: field methods in the study of crime and the criminal justice system* (New York: Free Press, 1978) p. 30.

38. Cf. C. Klockars, *The Professional Fence* (London: Tavistock, 1975) and F. A. J. and E. R. Ianni, *A Family Business: kinship and social control in organised crime* (London: Routledge & Kegan Paul, 1972).

39. H. Heclo and A. Wildavsky, *The Private Government of Public Money* (London: Macmillan, 1974) esp. chap. 3.

40. J. D. Douglas, op. cit. p. xiv.

41. M. Dalton, *Men Who Manage* (New York: Wiley, 1959).

42. H. Becker, 'The Culture of a Deviant Group: the Dance Musician', in *Outsiders* (Glencoe: Free Press, 1963) p. 84.

43. N. Polsky, op. cit. pp. 46—8.

44. K. T. Erikson, op. cit. p. 372.

45. Cf. S. Milgram *et al.*, 'The Lost-Letter Technique: a tool of social research', *Public Opinion Quarterly* 29, 1965, pp. 437—8.

46. For example, J. and I. Piliavain, 'Effects of Blood on Reactions to a Victim', *Journal of Personality and Social Psychology* 23, 1972, pp. 353—61.

47. A case described in E. Diener and R. Crandall, *Ethics in Social and Behavioral Research* (University of Chicago Press, 1978) p. 87.

48. J. Roth, 'Comments on "Secret Observation"', *Social Problems* 9, 1961, pp. 283—4.

48. C. W. M. Hart, 'Fieldwork Among the Tiwi 1928—29', in G. D. Spindler (ed.), *Being an Anthropologist* (New York: Holt, Rinehart & Winston, 1970) p. 151.

50. A. Sutherland, *Gypsies: the hidden Americans* (London: Tavistock, 1975) pp. 30—1.

51. Cf. S. Bok, op. cit. pp. 197 ff.

52. G. J. McCall, op. cit. p. 45.

53. W. F. Whyte, *Street Corner Society* (University of Chicago Press, 1955) Appendix.

54. F. Redlich, op. cit. p. 316.

55. K. Pryce, *Endless Pressure* (Harmondsworth: Penguin Books, 1979) pp. 282—7.

56. A Faraday and K. Plummer, 'Doing Life Histories', *Sociological Review* 27, 1979, pp. 791—2.

57. J. Patrick, op. cit. p. 16.

58. S. Cohen and L. Taylor, *Psychological Survival: the experience of long-term imprisonment* (Harmondsworth: Penguin Books, 1972) pp. 29 ff.

59. A. Sutherland, op. cit. pp. 20—5.

60. Cohen and Taylor, op. cit. pp. 38—9.

61. A. Sutherland, op. cit. p. 30.

62. J. Rubinstein, *City Police* (New York: Farrar, Straus & Giroux, 1973).

63. Ibid., Ballantine paper edition, 1974, pp. xii—xiii.

64. *The Handbook of Medical Ethics* (London: British Medical Association, 1980) p. 18.

65. M. Dalton, 'Preconceptions and Methods in *Men Who Manage*', in P. Hammond (ed.), *Sociologists at Work* (New York: Basic Books, 1964) pp. 50—95, at pp. 59—60.

66. Ibid. pp. 59—60.

67. G. Sjöberg and P. Miller, 'Social Research on Bureaucracies: limitations and opportunities', *Social Problems* 21, 1973, pp. 129—43, esp. pp. 136 ff.

68. See note 39 above.

69. J. Barnes, *Who Should Know What?* (Harmondsworth: Penguin Books, 1979) p. 127.

70. T. Kynaston-Reeves and D. G. Harper, *Employee Survey Research* (London: McGraw-Hill, 1980).

71. G. J. McCall, op. cit. chap. 6, 'Observing the Police'.

72. 'Toward a Code of Ethics', *The American Sociologist* 3, 1968, pp. 316–18.

73. British Sociological Association, 'Statement of Ethical Principles and their Application to Sociological Practice' (London: BSA, 1973) pp. 3, 2.

74. Wax and Cassell (eds), *Federal Regulations,* op. cit. note 4 above.

75. T. Duster, D. Matza and D. Wellman, 'Field Work and the Protection of Human Subjects', *The American Sociologist* 14, 1979, pp. 136–42.

76. 'Toward a Code of Ethics', op. cit. p. 318.

77. J. Barnes, op. cit. p. 126.